Questions & Answers

LAW OF TORTS

Keeping you afloat through your exams

QUESTIONS & Answers

Ask anyone for exam advice and they'll tell you to *answer the question*. It's good advice but the Q&As go further by telling you how to answer the questions you'll face in your law exams.

Q&As will help you succeed by:

- ✓ identifying typical law exam questions
- ✓ demonstrating how to structure a good answer
- ✓ helping you to avoid common mistakes
- ✓ advising you on how to make your answer stand out from the crowd
- ✓ giving you model answers to up to 50 essay and problem-based questions

Every Q&A follows a trusted formula of question, commentary, answer plan, examiner's tips, and suggested answer. They're written by experienced law lecturers and experienced examiners to help you succeed in exams.

'What a brilliant revision aid! With summaries, tips, and easy-to-understand sample answers, Q&As really help with exam technique and how to structure answers. A great help not only during the revision process, but also throughout the course.'

Kim Sutton, Law student, Oxford Brookes University

LAW OF TORTS
2013 and 2014

PUBLIC LAW
2013 and 2014

LAND LAW
2013 and 2014

LAW OF CONTRACT
2013 and 2014

EU LAW
2013 and 2014

FAMILY LAW
2013 and 2014

Titles in the series cover all compulsory law subjects and major options.

Buy yours from your campus bookshop, online, or direct from OUP

www.oxfordtextbooks.co.uk/law/revision

Questions & Answers

LAW OF TORTS

Seventh edition

David Oughton
Professor of Commercial Law,
De Montfort University, Leicester

Barbara Harvey
Principal Lecturer in Law,
De Montfort University, Leicester

2013 and 2014

OXFORD
UNIVERSITY PRESS

OXFORD

UNIVERSITY PRESS

Great Clarendon Street, Oxford, OX2 6DP,
United Kingdom

Oxford University Press is a department of the University of Oxford.
It furthers the University's objective of excellence in research, scholarship,
and education by publishing worldwide. Oxford is a registered trade mark of
Oxford University Press in the UK and in certain other countries

Fourth edition 2007
Fifth edition 2009
Sixth edition 2011
Impression: 2

British Library Cataloguing in Publication Data

Data available

ISBN 978–0–19–966190–9

Printed in Great Britain by
Ashford Colour Press Ltd, Gosport, Hampshire

CONTENTS

Key features

The Q&A series provides full coverage of key subjects in a clear and logical way. The book contains the following features:

- Questions
- Commentary
- Bullet-pointed answer plans
- Examiner's tips
- Suggested answers
- Further reading suggestions

 online resource centre

www.oxfordtextbooks.co.uk/orc/qanda/

Titles in the Q&A series are supported by additional online materials to aid study and revision.

Online resources for this title are hosted at the URL above, which is open access and free to use.

PREFACE

The degree of fear, apprehension, and circumspection felt by the authors prior to the publication of previous issues remains the same. One is always mindful of the response given to students who ask for the 'right answer' to a question on some aspect of law. As the common law is so rich and varied in its approach to legal issues, it is always the case that a novel set of facts can be approached from several different angles, so that in truth, it is almost impossible to say that there is a definitively correct final answer to a particular question. Nevertheless, we have attempted to give answers to questions of the type that students might expect to encounter in an examination on the law of torts, in the knowledge that there are others who might disagree with the approach that has been taken.

As with previous editions, in addition to the questions and accompanying suggested answers, each chapter seeks to provide readers with a selection of wider reading and a series of key points to be addressed in each of the questions in bullet-point or diagrammatic form. As far as possible, suggested answers have been reduced in size to what is roughly examination-answer length, although some longer answers have been retained as examples of extended coursework answers. Some of the more elaborate legal language has been adjusted to make the material more reader-friendly and there are flow charts and diagrams at certain points in the text. As ever, the unwitting support of students at various universities is gratefully acknowledged. Their questions, mistakes, and successes have all contributed to the content of this compilation of questions and answers by informing the authors of the areas of the law of torts that may give rise to some of the more difficult points of interpretation.

Lastly, but far from least, David Oughton would like to say thank you to Sue, Karen, and Gareth for their love, support, and encouragement. Barbara Harvey would again like to thank Jemima, Patrick, and David for all their love, support, and encouragement.

David Oughton
Barbara Harvey
August 2012

TABLE OF CASES

TABLE OF STATUTES

Introduction

1 The challenges of the law of torts

The law of torts is a subject you will have to take if you are pursuing a qualifying law degree, since it is one of the 'core' subjects, but it is a subject that most students think they have enjoyed. Unfortunately, appearances are deceptive. The law of torts might consist of some very interesting tales of human woe. It also addresses issues as diverse as the liability of public bodies for failings in their operational activities; the right to personal integrity; human rights; whether a business can recover economic losses it has suffered as a result of the alleged negligence or deliberate action of another business concern; whether a person can prevent the activities of a neighbouring landowner on his own land, on the basis that the activity constitutes an unreasonable interference with his own way of life; whether there is a right to privacy and whether damage to one's reputation is actionable.

Like its common law partner, the law of contract, the law of torts is a system of legal rules designed to compensate a person in respect of damage caused by another person. However, unlike contractual liability, the tortious liability of a defendant is potentially unlimited. While a defendant in a contract action is generally limited in his liability to the other party to the contract, tortious duties (or at least the duty of care imposed by the tort of negligence) are owed by every one of us to anyone we can foresee would be likely to be affected by our actions. As a result of this, there is a potential for indeterminate liability (as it was once put by Cardozo CJ in the USA—liability in an indeterminate amount, for an indeterminate time, to an indeterminate class of people (*Ultramares Corp v Touche* (**1931**) **174 NE 441**)). In response to this haunting prospect for the insurance industry in particular, the courts have sought to impose a variety of pure policy-based restrictions on some of the boundaries of the law of torts. As it was once observed in the House of Lords, it is necessary to place restrictions on developments that allow a claimant to allege negligence on the assumption that, Good Samaritans and Pharisees alike, we are all neighbours, and that someone solvent must be liable in damages (see *CBS Songs Ltd v Amstrad Consumer Electronics plc* [1988] 2 All ER 484 at 497, *per* Lord Templeman).

2 Examination preparation

Since the law of torts is likely to be a compulsory subject, it is assumed that you will face an unseen examination, in which you must prepare answers to about three or four questions in the space of about two to three hours. How you prepare your own revision work is a matter for you to decide on, since organizational preference is a matter of individual choice, but it is important to read as widely as possible. In general, you should gather together the materials you have accumulated in a logical order and learn both the principles of law and what you have picked up in tutorials etc. during the year on how to apply that law to the questions.

a) Before the examination

It is impossible to say how much time you will need to revise for the examination, because the requirements for each individual will differ. But it is worth remembering that while too little revision is fatal, too much is also dangerous since it is possible to reach a peak before the date of the examination. It is no use knowing everything perfectly two weeks before the examination, especially if you become stale thereafter. The key is to reach your peak on the day of the examination, which is all very well to say, but very difficult to put into practice.

A number of general points of common sense need to be made about the period prior to the date of your examination:

- Clarify the date, time, and place of your examination for yourself. Do not rely on what others have told you.

- Be aware of the form of your examination—is it unseen, open-book, based on a 'seen' scenario? How long is the examination? How many questions have to be answered? Is there part of the examination that is compulsory? Is there more than one part to the examination and how many questions from each part have to be attempted?

- Reading past examination papers can be quite revealing. Some examiners may 'recycle' papers used in the past. However, be careful not to assume that a question that appears similar to one you have seen before (perhaps with different dates or characters) will be identical to the one you have before you. It is fairly common practice to make crucial factual changes that redirect the whole focus of the question.

- Listen to your tutors during the course of the year. Of course, you can only do this if you have attended classes during the year, but that goes without saying! Your tutors may have implicitly given guidance on the importance of a particular topic.

- If your tutor has 'adjusted' the running order of materials dealt with in lectures/seminars/tutorials etc. in the period immediately before the date of the examination, you ought to be able to assume that the topics dealt with towards the end will be on the examination paper.

- If you have special needs of any kind, make sure that you claim any allowance to which you are legitimately entitled. Some students are entitled to use a word processor, may be given an extra time allowance, or may be entitled to sit the examination in a private room.

b) The examination itself

The most important general note of guidance is not to panic. If you have revised well there will always be a sufficient number of questions on the paper for you to answer if you think in a cool, calm, and collected manner. Moreover, the easy part about taking an examination for which you have prepared well is getting to pass standard. It becomes progressively more difficult to go from a pass mark to lower second, upper second, or first-class standard.

You are now sitting in front of a collection of pens, chewing gum (valium??), a watch, an answer book, and an examination paper and the invigilator says you may commence. Remember do not panic.

Again a number of general points of guidance can be given:

- Check the examination rubric—if it says answer two questions from part A and two from part B, do not be tempted to answer three questions from part A.
- Read the whole paper before you decide what to answer.

How long your examination will be may differ from institution to institution. In times past the examination might have been three hours in duration with instructions to candidates to answer four or five questions from a selection of eight or nine. However, in a world of modularity, generally the length of an examination has been reduced as has the number of questions you must answer. It should go without saying—make sure you know what is required of you before the date of the examination.

The questions you will encounter may be of two different types. Some will be hypothetical problem questions and some will be essay questions, usually based on quotations from either an academic text or from a judgment, sometimes followed by the unhelpful instruction, 'DISCUSS'.

You need to read the whole paper and decide which questions you wish to answer. Many institutions now give students reading time before the examination commences, but you will only have a limited time in which to answer these questions. It will usually pay dividends to sketch out a brief plan of each of your preferred choices. At this stage do not worry about the candidate next to you who has already filled two reams of paper. Content yourself that he/she is (a) writing irrelevant rubbish in a totally unplanned fashion and (b) will have to reconsider what he/she has written because he/she has no plan to work from and may have omitted important details.

The plan is time-consuming, but is worthwhile. The advantage of planning the questions you propose to answer is that what you write should be directly relevant and you will avoid the serious problem of writing irrelevant material about issues which do not form part of the answer to the question. Moreover, if you have time left at the end, you can check your answer against the plan you prepared earlier.

Time management is crucial. If you take 10 minutes to read the paper and plan your campaign, this leaves 42 minutes per question in a four-question examination. Remember to make corresponding adjustments for shorter examinations that require fewer questions to be answered. Do not be tempted to substantially overrun this time allocation. It is far better to hand in a script in which you have completed the required number of questions, albeit incompletely, than to spend 90 minutes on question 1, and then rush off the remaining questions in what time is left.

c) The questions you will encounter

The examination in the Law of Tort will consist of two types of question—hypothetical problems and essay questions.

A number of general points should be remembered:

- Use a conventional style consisting of paragraphs, a beginning, a middle, and an end.
- Try to avoid note-form and at all costs do not be tempted to write in 'Txt' language.
- Spelling and grammar are important. If you have any particular difficulties on this count, you should have taken action well before the date of the examination. Remember, universities provide a lot of general help for difficulties of this kind.
- The law of torts is a common law subject. As such, it is based on case law. It is crucial that you can cite authority to support the arguments you use in answering a question. The most important aspects of a case are the principle of law and, as appropriate, the facts of the case, related to the principle. Worry less about the name of the case and its date. Provided the examiner can recognize the principle you are seeking to apply, you will still get some credit.

(i) Essay questions

The key issue here is that if you do not understand precisely what the question asks you to do, do not answer it. Be honest with yourself when you ask what the question means. It is far too easy for a single word to be picked up from the quotation, taken in isolation, and misinterpreted. Not infrequently candidates take the opportunity to write everything they know on a topic regardless of its relevance. Candidates who do this invariably fail on the question to which that sort of approach is adopted. It is important to answer the question the examiner has set rather than the question you would have liked her to set!

In answering an essay question, you should produce a very brief introduction, identifying no more than the issues you propose to cover and any line of argument you propose to adopt. The main body of the essay will develop on those introductory issues and arguments and should relate them to the question which has been set and, at all costs, you should use cases to support your argument. Finally, you need to conclude your essay by relating your arguments to the specific question set.

(ii) Hypothetical problem questions

Problem questions are often easier to answer than are essay questions since if you are prepared to look carefully, much of the answer is actually discoverable from the question itself. They are very similar to a crossword puzzle. There are clues telling you what you must or must not write about—these are usually in the rubric at the end of each question. For example, if you are told to advise Dick do not be tempted to advise Dora instead! Moreover, in many instances the facts of the problem will preclude a discussion of certain issues but highlight the importance of discussing other issues. For example, if you are told that a particular individual has done something negligently, there appears little point in discussing the issues of duty of care and breach of duty so that the question is likely to be on remedies, defences, remoteness, or causation.

When answering problem questions, it helps to state the relevant law in relation to particular issues and then apply that law to the relevant issue, making reference to the relevant facts of the problem. Do not be tempted to discuss legal principles which bear no relevance to the question. Here a plan of your intended answer is particularly useful. As you go along, it helps to relate each point you make to the question set. In practice, it is far better to state a legal principle and immediately apply it rather than to regurgitate all the law first and then apply it at the end of your answer. The importance of applying the law as you go along is that you can demonstrate to the examiner that you know what the law is, you understand it and that you can relate it to the problem. The last two stages are easily lost if you separate the law from its application. Moreover, the law first, application later, approach is distinctly 'examiner-unfriendly' because he/she has to flip back two pages to discover what was said about the law when it was stated to see if it has been accurately applied.

At all stages, you must support your argument with references to relevant case law or statutory authority. Do not be tempted to say, 'see *Donoghue v Stevenson*' since the examiner has 'seen' the case on many previous occasions. What you must do is to show that you understand the principle of law established by a case and why it is relevant to the question. In this process it may be necessary to relate the facts of the case, but more often than not, the facts of a case will not be relevant. Moreover, do not use an ability to tell stories about what happened in a particular case to disguise your knowledge of the law. From an examiner's point of view there is little more annoying than having to wade through pages of case facts, only to discover, at the end, that the candidate has little or no knowledge of the legal principle established by the case referred to.

Having stated the law and applied it, you may come to a definite conclusion, but you do not have to. The nature of problem questions is that they will be riddled with ambiguities. The important point is that you must be able to see all the various possibilities raised by the question, explain them, and show how they affect the particular facts of the problem. It is far better to present several possible arguments than to dogmatically insist that there is a right answer not permitting of any alternatives. Given that you may have several lines of argument, reaching a definitive conclusion may be difficult. But this does not matter. If you have presented the arguments for each of the alternative lines of thinking and you have applied your argument to the question in a logical fashion, that will suffice. Occasionally, you can be forgiven if you decide to sit on the fence. After all, if the right answer is so obvious, we would not need courts or lawyers and you would not be revising for this examination! As you will have appreciated by following a tort law course, there are endless problems of policy which make the subject very uncertain at times.

Showing that you appreciate what law is relevant is an important feature. You can do this by highlighting, in block capitals, the cases you use. But examiners should also read what comes between the case names, so that has to be accurate and relevant as well!

3 Coursework preparation

Unseen, and to a lesser extent, 'seen' examinations test your ability to remember relevant facts and principles of law and apply them to the situation identified by the examination question. But examinations should not be the only way in which your ability in the law of torts should be assessed. If this was the only method of assessment, students would be adept at giving a number of brief, handwritten summaries of solutions to a limited range of situations (usually selected for the academic difficulties they raise), in a ridiculously short period of time, without any detailed research in the light of the known facts. How many professional lawyers would give extempore advice to a client without having, first, researched the problem before giving that advice?

This is where coursework comes into its own. Most law of torts courses will contain an element of coursework that probably counts for about 40 or 50 per cent of the overall mark for the subject as a whole. On the percentage value, you should check the course documentation at an early stage in the year.

What a piece of coursework tests is your ability to research a topic and reflect upon the issues it raises. As such, starting your coursework the night before it is due to be handed in is not likely to yield wonderful results, as you will not have had the time to research the issues and reflect upon them. The fact that a coursework title is available well before the date for submission will allow you to discuss the problem with your peers. However, you should not allow this discussion to convert into collective plagiarism. All universities have rules on plagiarism and it is advisable to make yourself familiar with what you can and cannot do. Remember, if you do commit an act of plagiarism, you could be required to leave the university with no degree at all.

The following general points apply to coursework:

- High marks are achieved by depth of understanding, which can only be developed through extensive research. If you rely on just one secondary source, e.g. Murphy and Witting, *Street on Torts* (Oxford University Press, 2010) or Lunney and Oliphant's *Tort Law, Text and Materials* (Oxford University Press, 2010), you probably have not done enough.

- Make use of primary sources and academic commentary other than basic student textbooks.

- Keep in mind, at all times, what question has been asked.

2

The role of the law
of torts

Introduction

This chapter seeks to place the law of tort (or the law of torts?) in context. This statement, perhaps, requires elaboration, since the tort of negligence (considered in **Chapters 4, 5, and 6**) and its specific off-shoots relating to employer's liability (**Chapter 7**), occupiers' liability (**Chapter 8**) and product liability (**Chapter 9**) have dominated the development of the law of torts in the twentieth and twenty-first centuries. Furthermore, much of the case law on general defences (**Chapter 13**) is specific to the tort of negligence, as is also the case with many of the rules on remedies and limitation of actions (**Chapter 14**). The key feature of the tort of negligence is that it holds a person liable for his personal carelessness by requiring him to behave according to the standard of reasonable care. The tort of negligence is mainly concerned with actions that cause physical harm, although, increasingly, liability has been extended to acts (and some omissions) that cause foreseeable economic harm.

Despite the dominance of the tort of negligence, there are other torts, which seek to protect other interests. There is a group of torts, loosely described in **Chapter 3** as trespass to the person, which focuses on personal integrity and may, to an extent, be relevant to the issue of individual privacy. Tort law also recognizes the interests and responsibilities of landowners, seeking to balance the right of a landowner to use his land as he wishes, against the right of neighbours to expect landowners to operate and maintain their land in a reasonable manner (**Chapters 8 and 10**). Other torts protect both personal and business reputations (**Chapters 11 and 12**). Thus, it is a tort to defame a person by seeking, intentionally, to lower that person's reputation in the mind of right-thinking persons generally. In relation to personal property and business interests, there is a range of torts, broadly based on intentional conduct, that protects the interests of a person who owns or is in possession against deliberate interference by others, and torts that guard against causing loss by unlawful means, conspiracy, and inducement of another to commit a breach of contract.

What can be seen from this is that there is a wide range of torts, protecting a wide range of interests and those different torts may be based on principles of liability that differ from case to case. Accordingly, it may be more accurate to speak of a law of torts than a singular, common-principled, law of tort.

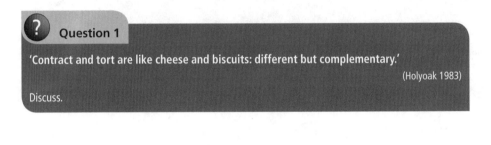

? Question 1

'Contract and tort are like cheese and biscuits: different but complementary.'

(Holyoak 1983)

Discuss.

Commentary

This question examines the relationship between tort law and the law of contract, since there are areas where these two core subjects overlap, such as the limited extent to which the tort of negligence can be used to recover economic loss. Some writers take the view that the juridical distinctions between the law of torts and other areas of common law civil liability have become so blurred that it might be better to speak of a law of obligations. However, there are features of the law of torts that serve to identify it as a set of ethical rules and principles of personal responsibility for one's actions that are primarily imposed by law.

 Answer plan

- The major differences between contractual and tortious liability.
- The generalizations which are said to distinguish the two branches of the common law, including the difference between the expectation interest and the status quo interest, the difference between fault-based and strict liability, and the view that contractual obligations are voluntarily assumed whereas tortious obligations are imposed by law.
- Whether there can be a concurrent liability in both contract and tort and whether contractual obligations override those which may be imposed by the law of torts.

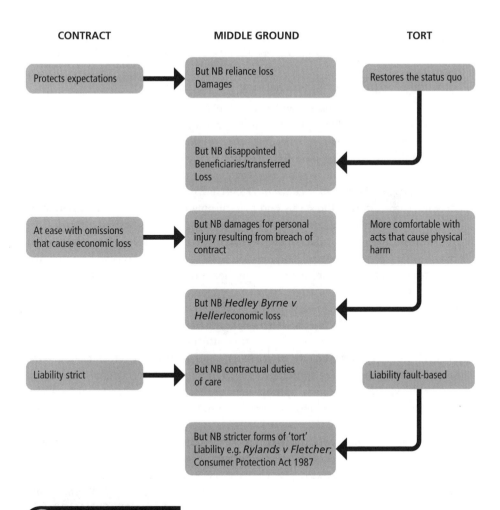

CONTRACT	MIDDLE GROUND	TORT
Protects expectations	But NB reliance loss Damages	Restores the status quo
	But NB disappointed Beneficiaries/transferred Loss	
At ease with omissions that cause economic loss	But NB damages for personal injury resulting from breach of contract	More comfortable with acts that cause physical harm
	But NB *Hedley Byrne v Heller*/economic loss	
Liability strict	But NB contractual duties of care	Liability fault-based
	But NB stricter forms of 'tort' Liability e.g. *Rylands v Fletcher*; Consumer Protection Act 1987	

Suggested answer

At first sight, the essential characteristics of contractual and tortious obligations are very different. The law of contract facilitates the process of making market transactions and provides a mechanism for the enforcement of promises by upholding legally binding agreements. However, it may also be argued that many contractual obligations are founded in the notion of reliance, since seriously made promises can cause the promisee to alter his position in the belief that the promise will be performed. Reliance is also an important feature in many tortious obligations, and it is in this arena that the closest similarities between the two types of obligation can be found.

Differences between tort and contract can be found in rules relating to remoteness of loss, quantification of damages, the difference between omissions and acts causing harm, and the law of limitation of actions. As the cause of action, in each case, accrues at a different time, possible problems may arise in cases of concurrent contractual and tortious liability: see *Midland Bank Trust Co v Hett, Stubbs & Kemp* [1979] Ch 384.

Protection of expectations and restoring the status quo

A number of generalizations are said to distinguish tortious and contractual liability, one of which is that the law of torts protects what a person already has, whereas the law of contract allows a person to become better off through the enforcement of promises, or that the law of contract protects the expectation interest by casting the claimant forward into the position he would have been in had the defendant performed his contractual promises (*Robinson v Harman* (1854) 1 Exch 850). In contrast, tort law is concerned with restoring the status quo by returning the claimant to the position he was in before the defendant committed his wrongful act (*Livingstone v Rawyards Coal Co* (1880) 5 App Cas 25). Rules of contract and tort both have a deterrent effect in that tort law deters people from engaging in acts that harm others, whereas contractual rules deter the breaking of promises, but this means that contract law is more attuned to dealing with omissions, whereas there are few instances in which the law of torts imposes a duty to act positively. While the typical loss in an action for breach of contract is the failure to make a gain which might otherwise have been made, the loss of profit representing the claimant's expectation also includes simple expenditure loss which, if included in the claimant's award of damages, will involve returning him to the position he was in before the contract was entered into. Moreover, where the contract is of a speculative nature, a more appropriate measure of damages may be the expense incurred by the claimant, thereby protecting the status quo interest alone (*Anglia TV Ltd v Reed* [1972] 1 QB 60).

While tort law is mainly concerned with protecting the status quo, there are instances in which it may also protect a person's expectation of gain, such as cases in which a solicitor has negligently advised a client so that a beneficiary fails to receive the bequest it was intended that he should receive (*Ross v Caunters* [1980] Ch 297; *White v Jones* [1995] 2 AC 207 and see also *Spring v Guardian Assurance plc* [1995] 2 AC 296). In these circumstances, the intended beneficiary has an expectation of gain which is not capable of protection by way of contractual rules, due to the restrictive effect of the doctrine of privity of contract. In these circumstances, the tort of negligence has been adapted to protect the intended beneficiary on the basis that the solicitor has voluntarily assumed responsibility for the accuracy of the advice given, even though this has the effect of giving the beneficiary the benefit of a contract to which he is not a party. Expectations can also be generated where there is a relationship between the defendant and the claimant that amounts to a bailment. In *Yearworth v North Bristol NHS Trust* [2009] EWCA Civ 37, prior to treatment for cancer, the claimant was advised that semen samples should be stored for possible future use. The defendants did not guarantee that the samples would be usable in the future, but they did undertake to look after the samples with all possible care. When the semen samples were allowed to thaw, the defendants were held to have unequivocally assumed responsibility for careful storage. As the relationship was akin to a contractual arrangement, it was held that damages could be awarded for the loss of enjoyment and other non-pecuniary family benefits.

The classic tort action, for damages for negligently inflicted personal injury, also takes account of expected future gains on the part of the claimant in the form of damages for lost earnings. Similarly, in an action for negligent misrepresentation damages are assessed according to principles applicable to the tort of deceit (**Misrepresentation Act 1967, s. 2(1)** and *Royscot Trust v Rogerson* [1991] 2 QB 297). However, in cases in which the misrepresentee has been induced to buy a business he may assert that he has failed to profit as much as he had expected. Where this has happened, the award of damages may take account of the profit the claimant might have made if he had acquired a notional similar business in the local area, but he must not be placed in the position he would have been in had the defendant's statement been accurate, since that would be tantamount to enforcing the defendant's 'promise': *East v Maurer* [1991] 2 All ER 773.

Cases in which a claimant has sought to recover damages for the loss of a chance have traditionally been regarded as contract actions, so that in *Chaplin v Hicks* [1911] 2 KB 786 the claimant was awarded damages in respect of the lost chance of progressing further in a beauty contest when she had been voted for by readers of the defendant's newspaper, but had not been contacted by the defendant regarding the next stage of the competition. As all of the final fifty contestants had about a one in four chance of being selected, the claimant was awarded 25 per cent of what she might have expected to gain had she been successful.

The issue of loss of a chance has also arisen in medical negligence cases where a claimant has been denied the chance of future good health due to a failed medical procedure (see *Hotson v East Berkshire Area Health Authority* [1987] 2 All ER 909; *Gregg v Scott* [2005] UKHL 2) or the chance of financial gain (see *Allied Maples Group Ltd v Simmons & Simmons* [1995] 1 WLR 1602). In the medical negligence cases, the courts have been reluctant to allow the claimant to succeed on the ground that the claimant must prove, on a balance of probability, that the defendant's act or omission was the cause of the claimant's condition and that if there is more than a 50 per cent chance that the claimant's condition would not have changed, the burden of proof cannot be said to have been satisfied.

Oddly, in *Allied Maples Group Ltd v Simmons & Simmons* [1995] 1 WLR 1602 the defendants incorrectly advised the claimants about the liabilities of a company that owned a chain of shops the claimants were interested in acquiring. Accurate advice would have given the claimants more than a speculative chance of protecting themselves from those liabilities, but there was no need for the claimants to show that the vendors would have consented to a contractual term protecting the claimants. In terms of the interests protected by the law of torts, it seems odd that loss of a chance of financial gain is treated more favourably than loss of the chance of a physical cure.

Voluntarily assumed and legally imposed obligations

A second distinction between tort and contract is said to be that contractual duties are voluntarily assumed via the terms of the contract and owed only to the other contracting party, whereas tortious duties are fixed by law, or owed to persons generally so that a duty can be owed to a complete stranger. However, in some contractual relationships the parties may not be directly known to each other, such as is the case with a typical hire purchase transaction in respect of a new car in which the car dealer fills out the paperwork but the contract is one between the customer and the finance company who make contact only by correspondence. While tortious duties are fixed by law, it should not be forgotten that some such duties arise out of a contractual relationship, as in the case of a supply of services where there is an implied term that the supplier will exercise reasonable care and skill in performing the contract (**Supply of Goods and Services Act 1982, s. 13**). Here, determining the extent of the supplier's duty to exercise reasonable care will require close attention to the specific undertakings which form the basis of the contract and it is important that any tortious duty found to exist should not undermine the express contractual undertakings of the parties: *Johnstone v Bloomsbury Health Authority* [1991] 2 All ER 293; *How Engineering v Southern Insulation* [2010] EWHC 1878 (TCC). However, the terms of the contract may also increase the level of care required of the supplier: see, e.g. *Greaves & Co (Contractors) Ltd v Baynham, Meikle & Partners* [1975] 3 All ER 99. The rule in *Hedley Byrne & Co Ltd v Heller & Partners Ltd* [1964] AC 465 requires the defendant to have voluntarily assumed responsibility for the accuracy of a statement communicated to the claimant. However, this meant that a defendant who disclaimed responsibility for the accuracy of the advice he gave, as in *Hedley Byrne,* could avoid liability. Subsequently, the requirement of voluntary assumption of responsibility came to be replaced by a requirement of reasonable reliance as the key indicator of liability on the part of the maker of a statement, as the concept of voluntary assumption of responsibility was thought to be inconsistent with the view that tortious duties are imposed by law: see *Smith v Eric S Bush (a firm)* [1990] 1 AC 831. Later case law has seen a revival of the requirement of voluntary assumption of responsibility, albeit explained differently to the way it was in *Hedley Byrne & Co v Heller & Partners Ltd*, where Lord Devlin required the relationship between the claimant and the defendant to be 'equivalent to contract' with the result that but for the absence of consideration there would have been a contractual relationship between the parties. In *Henderson v Merrett Syndicates Ltd* [1994] 3 All ER 506, it was considered that an insurance agent providing professional or quasi-professional services whose advice was relied upon by the claimant would owe a tortious duty of care to the claimant whether or not there existed between the parties a contractual relationship, provided the defendant had voluntarily assumed responsibility for the accuracy of the advice given. Moreover, it seems that this duty of care could be imposed despite the fact that the parties had chosen to structure their obligations through their contractual relationships. The difficulty this analysis presents, on the face of it, is that tortious duties are imposed by law rather than by way of any contractual arrangements. However, in *White v Jones* [1995] 1 All ER 691 Lords Goff and Browne-Wilkinson provided a more detailed explanation of the nature of the voluntary assumption of responsibility test, indicating that it was not the duty which was voluntarily assumed, since this must be imposed by law, but what must have been voluntarily assumed is the relationship between the defendant and the claimant, from which the duty can be inferred, especially in circumstances in which the claimant has reasonably relied upon the advice given by the defendant. The main problem with this particular analysis is that it is just as capable of applying to negligent acts, such as that of getting into a motor vehicle and driving it in a negligent fashion, which have traditionally been dealt with on the basis of an imposed duty not affected by considerations relating to the voluntariness of the defendant's conduct.

Henderson v Merrett Syndicates Ltd and *White v Jones* might be considered relevant only in the context of actions for negligently caused economic loss, but case law seems to suggest otherwise, especially where the defendant appears to have taken responsibility for a particular function, such as where an educational psychologist engaged by a local authority to advise on a child may be taken to have 'assumed responsibility' sufficient to owe a duty of care: *Phelps v Hillingdon LBC* [2001] 2 AC 619; see also *Watson v British Boxing Board of Control* [2001] QB 1134.

Strict and fault-based liability

A further distinction between contractual and tortious liability is said to be that contractual duties are strict whereas tortious duties are, generally, fault-based, but many contractual duties are fault-based, particularly those implied into contracts for the supply of services (**Supply of Goods and Services Act 1982, s. 13**). Moreover, where appropriate, collateral contracts have been used to impose liability on the maker of a misleading pre-contractual statement at a time when there was no liability in damages for negligent misrepresentation (*Esso Petroleum Ltd v Mardon* [1976] QB 801). In tort law the meaning of the term 'fault' is not easy to ascertain, but there are some torts that appear to impose strict liability, such as some duties imposed by the **Animals Act 1971, s. 2(1)**, maybe the rule in *Rylands v Fletcher* (1868) LR 3 HL 330, and the statutory torts created by the **Consumer Protection Act 1987, Part I**, and the **Nuclear Installations Act 1965**. Although there may appear to be some torts of strict liability, the way in which they have been interpreted may suggest the existence of a fault-based element. The non-natural use requirement of the rule in *Rylands v Fletcher* suggests that it is necessary to consider the general benefit to the community of the defendant's activity, the locality in which the accumulation took place, and the reasonableness of the precautions taken by the defendant to guard against the risk of harm to others (*Mason v Levy Auto Parts of England* [1967] 2 QB 530; *Cambridge Water Co v Eastern Counties Leather plc* [1994] 2 WLR 53). These elements are very similar to those relevant to an enquiry into the issue of breach of duty of care in negligence or reasonable user in nuisance; both of which are substantially fault-based enquiries. The concept of defectiveness in the **Consumer Protection Act 1987, s. 3** has been defined in terms of legitimate consumer expectations, which can serve to impose a standard markedly stricter than the requirement that a defendant should exercise reasonable care: see *A v National Blood Authority* [2001] 3 All ER 289. However, the presence of a development risks defence in the **Consumer Protection Act 1987, s. 4(1)(e)** substantially reduces the impact of the Act, since it is a defence for a producer to show that the state of scientific and technological development at the time a product was put into circulation was not such as to allow a product defect to be discovered. The best illustration of the complementary nature of contractual and tortious liability can be found in cases in which a person is concurrently liable in contract and in tort. Since tortious liability is regarded as parasitic (*Pacific Associates Inc v Baxter* [1990] QB 993), there is no sense in searching for liability in tort where the parties are in a contractual relationship (*Tai Hing Cotton Mill v Liu Chong Hing Bank Ltd* [1986] 1 AC 80). It follows that liability in tort cannot be any greater than that expressly or impliedly created by the contract between the parties: conversely, the mere fact that a contract exists between the parties and that they have chosen to structure their obligations by reference to that contract will not preclude the existence of a tortious duty of care where the contract remains silent on the matter which is in dispute (*Henderson v Merrett Syndicates Ltd* [1994] 3 All ER 506; cf. *National Bank of Greece SA v Pinios SA* [1990] 1 AC 637). As Lord Goff noted, it may be that the facts of *Henderson*, considered above, are unusual, since in most cases where there is a chain of contractual relationships, the imposition of a tortious duty of care might be inconsistent with the contractual undertakings of the parties. Thus it has been observed that in the case of a building contract under which there are contractual arrangements between the building owner and the main contractor and arrangements between the main contractor and the various subcontractors, it will not normally be the case that a subcontractor will owe any tortious duty of care to the building owner, since the subcontractor will not normally voluntarily undertake responsibility to the owner (*Barclays Bank plc v Fairclough Building Ltd* [1995] 1 All ER 289). Likewise the NHBC house building contract expressly creates staggered liability so as to be inconsistent with the creation of further tortious duties: *Robinson v PE Jones (Contractors) Ltd* [2011] EWCA Civ 119.

Furthermore, there may be circumstances in which the contractual undertakings of the parties are consistent with general tortious duties of care. Thus, if an employer fails to provide a safe system of work by requiring an employee to be available for work for an average of 88 hours a week, the contractual term requiring attendance may amount to a limitation of liability in respect of negligently caused personal injury, so that the provisions of the **Unfair Contract Terms Act 1977, s. 2(1)** may be invoked (*Johnstone v Bloomsbury Health Authority* [1991] 2 All ER 293).

In conclusion, it is clear that there are differences between contractual and tortious liability, but the two branches of the common law of obligations work together towards the provision of workable remedies for the claimant. However, where tort and contract intermix, the generality of the tort system will normally give way to the more specific inter-party obligations undertaken by way of contract.

⭐ **Examiner's tip**

Remember that tort does not trump contract—a duty of care will only be imposed if the parties are already in a contractual relationship if the tortious duty is consistent with the obligations arising under the contract.

Question 2

Consider the defects, if any, in the fault system of accident compensation and the case for reform of the means of accident compensation.

Commentary

Question 2 seeks to consider a function served by tort law, although it has to be said that the objective of accident compensation is primarily achieved through state intervention and private insurance. Many of the criticisms of the role of the law of torts in this regard must be read in the light of the more detailed consideration of remedies for breach of tortious obligations in **Chapter 14**. Although tort law does play a minor role in the overall picture of accident compensation, it should be appreciated that it is only a very small part of a broader range of state-provided compensation schemes, albeit somewhat more generous to those who are successful.

Answer plan

- Criticisms of the tort system based on cost, delay, the lump sum method of compensation, and general unpredictability of outcome.
- Alternatives to the tort system such as state insurance, no-fault accident compensation schemes, and private insurance.

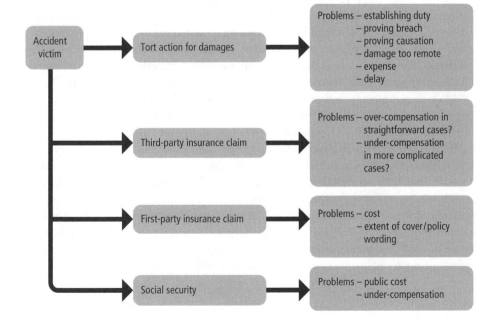

⇨ **Suggested answer**

In practice, much of the law of torts is concerned with compensating the victim of the defendant's accidental wrongdoing by providing a remedy (damages) in respect of the claimant's injuries, and not to punish the defendant. The same objective can also be achieved through private insurance, such as first-party insurance whereby the victim is insured against a specified type of accident or third-party insurance, whereby the accident causer is insured against harm that might be suffered by a third party. However, the insurance solution brings with it a number of problems, considered below. Finally, the compensation objective may be achieved through state social security payments, which tend to be lower than awards of damages. This is likely to be the most common source of accident compensation where no one can be blamed, as will be the case with accidents at home. However, state compensation suffers from the drawback that it must be paid for out of taxation which is a politically sensitive process and can deter governments.

Tort law is concerned with compensation for *wrongs*, namely some fault-based conduct on the defendant's part that causes the claimant harm, so that tortious rules are concerned with *loss shifting* by making the blameworthy defendant responsible for the loss suffered by the claimant. The insurance option has introduced the notion of *loss distribution* under which the question is not who is to blame for an accident, but who can most easily bear the loss caused by a particular accident (see, e.g. *Smith v Eric S Bush (a firm)* [1989] 2 WLR 790, *per* Lord Griffiths).

Where a potential cause of accidents is identified, such as the motor car or the work accident, insurance against the risk created may become compulsory or a regime of strict tort liability may be introduced by Parliament, e.g. the **Road Traffic Act 1988, ss. 143–5** and the **Employer's Liability (Compulsory Insurance) Act 1969**. Moreover, in relation to motor vehicle accidents, there is also a safety net provided by the Motor Insurers' Bureau (MIB) which has created a pool funded from insurance premiums to cover cases in which an accident is caused by an uninsured or untraced driver, including intentionally caused injuries (*Gardner v Moore* [1984] AC 548), but not accidents on private property, since the compulsory insurance scheme under the **Road Traffic Act 1988** is inapplicable (*Charlton v Fisher* [2001] EWCA Civ 112). A similar scheme does not apply to injuries at work and this does influence judicial decisions (*Dunbar v A & B Painters Ltd* [1986] 2 Lloyd's Rep 38, 42–3 *per* Balcombe LJ).

If an accident victim can successfully pursue a tort action, he stands to recover more than a person with no such claim, since English law adopts a system of 'full compensation' that takes account of the actual earnings of the claimant and pays in respect of both pecuniary loss (e.g. expense incurred) and non-pecuniary loss (e.g. pain and suffering). However, the number of successful tort claimants is relatively small because the claimant must be able to prove that the defendant caused the 'accident' (including disease or disability where man-made) by committing an actionable tort and, if there is no fault, no matter how serious the injury, no action will lie in tort and the victim will have to rely on such state benefits as might be available (see e.g. *Tomlinson v Congleton Borough Council* [2003] UKHL 47).

Other criticisms of the tort system as a means of accident compensation are those of cost, delay, unpredictability of outcome, the unbalanced way in which payments are made, and the problem of how compensation payments are used by the claimant after an award has been made.

In 1977, the administrative cost of tort compensation was said to be 85 per cent of the total amount paid out (Report of the Royal Commission on Compensation for Personal Injuries, Cmnd 7054, 1978). In contrast, the equivalent cost of the social security system came to only 11 per cent. Moreover, since a tort litigant must commence proceedings against the defendant, funds must be available at the outset. The development of 'no win, no fee' schemes for some personal injury cases, in which the legal adviser is only remunerated if the action succeeds, was allowed in order to facilitate the commencement of proceedings. These schemes appear to encourage settlements between the claimant's lawyer and the defendant's insurer, especially since insurers may prefer to settle a claim rather than litigate in order to avoid the costs associated with the latter. It is a popular conception that 'no win no fee' arrangements may lead to the development of a 'compensation culture' which in turn could promote an insurance crisis. However, the Better Regulation Task Force suggests that the number of personal injury claims has fallen since the introduction of such schemes: *Better Routes to Redress* (2004). The danger of a belief in the existence of a compensation culture is that potential defendants may become over-cautious. However, recent case law suggests that the judiciary is aware of that danger and has sought to assert the importance of personal responsibility for one's own actions: *Tomlinson v Congleton BC* [2003] UKHL 47. (See also **Compensation Act 2006, s. 1** which requires a court to have regard to the likely effect on desirable activity of requiring steps to be taken to guard against a breach of duty.)

Proving fault is a major cause of the cost of the tort system as the claimant must show who is to blame for the harm he has suffered. The assessment of damages requires the preparation of expert reports, and because of the adversarial system of trial legal costs are duplicated as both parties require their own experts and lawyers.

The tort system is also very slow in delivering compensation, especially in complicated cases in which obstacles thrown in the path of claimants might tempt them to give up the process. The Civil Justice Review (Cm 394, 1988) revealed that in 1987 an average High Court case took five years and a county court case three years. The Civil Justice Review (*Access to Justice*, 1996) or 'Woolf Report' suggested radical reforms designed to speed up the whole system of dispensing civil justice. There is a fast-track procedure for personal injury actions valued at £15,000 or less and a county court small claims procedure that covers personal injury where the award is unlikely to exceed £1,000. A trial must normally take place within 30 weeks of the date on which the writ was issued and trials are expected to last hours rather than days. In the case of complex claims, such as those for medical negligence and all claims valued at more than £15,000 there is a multi-track system subject to close judicial scrutiny for the purposes of time management. Judicial case management is intended to avoid time-wasting tactics on the part of defendants and their insurers that could lengthen proceedings. A claimant may make an offer of settlement, similar to the previous system whereby a defendant could make a payment into court. Importantly, an unreasonable refusal by a defendant to accept the offer of settlement may work against him.

The unpredictability of the tort system is notorious. Even where the claimant can show that he is owed a duty of care, he must also establish breach of that duty, factual causation, and hope that the loss he has suffered is not too remote and that the court does not regard his losses as having been exaggerated: *Painting v University of Oxford* [2005] EWCA Civ 161. Even where the claimant is successful, the final award may be less than was anticipated, which must be offset against the cost of bringing the action in the first place. Because of this pressure, claimants will often settle out of court, resulting in under-compensation in more complicated cases. At the same time, the cost incurred by insurance companies in processing smaller claims may lead to an over-generous settlement. The lump sum method of paying damages has been criticized as it requires the court to guess at what the future might bring and may fail to take account of events that exacerbate the claimant's loss. Courts can make an award of provisional damages where it is proved or admitted that there is a chance that the claimant will develop some disease or suffer serious deterioration in his physical or mental condition: **Senior Courts Act 1981, s. 32A.**

Given the uncertainties surrounding lump sum payments, it is not surprising that in the case of traumatic, long-term injuries, the accountancy-driven system of structured settlements has begun to prove popular (see **Damages Act 1996, s. 5**). Since the **Courts Act 2003, s. 100 and s. 101**, the **Damages Act 1996, s. 2(1)** has been amended so that, provided the continuity of payment under the order is reasonably secure, a structured settlement or periodic payment may be made, involving the substitution of an annuity-based pension in place of a lump sum payment. For these purposes continuity of payment is regarded as secure if there is a Financial Services Compensation Scheme in place or a government minister has provided a guarantee in respect of a designated body under the **Damages Act 1996, s. 6**, or where the defendant is a government department or health service body. The annuity, purchased by the defendant's insurers, can make provision for events which may affect the need for increased compensation at various stages in the continued life of the accident victim and avoids the problem of profligacy on the part of claimants following receipt of an award of lump sum damages. The court should have regard to the best interests of the claimant rather than give effect to what the claimant (or his family) wants. (See *Thompstone v Tameside & Glossop Acute Services NHS Trust* [2008] EWCA Civ 5.)

The decision to allow courts to order a means of compensation other than that asked for by the claimant is controversial. The periodic payment system also has, as its focus, the annual financial needs of the long-term accident victim. This different focus is argued to result in increased compensation in many cases that will have to be funded by the defendant's insurers. (See Lewis, 'The Politics and Economics of Tort Law' (2006) 69 MLR 418, 442.) The advantages of the structured settlement fall on both sides. Not only does the annuity system avoid payment of tax by accident victims (**Taxes Act 1988, ss. 329A and 329B,** added by the **Finance Act 1995, s. 142**) but it also results in substantial savings over the normal lump sum system so far as insurers are concerned. An immediate lump sum can be paid to the victim to meet identified need, e.g. the adaptation of a house. In contrast, probably the most serious criticism of the system of structured settlements is that a very small percentage of accident victims are deriving a substantial benefit at the expense of ordinary taxpayers, which effectively benefits such victims to an even greater extent than is already the case where an accident victim is successful in an action for damages. By way of contrast, there may be ordinary taxpayers who have subsidized the award to such a victim who are themselves injured, but unable to maintain an action for damages themselves because they have suffered a non-tortious injury.

Alternatives to the fault-based tort system include private insurance by the victim and the tortfeasor; the greater use of rules of strict liability based on an assumption that the potential tortfeasor should be insured against the possible risk of damage to others; public insurance schemes such as the social security system and more wide-ranging public insurance schemes such as that employed in New Zealand by virtue of the **Accident Rehabilitation and Compensation Insurance Act 1992** which effectively eliminates the need to have recourse to the law of torts as a system of accident compensation. A very limited scheme was also introduced by the **NHS Redress Act 2006,** which applies to low value medical negligence claims in order to avoid litigation, while also providing for a full investigation of the incident alleged to have caused the harm, so that lessons can be learned and improvements to procedures implemented.

Some types of accident damage can be insured against by means of life, permanent health, and personal accident policies. Moreover, some employers will take out occupational sick pay policies which go beyond state provision for short-term income replacement. The prevalence of such policies depends on the social class into which the accident victim falls and the nature of his employment. Before private insurance can replace the tort system, there must be a change in taxation policy so that all members of society are paid in such a way that they can afford to take out private insurance, and the problem remains that the low paid will not have the resources to cover themselves adequately. The fact that private insurance policies exist does not, at present, make any difference to an award of tort damages since the courts do not wish to discourage thrift, so payments out of privately arranged insurance will not be deducted from an award of tort damages (*Bradburn v Great Western Railway* (1874) **LR 10 Ex 1**).

The present social security system provides for payment in respect of a number of injuries which may or may not result from the fault of an identified defendant and some of which are based on nothing more than the means of the claimant (e.g. income support and housing benefit). Payments, generally, are based on subsistence levels rather than the total loss suffered by the claimant and, as such, will be considerably less than an award of tort damages.

Roughly, benefits can be divided into those relating to non-industrial injuries and those relating to injury suffered at work. The former include statutory sick pay, which is replaced by incapacity benefit after 28 weeks of illness, provided there have been sufficient contributions to the national insurance scheme. Claimants not qualifying for the latter, however, may claim severe disablement allowance. In severe cases, where constant care is required, a claim for disability living allowance may be permitted. In respect of industrial injuries, disablement benefit may be awarded to an injured employee. The important consideration concerning these benefits is that, at present, they are deductible from an award of tort damages, but they are not based on the principle of full compensation since the amount payable is based on average earnings rather than on the actual earnings of the accident victim. On the other hand, as has been observed, the social security system is more efficient in terms of the cost of making payments to individuals and can be geared to the needs of the claimant as and when new financial difficulties might arise.

? Question 3

'Economic analysis can never be an all-embracing explanation of the objectives of tort law… efficiency must at some point yield before…other guidelines.'

(Murphy and Witting, *Street on Torts*)

In the light of this statement, discuss the extent to which efficiency and justice are objectives of the law of torts.

Commentary

This question deals with the law of torts as a deterrent to harm-causing activities. It has been seen that the compensation system is concerned with the victim's loss. However, the mere existence of potential liability on the part of a defendant also serves as a deterrent to others that might persuade them not to engage in harmful conduct. In part, this raises the matter of the relationship between the law of torts and the criminal law, but also considers the increasing interest of economists in the use of tortious rules as a means of achieving efficient results. An answer should consider the various objectives of tort law, in particular whether the compensation objective is ever sacrificed at the hands of arguments based on economic efficiency, but other factors, such as justice, are also relevant in ascertaining the role of tort law.

Answer plan

- The primary objectives of economic analysis of legal rules.
- Efficiency versus justice as objectives of the law of torts.

- The distinction between loss shifting and loss distribution.
- The role of private first-party and third-party insurance.
- The different notions of justice across the whole range of tortious liability.

⇨ Suggested answer

The law of torts is primarily concerned with accidents which result in physical harm to the person or to property and occasionally some economic harm. The law of torts may deter wrongdoers from engaging in activities which harm others but it also provides a remedy for those who are harmed as a result of the defendant's wrongs.

On an economic analysis, the desire to deter a person from engaging in activities which cause harm to others is seen as a primary objective, since prevention is preferable to cure (see Calabresi, *The Cost of Accidents* (1970), Posner, 'A Theory of Negligence' (1972) 1 J Leg St 29; *The Economic Analysis of Law*, 6th edn (Aspen: 2003)). A legal rule is perceived to be efficient if it deters wrongdoing in a cost-effective manner, although efficiency should not be promoted to the extent that the plight of an injured person is forgotten. Somehow, in applying legal rules, the courts have to reach a suitable balance between efficiency and justice. If we have a rule that a claimant is entitled to sue a defendant for the losses caused by his wrongdoing, the costs and benefits of such a rule need to be balanced. Those costs include court and lawyers' costs, the cost of recovering damages once an award has been made, the cost of taking out liability insurance to protect against being sued, and the cost arising from defendants taking unnecessary defensive precautions. These costs have to be balanced against the fact that the public purse is relieved of the financial cost of treating the injured claimant, the fact that disruption to the claimant's life is minimized by the award, and the fact that others may be deterred from engaging in similar conduct to that of the defendant.

The deterrent effect of legal rules can be overstated as only a small number of torts require deliberate misconduct and, in particular, the tort of negligence is based on carelessness alone. However, tort law appears to operate as a deterrent when exemplary damages are awarded (see *Cassell & Co v Broome* [1972] AC 1027), but it is important that a victim of a tort should not be freely able to recover windfall damages at public expense: *Kuddus v Chief Constable of Leicestershire* [2001] UKHL 29.

The conflict between efficiency and justice can be seen most clearly in negligence cases when deciding if the defendant is in breach of a duty of care. An efficiency-based rule is that an act is only negligent if reasonable precautions have not been taken by the defendant (*Latimer v AEC Ltd* [1953] AC 643), since it is clear that taking every possible precaution to guard against a minor risk of harm would be uneconomic. The number of road traffic accidents could be reduced by imposing a mandatory speed limit of 10 mph, but this would hardly be socially acceptable or economically efficient.

Virtually every activity has some capacity for causing harm, but if its likelihood is minimal, such as damage caused by a cricket ball, when the evidence shows that only six balls have been hit from a cricket ground in 30 years, there is no need to take special precautions (*Bolton v Stone* [1951] AC 850). However, if the magnitude of risk created by the defendant is such as to expose a highly vulnerable claimant to increased risk of harm, greater care should be taken (*Paris v Stepney BC* [1951] AC 367), thereby illustrating the importance of practical justice in special cases. Risk assessment is an increasingly common practice in business and if a particular risk is a distinct possibility, precautions such as the provision of proper training for employees should be made: see *Davis v Stena Line* [2005] EWHC 420 (QB). However, to require a defendant to take precautions to guard against the crass stupidity of the claimant would be to go too far; see e.g. *Tomlinson v Congleton BC* [2003] UKHL 47.

If the law imposes liability for certain acts, this appears to have a deterrent effect if people realize they will have to pay damages and as a result refrain from conducting themselves in that way, but there are instances in which there may be little the defendant can do to avoid causing harm to others. For example, since the test of liability is objectively based, the defendant who does his incompetent best may still be liable since he is judged by the standards of the reasonable man and not by reference to his own ability (*Nettleship v Weston* [1971] 2 QB 691). Moreover, in many cases the defendant's fault amounts to little more than inadvertence, so that the defendant may not have foreseen the danger he creates, but the law may state that he has not acted in the same way as a reasonable man would have acted and is therefore liable.

The view that tort rules are deterrent in effect is understandable where liability is based on the notion of loss shifting, namely that there should be no liability without proof of fault and that a person who is at fault should pay for the losses he has caused. Modern tort law is now dominated by the presence of an insurance market and there has been a move towards a system of compensation based on loss distribution. The insurance market is such that major causes of accidents can be identified and those who engage in accident-causing activities, such as employers, drivers, and manufacturers, may be required or encouraged to take out insurance to cover potential risks of loss. Moreover, in most cases, the insured accident causer can pass on the cost of insurance to the consumers of his product or his service, thereby spreading the costs associated with the accident risk more broadly. Since the accident causer must be or ought to be insured the problem is that it is not the wrongdoer who pays damages but his insurer, and this undermines the argument that tort rules serve a deterrent purpose, since it is rarely the defendant who foots the bill. Insurers might be able to deter tortious misconduct, but there is little evidence that they do. It is possible to raise premiums in the case of bad risks, but this is never likely to deter mere inadvertence.

It is arguable that the threat of liability based on the notion of fault is likely to result in the adoption of defensive practices which might prove detrimental to the interests of the client or patient in professional negligence cases. The possibility that disproportionate measures might be taken is often put forward as a reason for not imposing a duty of care. But the concept of defensive practices is not confined to cases of medical malpractice and may extend into other areas such as the exercise of statutory powers by a public authority charged with a responsibility for protecting others (see *X (minors) v*

Bedfordshire County Council [1995] 3 WLR 152) or the police (see *Hill v Chief Constable of West Yorkshire* [1988] 2 All ER 238), or the Crown Prosecution Service (see *Elguzouli-Daf v Metropolitan Police Commissioner* [1995] 1 All ER 833). In contrast, there is some evidence to suggest that the fear of defensive practices is now given less emphasis: see *Fairchild v Glenhaven Funeral Services Ltd* [2002] UKHL 22, Lord Bingham; *Gregg v Scott* [2005] UKHL 2, Lord Nicholls (dissenting).

The deterrence and economic efficiency arguments are closely related as if an activity imposes costs on others, those costs should be reflected in the true cost of the harm-causing activity (see Calabresi, *The Cost of Accidents* (1970), p. 69). This would mean that the cost of a car not fitted with seatbelts, or one which is to be driven by a 17-year-old, would have to reflect the increased accident costs associated with the use of such a vehicle, but it is often difficult to identify the true cause of an accident. An efficient solution is not necessarily a fair solution as it may result in a decision to the effect that an accident victim is the best risk-bearer where he should have been insured, but that will leave the victim uncompensated.

Fairness or justice is seen by lawyers as the underlying purpose of tort rules. This may be rights-based justice under which the claimant is entitled to protection against unjustifiable interferences with his civil rights, such as rules which protect against battery, assault, and false imprisonment. However, although there is no common law rule protecting privacy (see *Wainwright v Home Office* [2003] UKHL 53), there is a right to prevent the wrongful disclosure of private information based on the **European Convention on Human Rights (ECHR)**, art. 8 (see *Campbell v MGN* [2004] UKHL 22; *McKennitt v Ash* [2006] EWCA Civ 1714; *Murray v Express Newspapers* [2008] EWCA Civ 446).

A second notion of justice is based on a balance of competing interests such as those of neighbouring landowners to be found in *Rylands v Fletcher* (1868) LR 3 HL 330 and the tort of private nuisance. These torts seek to balance competing ownership rights and take account of the notion of give and take. What matters is whether the defendant's use of his land is reasonable, having regard to matters such as the location of his property, the duration of the nuisance, whether the claimant's land use is unduly sensitive and, in relation to the remedy provided, whether the defendant's activity is socially useful.

Where a claimant is injured as a result of the defendant's tort, there is a primary need for the harm to be adequately compensated. It is generally accepted that victims of modern social conditions should not be left to bear all the costs. Thus in addition to liability rules under which most of the costs are borne by insurance, there are public compensation schemes to deal with matters such as invalidity payments, sickness benefit, and other forms of social security payment. The principal issue has become not who is to blame for a particular variety of harm, but who is in the best position to pay for the consequences of that harm? Instead of simply shifting losses from the claimant to the wrongdoing defendant, modern tort law and its accompaniments work on the basis of loss spreading. This notion is reflected in modern rules on vicarious and product liability which recognize that employers and producers are in a position to spread the cost of accidents by charging higher prices for their goods and services or by other cost-cutting measures combined with the secure knowledge that relevant insurance will cover any award of damages which might be ordered.

? Question 4

'The trouble with English tort law is that it fails to provide sufficient protection to each citizen's inalienable right to bodily integrity and freedom from interference.'

Discuss.

Commentary

This question centres upon the extent to which there is a right of privacy in English law and how various tortious rules have been manipulated, in the past, in an attempt to protect that right. The **Human Rights Act 1998** may be relevant where the alleged invasion of privacy is perpetrated, especially in the context of the wrongful disclosure of private information.

Answer plan

- Harassment as a tort.
- Limits of the tort of private nuisance.
- Limits of the torts of assault, battery and false imprisonment.
- Scope of the **Protection from Harassment Act 1997**.
- Effect of the **Human Rights Act 1998**.

Suggested answer

Common law rules do not overtly recognize a specific right to privacy (see *Wainwright v Home Office* [2003] UKHL 53; *Wong v Parkside NHS Trust* [2001] EWCA Civ 1721), nor is harassment a discrete tort (*Kaye v Robertson* [1991] FSR 62). However, aspects of several different torts do have the effect of protecting a person's privacy, provided the specific ingredients of that tort are satisfied. Moreover, one of the effects of the **Human Rights Act 1998** is to make it easier for a claimant to sue in respect of the wrongful disclosure of private information.

The tort of private nuisance, in certain circumstances, may provide a solution. In *Hunter v Canary Wharf* [1997] 2 All ER 426 it was held that an act of harassment might amount to a private nuisance if there was an unreasonable interference with the claimant's proprietary interest in the land subject to the act of harassment, however that action would not protect a person with no protected proprietary interest. However, it has been suggested in *McKenna v British Aluminium Ltd* [2002] Env LR 30 that a person with no proprietary interest might have an arguable case under the **Human Rights Act 1988** if there is an interference with family and private life.

The tort of assault requires the direct infliction of a reasonable apprehension of a battery (*Thomas v NUM* [1986] Ch 20), but this does not mean that persistent abusive telephone calls are incapable of being an assault, if the telephoned words or silences are threatening, especially as the claimant is unlikely to be aware of the whereabouts of the stalker: *R v Ireland* [1998] AC 147.

The rule in *Wilkinson v Downton* [1897] 2 QB 57 requires the defendant to have 'wilfully done an act calculated to cause harm to the claimant', but this may not cover cases in which harm is indirectly inflicted. Moreover, since *Wainwright v Home Office* [2003] UKHL 53 there is some doubt as to whether the rule in *Wilkinson* serves any useful purpose.

The **Protection from Harassment Act 1997** gives a remedy for harassing conduct that has injurious effects (**s. 3(2)**), but the Act does not apply to one-off incidents as there is a requirement that the conduct complained of should have occurred on at least two occasions (**s. 7(3)**).

The protection of a person's right to privacy has to be reconsidered in the light of the **Human Rights Act (HRA) 1998** which requires, where possible, that legislation must be interpreted in a way that is compatible with rights provided for in the ECHR (**HRA, s. 3**). Furthermore, it is also provided that it is unlawful for a public authority to act in a manner that is incompatible with a Convention right (**HRA, s. 6**). One of the rights provided for in the Convention is a right to respect for private and family life (**ECHR, art. 8**). This might suggest that the restrictive approach to the issue of privacy adopted at common law might change, at least where the actions of public authorities are concerned. Actions on the part of the Home Office would fit this description, but the Convention also covers 'persons whose functions are functions of a public nature' (**HRA, s. 6(3)(b)**), which appears to include the actions of universities, schools, and local authorities, and possibly a tabloid newspaper, insofar as information provision can be regarded as a 'public function'.

In *Campbell v MGN Ltd* [2004] UKHL 22 it was held that a newspaper commits a tort where it unjustifiably discloses to a third party any information about the claimant that the defendant newspaper knows or ought to know is private information. By publishing a photograph of Ms Campbell leaving a Narcotics Anonymous meeting MGN Ltd had committed this tort, which has its roots in the equitable wrong of breach of confidence, but is not constrained by some of the limits applicable to the long-established equitable wrong (see *Theakston v MGN* [2002] EWHC 137 (QB)).

The new tort requires the courts to perform an unusual balancing act in that it straddles two distinct human rights. On the one hand the publisher has a right to freedom of expression (**ECHR, art. 10**), but the claimant has a right not to have private information about him unjustifiably disclosed to a third party (**ECHR, art. 8**), and it is the balance between these two articles that forms the content of the new tort: *McKennitt v Ash* [2006] EWCA Civ 1714 at [11] *per* Buxton LJ. Thus a court will be faced with difficult questions such as how private is the information and how important is it that this aspect of the claimant's privacy should be protected? On the other side it will be necessary to ask whether, in disclosing the information, the defendant was expressing himself. If this is the case, it must then be asked how important is it not to restrict the defendant's right to do so?

According to Lord Nicholls and Baroness Hale in *Campbell* the test to apply is whether the claimant has a reasonable expectation that his privacy be protected. However, this is difficult to apply because of its circularity, and in other jurisdictions a test based on the reasonable person's reaction to publication has been used (see *Australian Broadcasting Corp v Lenah Game Meats* (2001) 208 CLR 199 at [99] *per* Gleeson CJ). However, the 'reasonable person's reaction test' may be criticized on the ground that it may not work where the information relates to a disturbed adult or a very young child (see *T v BBC* [2007] EWHC 1683 (QB); *Murray v Express Newspapers plc* [2008] EWCA Civ 446).

An important consideration is whether or not the information is of a type that the claimant would want to control the dissemination of (*Campbell v MGN* [2004] UKHL 22 at [51] *per* Lord Hoffmann). It would appear that information related to a person's sexuality or health, information that has been stored secretly, such as that in a private diary, information supplied consequent to a confidential relationship and, perhaps, financial information will normally fall within this reasonable expectation test: see e.g. *Mosley v News Group Newspapers Ltd* [2008] EWHC 1777 (QB). However, some such information may have become so widely available that the claimant can no longer claim to have a reasonable expectation of controlling its dissemination (*Lord Browne of Madingley v Associated Newspapers Ltd* [2007] EWCA Civ 295).

On the other side of the balance, it needs to be determined what constitutes freedom of expression. For these purposes, political speech in a democratic society is most deserving of protection. Other factors to consider include whether or not it is in the public interest to disclose the information. Some guidance on this matter may be found in the Press Complaints Commission's Code of Practice which indicates that the public interest includes (a) detecting or exposing crime or a serious demeanour, (b) protecting health and safety, and (c) preventing the public from being misled by some statement or action of an individual or organization. In interpreting the first of these factors, it would appear that the crime alleged to have been committed must be of a serious nature and will not include sexual misconduct which does not involve a significant breach of the criminal law (*Mosley v News Group Newspapers Ltd* [2008] EWHC 1777 (QB)). But if the sexual conduct is criminal in nature, disclosure may be justified: *LNS v Persons Unknown* [2010] EWHC 119 (QB).

Moreover, it would appear that public figures, including famous football players and other types of celebrity, may have to expect a greater degree of exposure as they have chosen to place themselves in the 'public eye', especially if the 'celebrity' has made untrue public denials relating to extra-marital affairs (see *A v B & C* **[2002] EWCA Civ 337**). However, the decision in *Campbell* does indicate that public figures cannot always expect information of any type concerning their private lives to be publishable.

Further reading

Atiyah, P. S., *The Damages Lottery* (Oxford: Hart Publishing, 1997), ch. 8.

Atiyah, P. S., and Stapleton J., 'Tort, Insurance and Ideology' (1995) 58 MLR 820.

Burrows, A., 'Dividing the Law of Obligations', ch. 1 in *Understanding the Law of Obligations* (Oxford: Hart Publishing, 1998).

Buxton, R., 'The Human Rights Act and Private Law' (2000) 116 LQR 48.

Cane, P., *Atiyah's Accidents: Compensation and the Law*? (Cambridge: Cambridge University Press, 2006), chs 16 and 19.

Cane, P., *The Anatomy of Tort Law* (Oxford: Hart Publishing, 1997), ch. 6, especially pp. 181–6 and 201–4.

Cane, P., *The Anatomy of Tort Law* (Oxford: Hart Publishing, 1997), ch. 7, 'Anatomy, Functions and Effect'.

Cane, P., *Tort Law and Economic Interests* (Oxford: Clarendon Press, 1996), ch. 10, 'The Province and Aims of Tort Law'.

Holyoak, J., 'Contract and Tort after *Junior Books*' (1983) 99 LQR 591.

Moreham, N., 'Privacy in the Common Law: A Doctrinal and Theoretical Analysis' (2005) 121 LQR 628.

Morgan, J., 'Tort, Insurance and Incoherence' (2004) 67 MLR 384.

Murphy, J., and Witting, C., *Street on Torts*, 13th edn (Oxford: Oxford University Press, 2010).

Smith, S., *Contract Theory* (Clarendon Law Series) (Oxford: Oxford University Press 2004), pp. 43–6, 72–4, and 96–7.

Whittaker, S., 'The Application of the Broad Principle of Hedley-Byrne as between Parties to a Contract' (1997) 17 LS 169.

Williams, G., 'The Aims of the Law of Tort' (1951) 4 CLP 137.

3

Trespass to the person

Introduction

Trespass to the person is one of the oldest torts and overlaps with the criminal law. Many of the wrongs which amount to a trespass to the person also amount to the commission of a crime, but be careful not to introduce Criminal Law concepts into answers on Tort. These torts are fault-based and require proof of intention; they are also actionable per se, that is, there is no need for the claimant to prove that damage has been suffered. Instead, it is sufficient that the defendant has infringed the claimant's interest in bodily security. However, the fact that there has been no damage may be relevant in determining the remedy. The interest primarily protected by the torts of battery, assault, and false imprisonment is the right of the individual to respect for bodily security. As such these are 'civil liberties' torts and have lost much of their practical importance due to the rise of the tort of negligence in the field of personal injury compensation. The three questions which follow cover a range of issues arising out of all three torts, as well as considering the possibility of liability arising under the principle in the case of *Wilkinson v Downton* [1897] 2 QB 57, a principle the relevance of which has been diminished more recently in light both of the availability of a claim in negligence, and of potential remedies under the **Protection from Harassment Act 1997**.

? **Question 1**

Harry, a scruffy-looking young man, is chatting in the street with his friend Terry. Both are drinking from bottles of lager.

Gino, accompanied by his 15-year-old daughter, Bella, passes by on the other side of the street and makes loud, offensive comments on Harry's and Terry's appearance. Harry moves towards Gino, swearing loudly and brandishing his bottle in a menacing manner, but is unable to cross the road due to the volume of traffic.

Gino returns ten minutes later, carrying a baseball bat. Gino takes a swing at Harry, but misses and strikes Terry instead, knocking him unconscious. Harry, fearing for his own safety, strikes Gino over the head with his bottle, which breaks, causing a splinter of glass to cut Bella, who runs home. David, a witness to these events, grabs Harry by the neck and restrains him by means of a stranglehold until PC Plod arrives. Terry, still unconscious, is taken to hospital where Dr John decides that emergency surgery is necessary, entailing a blood transfusion, to which Terry would have objected on religious grounds had he been conscious.

Bella is taken to hospital by her mother, Sophia. Dr John advises Sophia that it would be wise for Bella to have an antibiotic injection. Bella objects because she is passionately opposed to all drugs that have been developed using animal testing, but Sophia tells Dr John to ignore her daughter's objections. Accordingly, Dr John arranges for the injection to be given.

Advise all the parties of their potential liabilities in trespass to the person.

Commentary

The facts in the scenario raise issues of assault and battery, and relevant defences. One good way to approach it would be to identify all the potential assaults, and deal with them together so as to avoid the need for repetition—then adopt the same approach to the batteries. You should concentrate on the specifics raised by the facts, e.g. there is a distinction to be drawn between the offensive comments and the threats, or the significance of defences in relation to medical treatment. There is limited scope for addressing false imprisonment so a brief reference to this will suffice—sufficient to reveal that you know the core elements and how it overlaps with battery. Logically, defences should be discussed and applied only when the substance of the torts has been established.

Examiner's tip

The rubric (i.e. the instruction at the bottom of the problem) refers only to trespass to the person so do not be tempted to stray into coverage of other torts.

Answer plan

- State the core elements of trespass to the person.
- Identify and discuss capacity to carry out the threat and imminence of the harm threatened.

- Discuss the core content of battery.
- Identify the notion of transferred intent.
- Consider the ingredients of self-defence.
- Consider the possibility of lawful arrest.
- Discuss the role of consent and necessity in relation to emergency and other medical treatment.

⇨ Suggested answer

Trespass to the person comprises three torts: assault, battery, and false imprisonment. These torts involve intentional acts (but not omissions) and are actionable without proof of harm.

Harry's threatening attitude towards Gino and Gino's swinging of the baseball bat require consideration of assault, which is defined as an act which causes another person reasonably to apprehend the infliction of immediate, unlawful, force on his person (*Collins v Wilcock* [1984] 3 All ER 374). Gino's comments are unlikely to convey any threat of force and when Harry swears and waves a bottle in response to Gino's comments, it may be that the content of his words is insufficient to amount to a threat. Until recently, there was no clear legal authority that words alone could constitute an assault. Dicta went both ways (see *Meade's case* (1823) 1 Lew CC 184 (no assault); *R v Wilson* [1955] 1 WLR 493 (assault)). The House of Lords in *R v Ireland* [1997] 4 All ER 225 took the view that even a silent phone call could amount to an assault. Lord Steyn said, 'A thing said is also a thing done.' Accordingly it is now clear that the use of words alone may be an assault taking into account all the surrounding circumstances. What is clear is that where there are words accompanied by a threatening act or gesture, as in the question, there can be an assault (*Read v Coker* (1853) 13 CB 850).

So, if Harry's words together with his actions are capable of amounting in law and in fact to an assault, there remains the issue that there cannot be an assault unless the threat is immediate and gives rise to a reasonable apprehension of the imminent infliction of a battery. Thus a threat, no matter how violent, cannot be an assault if the claimant does not reasonably believe he is about to suffer a battery. In *Thomas v N.U.M. (South Wales Area)* [1986] Ch 20 the claimant was on a bus full of working miners during the miners' strike. Although the threats from striking pickets were violent and extremely threatening, there could be in law no reasonable apprehension of immediate battery due to the safety of the bus and the presence of a police escort. In the problem, the barrier posed by the volume of traffic on the road dividing Harry from Gino may suggest that there is no reason to believe that a battery was imminent.

Of course, when Gino returns with the baseball bat and takes a swing at Harry there may well be an assault as it would be reasonable for Harry to anticipate an immediate battery in the circumstances. In this circumstance the swing may also be an assault on Terry who receives the blow.

Battery was defined by Goff LJ in *Collins v Wilcock* [1984] 3 All ER 374 as 'the actual infliction of unlawful force on another person', and requires a direct intentional contact. In the problem the potential batteries are: first, when Gino strikes Terry with the baseball bat; second, the use of the bottle; third, the arrest; and fourth, the interventions by the doctor. In all of these instances there are direct intentional acts resulting in contact, that go well beyond anything that could be regarded as acceptable in everyday life.

It would seem, then, that the issue in the question is one of intention. Gino intends to hit Harry, but in fact strikes Terry. It is important to remember that for trespass, the intention should relate to the act rather than to the consequences of the act. But there still remains the issue of whether English tort law recognizes the notion of transferred intent. This concept is recognized in English criminal law: *R v Latimer* (1886) 17 QBD 359 and in the civil law of the USA. More recently, the High Court in *Bici v Ministry of Defence* [2004] EWHC 786 (QB) adopted the principle, applying dicta in the Northern Irish case, *Livingstone v Ministry of Defence* [1984] NI 356. The decision is not without its critics, but it seems logical enough that if Gino intends to strike Harry he should also be liable in damages for the infringement of Terry's personal security.

It is unlikely that Gino can successfully plead self-defence, not least because his act occurs some time after the event when the threat, if any, has disappeared. Also, this defence requires that actions taken in self-defence should be proportionate to the threat. In *Cross v Kirby* (2000) *The Times*, 5 April the defendant was attacked by the claimant (a baseball bat wielding anti-hunt protestor). After having been struck several blows he wrestled the bat from the claimant and struck him with it, fracturing the claimant's skull. The Court of Appeal held that, in all the circumstances, the trial judge had weighed the conduct too finely and that the use of force was not disproportionate. In Gino's case, the use of an offensive weapon is probably out of proportion to the threat posed by a bottle in the hands of two abusive delinquents on the other side of a busy street.

By contrast, Harry's response to the threat posed by Gino may be justified in self-defence. In light of the threat posed by a person wielding a baseball bat, it is possible that the use of a bottle may be regarded as proportionate and he may be taken to have acted reasonably in all the circumstances.

There remain the issues of consent and public policy, which are relevant to the fight between Gino and Harry. It has been said that in the case of an ordinary fight with fists, none of the participants will be permitted an action for damages on the ground that they all consent to their injuries, though if the claimant's conduct is trivial and the defendant's conduct is totally out of proportion the defences referred to will not be available. This was the gist of *Lane v Holloway* [1968] 1 QB 379 where the defendant's response was grossly excessive compared to the conduct of the claimant. That case also rejected provocation as a defence; so here the perceived insult would not deprive Harry of his action in assault. Moreover, a person who sets out to attack another but who 'gets more than he bargained for', as seems to be the case with Gino, may also find his claim barred on grounds of public policy as in *Murphy v Culhane* [1977] QB 94. The so-called 'illegality defence', or *ex turpi causa non oritur actio*, operates to prevent a successful action by an individual whose claim depends for its success on an unlawful act of the claimant of a very serious nature. As a matter of public policy the courts will not be seen to be supporting a claim in such circumstances. Lastly, despite the fact that, prior to the enactment of the **Law Reform (Contributory Negligence) Act 1945**, it was disputed whether the defence of contributory negligence applied to the tort of trespass, it was held in *Barnes v Nayer* (1986) *The Times*, **19 December** that a claimant's contributory negligence can amount to fault for the purposes of the 1945 Act.

Applying a stranglehold is capable of amounting to a battery, and if it constitutes an 'unlawful imposition of constraint on another's freedom of movement from a particular place' (*Collins v Wilcock* [1984] **3 All ER 374**) it may be a false imprisonment. The circumstances suggest that David does this by way of a citizen's arrest. **Section 24A of the Police and Criminal Evidence Act 1984 (PACE)** excuses a private individual who makes an arrest provided certain conditions are met. A person other than a police officer may arrest a person actually committing or reasonably suspected of committing an indictable offence, provided such an offence has taken place. A serious assault on an individual is an indictable offence and it is reasonably clear that an offence has been committed as David has witnessed the events. **Section 24A** also requires that arrest is necessary to prevent injury to another or to prevent the suspect escaping, and that it is not practicable to wait for a police officer to make the arrest. Under **s. 28**, the person arrested must be told that he is under arrest and the reason for his arrest, either at the time, or as soon as practicable thereafter. If the arrest is made by a person who is not a constable, as here, the common law rule is that the arrested person does not have to be informed of the reason for his arrest if the circumstances make the reason obvious—in *Christie v Leachinsky* [1947] **AC 573** the House of Lords suggested that this would be so if someone were caught red-handed. All of these requirements seem to be satisfied with the result that David probably has not committed a tort.

David may also invoke the right in a citizen to take reasonable steps to prevent an actual or imminent breach of the peace—as occurred in *Albert v Lavin* [1981] **3 All ER 878** where an off-duty police officer was held to be entitled to restrain someone who was a threat to the peace—provided reasonable force was used and the restraint was for no longer than necessary. David seems to meet these conditions.

Dr John's surgical treatment of Terry is, prima facie, a battery within the definition given above, and the usual defence in relation to medical treatment—consent—is not an option since Terry is unconscious. Clearly, it would not be in the public interest for the treatment of patients incapable of consenting to be an actionable battery, so there must be some other justification. In *F v West Berkshire Health Authority* [1989] **2 All ER 545**, Lord Goff explained the nature of the defence of necessity, which permits, in the case of an emergency concerning a temporarily incapacitated patient, such treatment as is necessary in order to save life, ensure improvement, or to prevent physical or mental deterioration, and no more. The scope of the intervention is to be tested according to the *Bolam* test used in considering the appropriate standard of care in medical cases (*Bolam v Friern Hospital Management Committee* [1957] **1 WLR 582**). This approach is consistent with public policy, which recognizes a presumption in favour of the preservation of life. Since the operation on Terry is considered to be essential, the defence of necessity would seem to apply unless Dr John can be taken to have been aware of Terry's objection to receiving blood other than his own. On the facts, there is nothing to suggest that Dr John is aware of Terry's religious objections so his actions will probably be justified.

The injury to Bella, though not intentional in the ordinary sense, may be a further battery if the same reasoning is applied as when Gino struck Terry, subject only to whether or not Harry is able to plead successfully that he was acting proportionately in self-defence. A further battery may occur when Dr John proceeds to administer an injection. Here, the defence of necessity is not appropriate as there are several potential sources of consent by which the act may be rendered lawful. First, there is parental consent by Sophia, Bella's mother. As Bella is 15 years old, and therefore a minor, her mother's consent is valid. Then there is Bella herself. If Bella had been aged 16, she would be presumed, by virtue of **s. 8(1) of the Family Law Reform Act 1969**, to have the capacity to consent to medical treatment. As Bella is 15, the question of capacity will be determined by reference to the *Gillick* test. In *Gillick v West Norfolk and Wisbech Area Health Authority* **[1986] AC 112**, a mother sought judicial review of a policy that children under 16 could be given contraceptive advice without parental consent. The House of Lords said the issue was whether the minor had sufficient maturity and understanding of the issues involved in treatment. Under this test, provided Bella was of sufficient maturity to understand what is involved in having an injection, she could consent for herself.

In the question, however, Bella is refusing to consent, so Dr John has a consent (from the mother) and a refusal (from the patient). In *Re R (a minor)* [1991] 4 All ER 177, a 15-year-old girl who suffered phases of disturbed behaviour had refused sedative treatment and wardship proceedings were commenced by a local authority. The Court of Appeal considered that a court has wider powers than a parent and can override a withholding of consent if this is in the patient's best interests. It appeared from the case that some kind of balancing process was to be undertaken, between the respective strengths of the child's refusal and the opposing consent. In *Re W (a minor) (medical treatment)* [1992] 4 All ER 627, Lord Donaldson reconsidered and rejected his analogy in *Re R* that those capable of giving consent could be regarded as 'keyholders', as this implied that the status of refusal was equal to that of consent. On reflection, he said that a better analogy was that of a 'flak jacket', since 'anyone who gives [a doctor] a flak jacket (i.e. consent) may take it back, but the doctor only needs one and so long as he continues to have one he has the legal right to proceed'. In the problem, provided Dr John has valid consent from Bella's mother he commits no battery on Bella.

? Question 2

Eric had just won a darts game in the Dog & Duck public house. As he returned to his seat he was cheered on by his friends; Jockey, his opponent, slapped his shoulder in a hearty fashion to congratulate him on his victory. Eric was off balance at the time and tumbled over, injuring himself. Eric shouted at Jockey, 'You swine, you did that on purpose, I'll see you outside in two minutes.'

Fearing the worst, Sid, the owner of the Dog & Duck, grabbed Eric by the shirt collar and frog-marched him to his office. Eric resisted violently and aimed a punch at Sid, but missed.

Sid managed to calm Eric and persuaded him to remain in the office in order to avoid further trouble. Having left the office, Sid asked two burly friends, Peter and Phil, to ensure that Eric did not leave the ground floor room. Four hours later, Sid called the police. In the meantime, Eric slept off the effect of the alcohol and was unaware that Peter and Phil were there.

Consider whether or not any causes of action in trespass to the person are revealed by these facts.

Commentary

The rubric clearly indicates you are dealing with trespass so it would be wrong to deal with other potentially applicable torts such as negligence. Your introduction may be used to summarize the common elements of the forms of trespass, and comment on the underlying rationale. By dealing with matters thematically much repetition can be avoided, e.g. take all the possible instances of battery together, then all the instances of assault and so on. Deal with the application of each tort or defence as you work your way systematically through the answer.

Answer plan

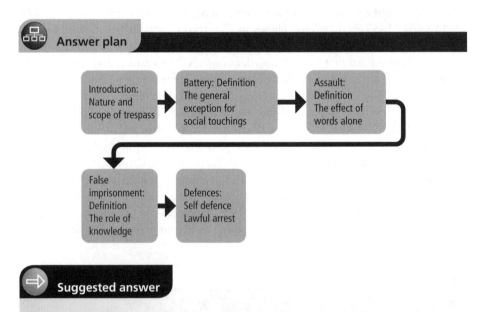

Introduction: Nature and scope of trespass → Battery: Definition The general exception for social touchings → Assault: Definition The effect of words alone

False imprisonment: Definition The role of knowledge → Defences: Self defence Lawful arrest

Suggested answer

Trespass to the person comprises three distinct torts (battery, assault, and false imprisonment) which have certain characteristics in common. They all require direct, intentional acts as opposed to omissions ('not doing is no trespass': *Case of the Six Carpenters*

(1610) 8 Co Rep 146a), and are actionable per se, i.e. complete without the need for proof of actual harm which makes them very effective as a means of controlling invasions of liberty (especially by those in authority).

What batteries are revealed by these facts?

Battery may be defined as the intentional application of direct force to the person which is undesired by the claimant. Thus, for Eric to succeed in battery it would be necessary to demonstrate that Jockey and Sid intended the contact, though, according to the Court of Appeal in *Wilson v Pringle* [1986] 2 All ER 440, he need not show that they intended the harm which results.

On the face of it, slapping on the shoulder is a battery: there has been an intentional touching without the consent of the claimant. The law was clearly stated in *Collins v Wilcock* [1984] 3 All ER 374 that the merest touching would suffice because the law could not be expected to distinguish between varying degrees of force. Goff LJ explained that this general principle was designed to protect the value that the law placed on the liberty of the subject and the inviolability of the human body, but went on to say that the broad principle was a starting point. In addition to the usual defences, he identified a general exception to cover all touchings which were generally acceptable as part and parcel of everyday life, e.g. tapping someone on the shoulder to gain their attention. Lord Goff reiterated this view in *F v West Berkshire Health Authority* [1989] 2 All ER 545, 'respectfully doubting' Croom-Johnson LJ's attempt in *Wilson v Pringle* to introduce a requirement of hostility. The lack of any legal definition of 'hostility' and the circularity of Croom-Johnson LJ's attempt to explain it (he described the touching in *Collins v Wilcock* as unlawful and therefore hostile and a battery) mean hostility contributes nothing as a test. Lord Goff further suggested, obiter, that such things as a prank that gets out of hand, an over-friendly slap on the back, or an operation where the surgeon mistakenly thinks that there is consent when there is none, could not be categorized as hostile but could still be held to be unlawful. So here it would have to be decided whether or not the contact went beyond general touching acceptable in everyday life. It may well be that hearty congratulations, even from an opponent, could be seen as generally acceptable within a sporting context.

Whether the grabbing of Eric by Sid and the frog-marching amounts to a battery will be tested by reference to the approach in *Collins v Wilcock*. It is likely that the type of touching goes beyond what is generally acceptable in everyday life, as indeed was the detention for questioning in that case. If this is so, Eric may have a defence, see later.

What assaults are revealed?

An assault was defined by Goff LJ in *Collins v Wilcock* as 'an act which causes another reasonably to apprehend the infliction of immediate, unlawful force on his person'. In the course of resisting violently, Eric aims a punch at Sid, but misses. The fact that there is no contact means that there cannot be a battery, but there is the possibility of an assault since a violent punch is likely to cause Sid to fear, quite reasonably, for his own safety.

Eric shouts abuse at Jockey and threatens to see him outside in two minutes. The words alone may be no more than mere abuse but may amount to an assault provided that they would arouse in a reasonable person the apprehension of the immediate infliction of a battery. Despite earlier contradictory dicta in *Meade's case* (1823) **1 Lew CC 184** (no assault) and *R v Wilson* **[1955] 1 WLR 493** (assault), the House of Lords held in *R v Ireland* **[1997] 4 All ER 225** that a silent telephone call (or one where words are spoken) may be an assault where it creates the necessary element of apprehension in the mind of the claimant. Jockey would have to show that the words used and Eric's general behaviour disclose an immediate threat. He says he wishes to speak with Jockey in two minutes' time but the whole of the behaviour has to be examined in light of its impact on a reasonable person in the claimant's position. Thus, it is clear that the language used by the threatener will have to be examined to determine whether his words contain an immediate threat of a battery or whether the words used negate the threatening nature of the rest of the defendant's language, as in *Turbervell v Savadge* (1669) **1 Mod Rep 3** where the defendant was held in essence to have said, 'Much as I would like to, I will not attack you now.'

Moreover, before anything can be done to carry out the threat, Sid intervenes. A threat, no matter how violent, cannot be an assault if the claimant does not believe he will be battered; for example, if the defendant is, to the claimant's knowledge, unable to carry out the threat, as in *Thomas v N.U.M. (South Wales Area)* **[1986] Ch 20** where the claimants, although violently threatened, were safe inside a bus with a police escort. Accordingly, while Eric remains in Sid's office there seems little for Jockey to fear.

Are there any false imprisonments?

In taking hold of Eric and frog-marching him into his office Sid may commit not only a battery but also a false imprisonment, and by detaining Eric in the office, he may also be committing false imprisonment. This was defined by Goff LJ in *Collins v Wilcock* as 'the unlawful imposition of constraint on another's freedom of movement from a particular place'. The restraint must be total: in *Bird v Jones* (1845) **7 QB 742** the fact that the claimant could proceed by an alternative, though more lengthy, route meant that he had not been subject to a tort and was not justified in using force to make his way past an obstruction. On the facts, Eric does not know that if he tries to leave the office, he will be prevented from doing so by Peter and Phil. The House of Lords in *R v Bournewood Community and Mental Health NHS Trust ex parte L* **[1998] 1 All ER 634** concluded that there must be circumstances amounting to a factual detention of the claimant. The case concerned a voluntary mental health in-patient who would have been restrained had he attempted to leave a hospital and who was subject to ongoing supervision. This was held by the majority not to be false imprisonment, though subsequently the European Court of Human Rights in *HL v UK* **45508/99 (2004) ECHR 471** held the same patient's detention to have been in breach of his Article 5 rights.

As Eric is first unaware of the men outside the office, and later falls asleep, it must be considered whether a claimant must be aware of the fact of restraint in order for the tort to be committed. The House of Lords in *Murray v Minister of Defence* **[1988] 1**

WLR 692 resolved a conflict between two earlier cases and decided this point in favour of the view that the claimant need not know of the fact of restraint. In *Herring v Boyle* (1834) 149 ER 1126 a mother had twice gone to school to collect her son but was refused because the fees had not been paid. The son was not aware of what was going on and the equivalent of the Court of Appeal held that in the absence of knowledge there was no false imprisonment. The House of Lords in *Murray* described this decision as 'extraordinary' and preferred the approach of Atkin LJ in *Meering v Grahame-White Aviation* (1919) 122 LT 44 (although that decision was arguably *per incuriam* since the Court of Appeal omitted to consider the binding decision in *Herring's* case). In *Meering*, the claimant was detained in an office pending the arrival of the police. He was unaware that security guards had been placed outside who would have detained him if he had tried to leave. Atkin LJ concluded that this amounted to false imprisonment and that someone could be falsely imprisoned when asleep, or drunk or insane, or only an infant.

The House of Lords in *Murray* concluded that there were good policy reasons why the tort should continue to protect the claimant irrespective of his knowledge of the detention. This analysis suggests that the basic elements of false imprisonment are made out.

What defences are available to Eric?

Section 24A of the Police and Criminal Evidence Act 1984 provides two defences in respect of 'citizen's arrest'. They permit any person to arrest without a warrant anyone who is either committing an indictable offence, or who is reasonably believed to have committed an indictable offence. In the problem there is no indication such an offence has been committed.

Alternatively, Eric may seek to invoke the common law power permitting citizens to deal with actual or reasonably apprehended breaches of the peace: see *Albert v Lavin* [1981] 3 All ER 878. If Eric's behaviour gives rise to a threat to the peace then the consequent detention may be lawful provided it is not for an unreasonable period. On the facts, the delay of four hours may well take the action beyond what is reasonable and turn a justified detention into a false imprisonment.

? Question 3

During a party at Yasser's house, Barney, a house guest and known prankster, jumped from the doorway in a darkened corridor, with a sheet over his head just as Wilma, another guest, was passing but he did not make physical contact with her. Wilma fainted with shock and banged her head causing bruising. Barney carried her into a room and left her there to recover.

One hour later, Barney went to see if Wilma had recovered, but found Wilma asleep. Barney shook her gently to ask if she was feeling better. Wilma awoke, and believing she was being attacked, struck violently at Barney with a poker from the fireplace. Barney suffered a fractured skull.

Consider the potential liability of the parties in trespass to the person and under the principle in *Wilkinson v Downton*.

 Commentary

This question centres on the constituent elements of the intentional torts relating to trespass to the person—assault, battery, and false imprisonment—and calls for some comment on the principles underpinning the various torts. The rubric also includes reference to the principle in **Wilkinson v Downton**, so your answer should identify the original principle but also show how it has undergone more recent developments. If you deal with each tort distinctly, e.g. all the possible batteries should be examined together, you will avoid the need for repetition. The question also highlights self-defence.

⭐ **Examiner's tip**

Two of the issues in this problem involve significant recent development through case law. Your answer will therefore be much stronger if it demonstrates an awareness of the Court of Appeal's decision in **Wong v Parkside Health NHS Trust [2001] EWCA Civ 1721** and that of the House of Lords in **Wainwright v Home Office [2003] UKHL 53**; and detailed knowledge of the principles in **Ashley v Chief Constable [2008] UKHL 25** relating to self-defence and mistake of facts.

 Answer plan

- Brief description of the relevant torts.
- The content of assault.
- *Wilkinson v Downton*.
- The content of battery.
- The requisite intent.
- False imprisonment and awareness of the fact of detention.
- Omissions.
- Defence of necessity.
- Self-defence.

Suggested answer

Trespass to the person comprises three distinct torts (battery, assault, and false imprisonment) which have certain characteristics in common. They all require direct, intentional acts as opposed to omissions ('not doing is no trespass': *Case of the Six Carpenters* **(1610) 8 Co Rep 146a)**, and are actionable per se, i.e. complete without the need for proof of actual harm which makes them very effective as a means of controlling invasions of liberty (especially by those in authority). The principle in *Wilkinson v Downton* **[1897] 2 QB 57** as currently explained by the House of Lords in *Wainwright v Home Office* **[2003] UKHL 53** requires actual harm that was intentionally caused, though it differs from trespass in that the harm may arise indirectly.

Will an action lie in assault in respect of the prank where Barney jumps out? Assault was defined by Goff LJ in *Collins v Wilcock* **[1984] 3 All ER 374** as an act that causes another 'reasonably to apprehend the infliction of immediate, unlawful force on his person', so the question here is whether or not Wilma was placed in such a fear. If she was then she may succeed in assault. Although Barney may well say that he did not intend any harm, in line with the view on battery, while the act must be intentional, an intention to harm is not required. Barney may also say that his action was only a joke. But, again motive is irrelevant and the action should be judged objectively.

It may also be possible to establish that in respect of Barney's prank an action may lie under the rule in *Wilkinson v Downton* even though more harm resulted than was intended, as in *Janvier Sweeney* **[1919] 2 KB 316**, where some harm had been intended but greater harm resulted. The principle states that a person may be liable for 'wilful conduct calculated to cause harm' from which actual harm results. A problem with the law at the time of *Wilkinson v Downton* was that the psychiatric injury suffered by the victim was not recoverable under the law of negligence. The court therefore adopted the wording 'calculated to cause harm' to ensure that recovery was possible. Although a negligence action may now be available, the principle remains useful insofar as indirect intended harm is concerned, and a case such as *Wilkinson v Downton* itself might be decided the same way.

For many years, the scope of the tort was open to debate both as to the meaning of harm, and as to the required degree of intention. These issues have been resolved in recent cases. In *Wainwright v Home Office* **[2003] UKHL 53**, the House of Lords has now held that liability under this rule is dependent upon an actual intention to cause harm. The House of Lords also confirmed that anything less than actual physical damage or recognizable psychiatric damage was unlikely to be recoverable under the principle in *Wilkinson v Downton* and neither Lord Hoffmann nor Lord Scott were keen to see the tort extended. To recover under the principle it would have to be shown that Barney had actually intended to cause harm to Wilma even though this might have occurred indirectly. Here, it may well be the case that Barney was merely engaging in well intentioned horseplay so as to contribute to the party atmosphere. Also, one might question whether or not the faint would be sufficient harm for these purposes, though her head injury may qualify.

Battery was defined by Goff LJ in *Collins v Wilcock* **[1984] 3 All ER 374** as 'the actual infliction of unlawful force on another person', and requires a direct intentional contact. As there was no initial physical contact with Wilma no battery has been committed by Barney at that stage.

On the other hand, there was some physical contact between them when Barney picked Wilma up and, later, when he shook her. Wilma may have an action for battery in respect of these touchings no matter how slight unless a defence applies. In *Cole v Turner* **(1704) 6 Mod 149**, Holt CJ said that 'the least touching of another in anger is a battery'. The Court of Appeal in *Wilson v Pringle* **[1986] 2 All ER 440**, held that for an action in battery to succeed, the 'touching must be proved to be hostile touching'. The requirement of hostility, and more particularly its meaning, has generated controversy. This view is inconsistent with the earlier comments of Goff LJ in *Collins v Wilcock* and the later comments of Lord Goff in *F v West Berkshire Health Authority* **[1989] 2 All ER 545**. These were that, as a general principle, all touchings no matter how slight were capable of amounting to battery, subject to the general defences and a further 'general exception' in respect of all touching acceptable as part and parcel of everyday life. The view of Lord Goff is preferable given the lack of clarity as to the legal meaning of hostility and that the only explanation of this in *Wilson v Pringle* was largely circular. Lord Goff 'respectfully doubted' whether there is any requirement that the physical contact must be hostile and stated that a prank that gets out of hand, or an over-friendly slap on the back could amount to battery even though they are not hostile acts. Similarly, a person who pushes another into a swimming pool by way of a joke would also be liable for battery, as in *Williams v Humphrey* **(1975)** *The Times,* **20 February**. On this basis, Barney could be liable unless he can show that picking Wilma up as a consequence of the prank was 'generally acceptable in the ordinary conduct of daily life'. Similarly, when Barney shook Wilma, the gentleness of the shake is not the key point, but whether the shake could be described as generally acceptable in everyday life. In *Mepstead v DPP* **[1996] COD 13** the gentle holding of the arm of a motorist to calm him down when a fixed penalty notice had been given was not sufficient to amount to a battery.

Of course, when Wilma lashes out violently at Barney and causes substantial harm to him there is, on the face of it, a battery. The real issue here is the availability of self-defence, which will be discussed shortly.

Are any defences available to the parties? Undoubtedly the touching of Wilma by Barney when he picked her up amounts on the face of it to a battery, but was it justifiable? The only defence that seems to be relevant is that of necessity. This was explored in *F v West Berkshire Health Authority* which concerned the legal basis on which the sterilization of an adult with significant learning difficulties could be justified when neither she nor anyone else was able to give or withhold consent to this treatment. The House of Lords held that the principle of necessity could operate to justify the procedure. The case acknowledged a distinction between permanently incapacitated patients, for whom the guiding principle was what was in the best interests of the patient judged according to the principle in *Bolam v Friern Hospital Management Committee* **[1957] 1 WLR 582**, and the temporarily incapacitated where the principle justifies only such treatment as is necessary for saving and conserving life. For such patients, the principle of autonomy dictates that they should not be deprived, e.g. while unconscious, of their overriding right to self-determination. On this basis, Barney's actions may appear to be justified. On the other hand, it was held in *Rigby v Chief Constable of Northampton-shire* [1985] 2 All ER 985 (a case on trespass to land) that the defence of necessity cannot be relied on where that necessity arose from the defendant's tortious behaviour. If Barney's original act of scaring Wilma was a tort then necessity may not be available as a defence.

As regards self-defence and Wilma, there are two distinct issues. Is self-defence available where there is a mistake as to the facts? What degree of force is available to the victim? In *Ashley v Chief Constable of Sussex Police* [2008] UKHL 25 the House of Lords addressed the first question. A police officer was part of a group of armed officers executing an arrest of the claimant's brother. The police officer mistakenly thought that he was under threat of attack and fired his weapon, killing the brother. There was a preliminary issue as to whether or not the case should be allowed to go for trial and, if so, what was the test which governed the use of violence in such circumstances. The House of Lords confirmed the decision of the Court of Appeal that the necessity must be judged on the facts as the defendant honestly believed them to be, but if he made a mistake of fact then it would have to be shown to be a reasonable mistake. In the problem, the circumstances might suggest that it was reasonable to suppose that there was an attack in progress and there is no suggestion this was not an honest belief.

As regards the degree of force used, the law demands that this should be reasonable and proportionate to the perceived threat but the courts are keen to ensure that this is not weighed too finely. For example, in *Cross v Kirby* (2000) *The Times*, 5 April, the Court of Appeal held that a defendant who had been struck several times by a baseball bat wielding assailant had not reacted disproportionately by using the bat to strike the claimant, breaking his skull. So, although Wilma's use of the poker has caused a serious injury this may be regarded as reasonable in all the circumstances.

Further reading

Bailey-Harris, R., 'Pregnancy, Autonomy and Refusal of Medical Treatment' (1998) 114 LQR 550.

Bridge, C., 'Religious Beliefs and Teenage Refusal of Medical Treatment' (1999) 62 MLR 585.

De Cruz, P., 'Adolescent Autonomy, Detention for Medical Treatment and Re C' (1999) 62 MLR 595.

Johnson, A., 'Putting the Cart before the Horse? Privacy and the Wainwrights' (2004) 63 CLJ 15.

Seabourne, G., 'The Role of the Tort of Battery in Medical Law' (1994) 24 Anglo-Am LR 265.

Tan, F. K., 'A Misconceived Issue in the Tort of False Imprisonment' (1981) 44 MLR 166.

4

Negligence I: duty of care

Introduction

Modern tort law is dominated by the tort of negligence. The principal requirements of the tort are that the defendant should owe the claimant a duty of care, that there should be a breach of that duty, and that the breach of duty should factually cause actionable damage to the claimant which is not legally too remote.

The duty issue is primarily based on the notion of reasonable foresight of harm to the claimant. This involves foresight of harm occurring at all, and that this particular claimant should fall within the class of persons who could foreseeably be affected—a factor usually referred to as proximity, describing the legal relationship between defendant and claimant. A further factor has evolved, namely that it should be 'fair, just, and reasonable' for a duty to be owed by the defendant to the claimant. This last factor allows a full range of policy considerations to be taken into account, not the least of which is the effect on the public at large were a duty to be found to exist.

As negligence as a tort has evolved to apply to more than just carelessly inflicted personal injury and property damage, policy considerations have become relevant so as to prevent the tort from running out of control into areas it was never intended to enter.

(1) General principles

> **?** **Question 1**
>
> '[T]he only necessary function performed by the duty of care concept in the present law is to deal with those cases where liability is denied not because of a lack of foreseeability, but for reasons of legal policy ...'
>
> *(Rogers, Winfield & Jolowicz on Tort)*
>
> Discuss.

Commentary

This question calls for an exploration of the relationship between foreseeability of harm to a foreseeable claimant and overriding (potentially) considerations of public policy that may act to deny a duty.

Examiner's tip

A good answer will make use of examples of policy reasoning that has changed over time to meet the perceived current needs of society.

Answer plan

- The basis on which **Donoghue v Stevenson** was decided.
- The relationship between the elements of reasonable foresight of harm, proximity of relationship, policy, and justice.
- The meaning of policy and the range of factors which may influence a decision on the duty issue for reasons of policy.
- How policy considerations affect different types of negligence action in specific ways.

Suggested answer

This question is concerned with the requirements for the establishment of a duty of care in the tort of negligence. In particular, it requires discussion of the extent to which the criteria for the existence of a duty situation have changed since the time prior to *Donoghue v Stevenson* [1932] AC 562 when duty situations were identified by reference to specific relationships between the parties and were limited in number (e.g. occupier/visitor, doctor/patient, employer/employee). Since that time, the tort of negligence has undergone substantial periods of change and in many situations the role of policy has become crucial in identifying when a duty of care is owed.

Donoghue v Stevenson established the principle that a defendant owes a claimant a duty of care if there is a relationship of neighbourhood in the sense that the claimant can be reasonably foreseen as likely to be affected by the defendant's act (or, in limited circumstances, omission). What this test does is to identify the person to whom a duty of care may be owed, but it says little about when or in what circumstances the duty is owed. The Privy Council, in *Yuen Kun Yeu v Attorney-General for Hong Kong* [1988] AC 175, concluded that a test based solely on reasonable foresight may omit essentials or take into account non-essential issues. They preferred the approach proposed by Brennan J in the High Court of Australia in *Sutherland Shire Council v Heyman* (1985) **60 ALR 1**, which requires an incremental development of the duty issue by reference to or by analogy with established categories of recognized duty situation; a position subsequently adopted by the House of Lords in *Caparo plc v Dickman* [1990] 2 AC 605.

The modern position was stated in *Marc Rich v Bishop Rock Marine Co Ltd* [1995] **3 All ER 307**, in which it was held by Lord Steyn that, in all cases of negligence, the main considerations in a duty enquiry are the '*Caparo* three requirements': reasonable foresight of harm; proximity of relationship; and whether it is fair, just, and reasonable to hold that the defendant owes the claimant a duty of care. Crucially, what the court regards as fair, just, and reasonable will be much influenced by questions of policy, especially any effect that a finding of liability in an individual case may have on the development of the law and on the wider public interest. Moreover, in appropriate cases, particularly those which fall within the general scope of the rule in *Hedley Byrne & Co Ltd v Heller & Partners Ltd* [1964] AC 465 concerning economic loss resulting from the provision of negligent advice, it has become apparent that an additional consideration is whether the defendant has voluntarily undertaken a responsibility towards the claimant for the accuracy of the advice given (see *Spring v Guardian Assurance plc* [1994] 3 All ER 129; *Henderson v Merrett Syndicates Ltd* [1994] 3 All ER 506; *White v Jones* [1995] 1 All ER 691).

These criteria form part of a composite test based on the necessary relationship between the parties, though Lord Oliver in *Caparo* describes them as, 'in most cases, in fact, merely facets of the same thing'. For example, what is foreseeable depends on issues of policy, justice, and proximity. But what is a proximate relationship depends on the other criteria and so on, and it is for this reason that Lord Wilberforce in *Anns v Merton LBC* [1978] AC 728 is now regarded as having oversimplified the process in separating the issues of foresight of harm and policy in his two-stage test.

The question refers to the fact that a relationship of proximity alone is not conclusive. So, for example, *Donoghue v Stevenson* shows that there is a sufficient relationship of proximity between a manufacturer and a consumer in respect of *physical harm* caused by a negligently produced article. But the existence of such a relationship is inconclusive if the consumer suffers *pure economic loss* (*Muirhead v Industrial Tank Specialties* [1986] QB 507; *Murphy v Brentwood DC* [1991] 1 AC 398). This is because the length of the chain of distribution is so long that it would be unreasonable to hold the defendant liable when the claimant has a more direct claim against his retail supplier.

As the question suggests, the real issue is one of policy, namely, is it right that the law should impose a duty of care in the particular circumstances of the case? The main policy issues are, first, the floodgates argument; second, is this a field that would be better legislated by Parliament; third, has Parliament already legislated; fourth, what practical effects might the imposition of a duty of care have; and finally, should the claimant do something other than sue the defendant? There may also be human rights issues to be taken into account.

The floodgates argument asks the question: would the establishment of a duty situation raise the spectre of a large number of, possibly unwarranted, claims? This was probably at issue in *Alcock v Chief Constable of South Yorkshire Police* [1992] 1 AC 310 and characterizes the development through case law of the legal principles in relation to psychiatric harm negligently inflicted on 'secondary' claimants, i.e. those who were not themselves at risk of physical injury, but whose claim is based on psychiatric injury caused by negligent harm to a third party. In respect of this kind of harm there has been a past fear of the 'gold-digging claimant' (though arguably this should be met by the requirement that a medically identifiable psychiatric illness has been suffered). In the case of such secondary claimants, the potential numbers of claims arising out of any incident are limited by the so-called control mechanisms set out in *Alcock*, which allow any person with a close tie of love and affection with the victim of the defendant's negligence to sue, provided they were present at the scene of the accident or came upon its immediate aftermath. This serves to eliminate more remote claimants such as those who read of an accident in a newspaper, or are told of it by friends. But arguably, this goes too far by preventing any person not at the scene of the accident from recovering at all, which could cause injustice in exceptional cases. These cases would have been met by the more flexible reasonable foresight test applied by Lords Bridge and Scarman in *McLoughlin v O'Brian* [1983] AC 410. (See also the proposals of the Law Commission, *Liability for Psychiatric Illness* (Law Com 249, 1998) which recommends that the requirement of spatial and temporal proximity should be dispensed with provided a close relationship with the victim can be established.)

In *Page v Smith* [1995] 2 All ER 736, Lord Lloyd recognized that these concerns do not arise in psychiatric damage cases where the claimant is a 'primary' claimant in the sense of being objectively placed at risk of physical injury by the defendant's negligence. Generally, the number of 'primary' claimants would be relatively small, though it is not impossible to envisage negligently triggered disasters in which the casualty list might be substantial. This reasoning reflects the second aspect of 'floodgates': namely that the principle is concerned not only with the potential size of the class of claimants, but also with the possibility of ascertaining with certainty the limits of that class. It is not considered fair or reasonable for a defendant to be burdened with liability in negligence to individuals who cannot be accurately, and reasonably promptly, identified.

The floodgates issue is also pertinent in many economic loss claims, especially where negligent advice is concerned, since words spread more rapidly and widely than actions. Any number of people may hear and act on advice originally given by the defendant. Accordingly, in such cases, it is important to consider why the advice was prepared and communicated and who can reasonably be expected to rely on it. Thus, in *Caparo v Dickman* [1990] 2 AC 605, advice prepared by an auditor could conceivably have been acted on by anyone who read the public document in which it was contained. But the advice was only intended for consumption by the company to which the report was directed. It was not intended that potential investors should take account of the contents of the document, even though many such people might choose to consult. In contrast, the advice prepared in *Morgan Crucible v Hill Samuel Bank* [199

142 was specifically directed at inducing the claimant to make an investment, with the result that he was owed a duty of care by the advice giver.

The issues of prospective or actual Parliamentary intervention are often related to matters of consumer protection, which may impinge on the general issue of freedom of contract. Here the court may be disinclined to restrict that freedom by imposing a tortious duty of care. Moreover, if Parliament has already acted, the courts may be disinclined to impose a common law duty which goes further. This seems to have been one motivating factor in *Murphy v Brentwood DC* [1991] 1 AC 398 where the **Defective Premises Act 1972** was thought to be the appropriate route, despite the fact that it was so narrow in scope as to be almost useless!

There is the question whether the claimant should proceed in some way other than via the tort of negligence. Often the claimant may sue for a breach of contract or may be expected to insure himself against the risk of loss created by the defendants, e.g. where economic loss is caused by a defective product. Also in cases of negligence by builders, there may be a clear expectation that the building owner should be insured against risks created by a subcontractor (*Norwich City Council v Harvey* [1989] 1 All ER 1180). In some instances, the claimant himself may be expected to guard against the risk of harm rather than the defendant. For example, it would be unreasonable to impose a duty on the Civil Aviation Authority to ensure that the owner of an aeroplane has properly maintained it, since the role of the CAA is to protect the public, not to protect individuals from their own failures (*Philcox v Civil Aviation Authority* (1995) *The Times*, 8 June).

A related matter is whether an alternative remedy already exists. For example, in the case of alleged negligence on the part of a public body or official, there may be an existing remedy in the form of judicial review (*Rowling v Takaro Properties Ltd* [1988] 1 All ER 163) or some other source of compensation such as a claim against the Criminal Injuries Compensation Scheme (*Hill v Chief Constable of West Yorkshire Police* [1989] AC 53). Similar considerations apply where there exists an action for breach of contract, even where the contractual defendant may not be the same person as the claimant could have sued in tort (*Banque Financière de la Cité v Westgate Insurance Ltd* [1988] 2 Lloyd's Rep 513).

Policy is overtly relevant when the courts consider the practical effect of a decision to impose a duty. For example, *Hill v Chief Constable of West Yorkshire Police* [1989] AC 53 and *Marc Rich v Bishop Rock Marine Co Ltd* [1995] 3 All ER 307 reflect the House of Lords' concern that risk of civil liability might cause organizations whose primary duty was to protect the collective welfare of the public to introduce defensive practices which, in the long run, might slow down the investigation process (police) or cause them to impose overly burdensome safety requirements (marine surveyors). It might also deter local authorities from undertaking certain safety inspections. This detrimental effect on the public interest is sufficient, it is argued, to outweigh the injustice of denying a small number of injured individuals their

This idea of the public interest as an overriding policy consideration developed across a wide range of activities during the 1990s, including child protection agencies (*X (minors) v Bedfordshire County Council* [1995] 3 WLR 152), the Crown Prosecution Service (*Elguzouli-Daf v Metropolitan Police Commissioner* [1995] 1 All ER 833), coastguards (*OLL Ltd v Secretary of State for Transport* [1997] 3 All ER 897) and the fire brigade (*Capital and Counties plc v Hampshire County Council* [1997] 2 All ER 865), sometimes being described merely as a policy issue and a factor to be taken into account, but sometimes as an 'immunity' effectively barring any possibility of a claim. An extreme example of the immunity related to advocates in respect of the conduct of litigation. If an advocate were to owe a duty of care, it was said, this might result in endless numbers of cases being retried at the instance of dissatisfied litigants (*Rondel v Worsley* [1969] 1 AC 191). The prospect of the **Human Rights Act 1998** coming into force in 2000 prompted a number of actions challenging the legality of such immunities in negligence and may well have been influential in the modern approach, which requires a balancing of all the policy issues relevant to any individual case. In particular, the blanket immunity enjoyed by advocates was abolished by the House of Lords in *Arthur J. S. Hall & Co (a firm) v Simons* [2000] 3 All ER 673—arguments that had previously been thought overwhelming were now seen, by reference to experience from other jurisdictions and by comparison with other professionals to whom they might equally apply, to be overcautious and unnecessary.

A somewhat different aspect of public policy influenced the outcome in *Greatorex v Greatorex* [2000] 4 All ER 769, in which a father whose motorist son had been injured by his own negligence suffered psychiatric illness consequent on attending the accident. Part of the justification for denying liability was a public interest in protecting the integrity of family life, which would, the judge reasoned, be put at risk were the distress of such an accident to be exacerbated by litigation. Direct physical injury inflicted by one family member on another is actionable, but mental suffering, he concluded, must be accepted as part of ordinary family experience unless inflicted by a third party.

In summary, policy considerations feature strongly in determining whether a duty of care is owed and the simple fact of a particular type of relationship is not conclusive. This is because regard must be had both to the kind of harm suffered and to the way it was caused. The use of a criterion of reasonable foresight of harm on its own might, in some cases, create a range of problems including the danger of indeterminate liability or an unacceptable depletion of public funds otherwise destined for the benefit of a wider public. In the end, as Lord Oliver observed in *Caparo*, notions such as foreseeability and proximity are merely convenient labels describing circumstances 'from which, pragmatically, the courts conclude that a duty of care exists'. While the courts may be disinclined to take on the role of legislators, they do have to take steps to keep the tort of negligence within reasonable bounds and it is the use of policy considerations which allows them to do this.

(2) Psychiatric harm

Question 2

Don, the driver of a stock car, negligently fails to maintain his vehicle. In the course of a race, which is being televised, Don's brakes fail and his car crashes into a crowd of spectators. The car narrowly misses Albert but strikes and kills Bob. Bob's daughter, Claire, is very badly injured, but survives and is taken to hospital.

Albert, a person of unusually nervous disposition, develops an anxiety neurosis.

Freda, a friend of Bob, is present at the scene of the accident. At first, she attempts to help, but realizing that Bob is dead and that Claire is being dealt with by professionals, Freda rushes back to tell Bob's wife, Glenda, what has happened. Some time later, Glenda, who is also Claire's stepmother of six months' standing, drives to the hospital and asks to see Bob and Claire. Glenda is shown Bob's body, and sees Claire on a hospital trolley, awaiting treatment, crying in pain and in a badly disfigured state.

Harriet, Bob's mother, sees a live television broadcast of the events, recognizes her son in the crowd and realizes that Don's car has crashed into the area where her son is standing.

Freda, Glenda, and Harriet are all horrified by what has happened. Both Freda and Glenda suffer from reactive depression. Harriet helps care for Glenda and Claire following the accident and becomes a recluse because of her inability to come to terms with the psychological suffering of Glenda and the physical injuries suffered by Claire.

Advise Albert, Freda, Glenda, and Harriet.

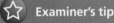

Commentary

This question involves a discussion of the principles relating to negligently inflicted psychiatric harm. It is essential to explain the distinction between primary and secondary claimants, and its effect on the likely success of any claim. It is also important to explain in detail, and apply, the various control mechanisms in *Alcock* and subsequent cases.

Examiner's tip

A good answer will deal with the law as it currently stands, drawing on past developments as necessary to explain the reasoning. Your notes may well start with cases before this type of damage was recognized in law, but these older cases have no real place in connection with a modern problem. You will have studied them simply to understand the way the courts' approach has evolved.

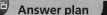

Answer plan

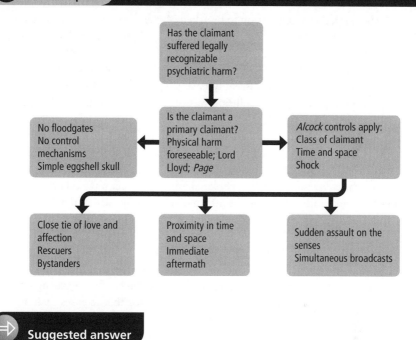

Has the claimant suffered legally recognizable psychiatric harm?

Is the claimant a primary claimant? Physical harm foreseeable; Lord Lloyd; *Page*

No floodgates
No control mechanisms
Simple eggshell skull

Alcock controls apply:
Class of claimant
Time and space
Shock

Close tie of love and affection
Rescuers
Bystanders

Proximity in time and space
Immediate aftermath

Sudden assault on the senses
Simultaneous broadcasts

Suggested answer

Since the scenario states that Don is negligent in maintaining his vehicle, there is no need to consider the issues of duty and breach of duty in respect of the harm to Bob and Claire. Assuming the death of Bob and the injuries to Claire are caused by Don's negligence and that harm is not too remote, Don will be liable in damages to both Claire and Glenda, the latter representing the estate of the deceased and the former being a dependant, thereby being able to recover damages under the **Law Reform (Miscellaneous Provisions) Act 1934** and the **Fatal Accidents Act 1976**, respectively.

When considering the issue of psychiatric damage, it is important to acknowledge that not every form of mental suffering will be sufficient to establish a duty situation. It is a requirement of English law that the claimant has suffered identifiable recognizable psychiatric illness. *McLoughlin v O'Brian* [1983] 1 AC 410 is authority that mere grief, sorrow, or upset are normal human emotions in respect of which no duty of care is owed. Moreover, in *Bourhill v Young* [1943] AC 92 the House of Lords held it is expected that people should possess sufficient 'phlegm' and fortitude to be able to overcome the normal distress at witnessing an accident. On this basis, the fact that Freda, Glenda, and Harriet are 'horrified' will not suffice. By contrast, the reactive depression suffered by Freda and Glenda, as a recognizable psychiatric illness, will be sufficient, as will Albert's anxiety neurosis. Harriet's personality change and inability to cope with everyday life would seem to indicate a qualifying condition, but her claim will fail because the condition was caused not by shock, a sudden assault on the senses, but by the long-term effects of caring for the other victims—a scenario specifically excluded by Lord Keith in *Alcock v Chief Constable of South Yorkshire Police* [1992] 1 AC 310.

For each claimant, the next question to be asked is whether they are to be regarded as a primary or secondary claimant. Primary claimants are those described by Lord Oliver in *Alcock* as being 'involved, mediately or immediately, as a participant', and by Lord Lloyd in *Page v Smith* [1996] AC 155 as being within the class of persons who, without the benefit of hindsight, might foreseeably have suffered physical injury. In *Page*, the driver of a car involved in a minor collision was physically unhurt but nonetheless suffered a recurrence of ME (myalgic encephalomyelitis, also known as CFS or chronic fatigue syndrome), a condition he had suffered from intermittently over many years, but from which he was in remission at the time of the accident. The test applied in the House of Lords was to ask whether it was foreseeable to the defendant that her conduct would expose the claimant to a risk of personal injury, whether physical or psychiatric. If the answer to that question was in the affirmative, it was irrelevant that the claimant did not suffer physical injury or that the claimant's actual injury was due to his 'egg-shell personality', since the defendant was required to take the claimant as he found him. However, where the claimant has an 'egg-shell skull' personality, the quantum of damages he receives may be reduced to take account of the fact that the claimant might have suffered the illness complained of even without the defendant's negligent act (*Page v Smith (No. 2)* [1996] 1 WLR 855). Lord Lloyd indicated that in cases such as these there is no floodgates risk, and therefore no policy need for the control mechanisms that are used in the case of secondary claimants to limit the number of claims.

If Albert, having been 'narrowly missed', can show that he falls within a class who could foreseeably have been physically injured his claim will succeed, despite the fact that he is a person of unusually nervous disposition. Alternatively, he may seek to rely on those cases in which the claimant fears for his own safety as a result of what the defendant has done, and in consequence suffers psychiatric harm (*Dulieu v White* [1901] 2 KB 609). Although this sounds as though it offers an additional line of argument, recent cases have shown that a very restrictive approach is taken to the question whether the claimant's fear, even where it is accepted as genuine, is to be regarded, in law, as reasonable (*McFarlane v EE Caledonia Ltd* [1994] 2 All ER 1; *Hegarty v EE Caledonia Ltd* [1997] 2 Lloyd's Rep 259). If Albert cannot show that he is a primary claimant, he must satisfy the requirements for a secondary claimant, as with Glenda, Freda, and Harriet.

Secondary claimants are those whose psychiatric harm stems from their reaction to physical harm caused to someone else by the defendant's negligence. Clearly, for every physically injured primary victim there may be a great number of potential claims from relatives, friends, and witnesses of the event, all saying that they have been affected by the defendant's negligence. It is concern about this potential for a great number of claims, the floodgates issue, that has driven the courts' restrictive approach to the existence of a duty in such cases. This approach manifests itself in the so-called 'control mechanisms', a series of tests set out by the House of Lords in *Alcock*, following the Hillsborough tragedy. These tests represent a modification of the three *Caparo* requirements for the existence of a duty in negligence, namely foreseeability, proximity and fairness, justice and reasonableness, not replacing them, but recasting them in a form more readily applicable to psychiatric injury cases.

Although there are variations in their Lordships' speeches, some general consensus has emerged and has been applied in subsequent cases. First, as regards the class of persons who may claim it would seem that the test is that of a 'close tie of love and affection' with the primary victim. This might be presumed in the case of parents/children, spouses, and (perhaps) engaged couples, though evidence might be brought by the defendant to rebut the presumption. For all others, a relationship qualitatively similar to those listed must be proved. It was held that the closeness of the relationship was what made it foreseeable that the claimant would suffer psychiatric damage, while those with a lesser tie fall within the *Bourhill* expectation of 'phlegm and fortitude'. Secondly, the claimant must be proximate in time and space to the incident (i.e. actually be there), though their Lordships approved an extension in *McLoughlin* to a claimant who comes upon the 'immediate aftermath'. In that case, a mother arrived at hospital, some two hours after a road traffic accident involving her husband and children, and was faced with one dead child and the rest of her family injured and not yet cleaned up or treated. The impact of the scenes to which she was exposed, and within such a short timescale, was held to be equivalent to having been present at the accident. The last factor is the manner in which the claimant learned of the incident, which must cause actual shock, a 'sudden assault on the senses', and learning of events through a third party will not be enough.

Turning back to the claimants, Albert, if his claim as a primary claimant is rejected, will not be able to establish the requisite close tie of love and affection with the victims, which places him in the class of 'bystander'. Under *Alcock*, it appeared that a bystander might be able to claim if something sufficiently gruesome happened sufficiently close to him; the scenario that had been suggested in *McLoughlin* was of a situation in which a petrol tanker crashed into a school in session and exploded in flames. In such a situation, it was thought, it was foreseeable that even a bystander might suffer psychiatric damage. This line of reasoning was rejected in *McFarlane v EE Caledonia* [1994] 2 All ER 1, a case arising out of the Piper Alpha disaster, both on grounds of practicality (how does one measure gruesomeness?), and of principle—to accept it would, it was said, be to base liability solely on a test of reasonable foreseeability. Although critics have challenged the latter assertion, this approach to bystanders has been endorsed by the House of Lords in *White v Chief Constable of South Yorkshire Police* [1999] 1 All ER 1. As a secondary claimant Albert's claim is doomed to fail.

Although Freda was present at the scene of the accident, there is no suggestion that she was close enough to be a primary claimant. As a secondary claimant, she must first establish that she has a close tie of love and affection with the victims. Merely being a friend of Bob will not be enough, unless she can prove that their friendship was equivalent to a close familial tie. If she can do so, she will certainly satisfy the other requirements having been proximate in time and space to the shocking event and having experienced it with her own unaided senses. If she cannot establish the requisite tie, then she is a bystander. Under *Alcock*, a person who performed the role of rescuer was seen, based on *Chadwick v British Transport Commission* [1967] 1 WLR 912 and for policy reasons, as an exception to the bystander class in much the same way as rescuers enjoy a special position in relation to the rules of negligence in all other cases. The problem, however, with acts of rescue leading to psychiatric injury is that it is very difficult for courts to identify exactly what an individual must do in order to claim the special status, bearing in mind the essentially restrictive approach that is taken to secondary claimants generally. For example, in *McFarlane* the claimant had assisted with survivors by handing out blankets, which was not held to be sufficient to make him a 'rescuer'. The problem for the law became acute in *White v Chief Constable of South Yorkshire Police* [1999] 1 All ER 1, where the rescuers in question were police officers working with the dead and injured at Hillsborough. A majority of the Court of Appeal had held that the activities of certain of the officers sufficed to warrant the label of rescuer and hence the special treatment. This analysis was rejected by the majority in the House of Lords, on the basis that a class incapable of being defined in law cannot be sustained, and that justice would be better served by applying the ordinary rules in all cases, with the result that any claimant lacking a close tie with the victims must either be objectively at risk of physical injury or reasonably believe himself to be so (i.e. be a primary claimant). This decision is fatal to any claim by Freda based solely on rescuing activities since, although the defence of *volenti* continues to be defeated in the case of rescuers in respect of their voluntarily leaving a safe place in order to assist (as in *Chadwick*), on the facts given there is no suggestion of any ongoing risk to people at the scene.

Glenda, as Bob's wife, will be presumed to have a close tie of love and affection, and as a stepmother of six months' standing may have begun to develop the required bond with Claire. She was not at the scene of the accident when it happened, and being told of the incident by Freda will not be sufficient to establish the existence of a duty of care (*Hambrook v Stokes Bros* [1925] 1 KB 141).

Although she was not at the scene of the accident, Glenda's experience at the hospital may suffice provided it may be categorized as the immediate aftermath. She arrives 'some time later', and it is not clear what length of delay may still qualify as immediate—a time lapse of eight hours in *Alcock* and one of five hours in *Chester v Waverley Municipal Council* (1939) 62 CLR 1 was considered too great, while two hours was accepted in *McLoughlin*. As well as immediacy, the word 'aftermath' must be considered since in *McLoughlin* it was the state of the victims and the impact on the claimant's mind that was important. In *Alcock*, it was considered relevant that the relatives had turned up at a mortuary in order to identify the bodies of their loved ones. While Lord Ackner was prepared to regard this as part of the 'aftermath' of the accident, it was not part of the *immediate* aftermath, but Lord Jauncey opined that the experience of going to identify a body is not the same as attendance at the aftermath of an accident for the purpose of providing comfort and care to a person who may still be alive (see also Handford, 'Compensation for Psychiatric Injury: The Limits of Liability' (1995) 2 *Psychiatry, Psychology and Law* 37). Provided Glenda arrives at the hospital very soon after the incident at the race track, and is confronted by a sufficiently shocking scene, she should be able to recover damages in respect of the reactive depression she suffers. On the facts, it seems Glenda is already aware that Bob is dead, but her claim in respect of Claire may succeed.

Harriet is probably ineligible due to her psychiatric illness being gradual and not caused by shock. Her claim also faces another difficulty. Although, as Bob's mother, there will be a presumption of love and affection, Harriet is not present at the scene of the accident, but she observes the events on a live television broadcast. In *Alcock* it was emphasized that it is also necessary to look at the means by which the shock is caused. In that case, it was considered relevant that the police were aware that the football match was being televised (thus eliminating any argument that broadcast by a third party was a *novus actus interveniens*), but they were also aware of a code of ethics which forbade the showing of pictures of suffering by identifiable individuals, and which they were entitled to rely on. There was also doubt as to whether scenes viewed on a television screen could ever be 'equiparated with the viewer being within sight or hearing of the event...or as giving rise to shock, in the sense of a sudden assault on the nervous system' (*Alcock*, *per* Lord Keith). This would suggest that Harriet would not have a claim.

(3) Economic loss

? Question 3

Badman Batty, construction contractors, are engaged by Crumbridgeshire County Council to resurface a 10-mile stretch of the Crumbridge ring road. Badman Batty hires a surface stripping machine in order to facilitate the work.

Bob, a surveyor employed by the County Council but on loan to Badman Batty, decides he is capable of using the surface stripping machine but sets the controls in such a way that too deep a cut is made, so that the machine severs a water main which floods the road and a nearby power generator. The following parties claim damages for negligence:

(a) Peter, a businessman, was driving on the ring road at the time of the incident and claims he has been prevented from attending a meeting at which he had high hopes of securing a £500,000 contract with another business.

(b) Power-Green Ltd, owners of the generator engulfed in water from the severed main, claim the cost of repairing their damaged generator and the profit they would have made had the generator been operative during the five days it takes to effect repairs.

(c) Plasticraft Ltd, the beneficial owners of a factory on an industrial estate supplied with electricity generated by Power-Green's incapacitated generator, complain that their operations were interrupted for five days. Plasticraft Ltd occupy these premises pursuant to a contractual arrangement with the legal owners, Property Holdings Ltd, a subsidiary company in the same group of companies as Plasticraft Ltd. Plasticraft say they had to dispose of a batch of plastic plates, valued at £10,000, as the plastic congealed when the power supply failed. The cost of cleaning congealed plastic from their machines is assessed at £2,500. Plasticraft Ltd also claim damages for loss of business profit on operations they could have carried on during the remainder of the five-day interruption to their power supply.

Advise Badman Batty of their potential liability in tort.

 Commentary

This question is concerned with economic loss caused by a negligent act. Generally, the courts have been reluctant to allow an action in this area and have imposed restrictions at the duty stage of the enquiry. However, the economic loss may or may not have been caused by a person who is an employee of the defendants and thus raises the issue of the vicarious liability of an employer.

 Answer plan

(1) Identify the reasons for limiting duties of care in respect of economic losses.

(2) Is the property damaged by the defendant either owned or in the possession of the claimant—if so direct economic loss consequent on that damage may be recoverable.

(3) Is the principal employer or the borrowing employer responsible for the actions of a 'loaned' employee?

(4) When does an employee act in the course of his employment—features of the close connection test.

⇨ Suggested answer

Bob's actions result in physical damage to the water main, to which the rule in *Donoghue v Stevenson* [1932] AC 562 will apply, but only in favour of a person with a proprietary interest in the water main itself. However, a further consequence of Bob's act is that others suffer economic losses that may not be recoverable for policy reasons.

The economic loss issues

Peter's failure to secure a lucrative contract is a form of pure economic loss which is not directly related to the severance of the water main. This raises a 'floodgates' problem, or 'liability in an indeterminate amount to an indeterminate class for an indeterminate time' (*Ultramares Corp v Touche* (1931) 174 NE 441 *per* Cardozo J).

Peter's problem is that any number of other motorists could be affected in the same way, so there may be an indeterminate class of claimants and no duty of care. In *Spartan Steel & Alloys Ltd v Martin & Co (Contractors) Ltd* [1973] 1 QB 27 the Court of Appeal held that a defendant will be liable for negligently caused physical harm and for economic loss directly consequent on that physical harm; there is no liability for pure economic loss which flows indirectly from a negligent act. The loss of the £500,000 contract must be regarded as falling within this principle and is therefore loss in respect of which no duty of care is owed.

In any event, the loss suffered by Peter is speculative, so that all he has lost is the chance to secure a lucrative contract. In *Hotson v East Berkshire Health Authority* [1987] 2 All ER 909 it was held that a claimant must prove, on a balance of probability, that the defendant was the cause of the harm complained of and Peter may find it difficult to discharge the onus of proof. However, since Peter has suffered economic loss, he may be assisted by the decision in *Allied Maples Group Ltd v Simmons & Simmons* [1995] 1 WLR 1602 where it was held that if the claimant can prove that he had a real or substantial chance of making a gain rather than merely a speculative chance, that chance can be evaluated as part of the quantum of damages. The question states that Peter had 'high hopes' of securing this contract, so if he has some evidence, e.g. a signed 'letter of comfort', to show that he expected to secure the contract the loss of that chance may be taken into account in any award of damages.

Power-Green Ltd have suffered physical damage to their generator so, applying ordinary *Donoghue v Stevenson* principles, Bob will be liable for that damage. The loss of profit flowing directly from the damage to the generator that is owned by Power-Green Ltd seems to fall within the *Spartan Steel v Martin* principle, so a duty of care should be owed.

Plasticraft's batch of plastic plates that congealed when the power supply was interrupted is another example of physical harm caused by Bob's negligence. This also resulted in the additional cost of cleaning plastic from their machine, which will be classified as physical harm, similar to the additional labour costs incurred in *Muirhead v Industrial Tank Specialties Ltd* [1985] 3 All ER 705. Moreover, any economic loss directly consequent on this physical damage, such as the resale value of the plates in process at the time of the interruption to the electricity supply will be recoverable: *Spartan Steel & Alloys Ltd v Martin (Contractors) Ltd* [1973] 1 QB 27. However, Plasticraft Ltd must have a sufficient possessory or proprietary interest in the property affected by Bob's negligent act to be able to sue. In *Leigh & Sillavan Ltd v Aliakmon Shipping Ltd* [1986] AC 785, due to the terms of the contract he had made with a seller, the claimant was neither the owner nor the possessor of property damaged by the defendant carrier's negligence and, as a result, was unable to sue. In the present case, if Plasticraft Ltd are not the legal owners of the affected premises this might affect their ability to sue. However, in *Shell UK Ltd v Total UK Ltd* [2010] EWCA Civ 180 it was held that the beneficial owner of a pipeline damaged by the defendant's negligence could sue by joining the legal owner of the pipeline as a party to the proceedings either as an unwilling defendant or as a willing joint-claimant. As Plasticraft Ltd and Property Holdings Ltd are part of the same group of companies, it seems likely that Property Holdings Ltd will agree to lend their name to any action brought by Plasticraft Ltd.

Both Power-Green and Plasticraft sue in respect of loss of general business profits resulting from the inability to continue operations following the power cut, but these losses are indirect and therefore not recoverable under the *Spartan Steel & Alloys Ltd v Martin (Contractors) Ltd* principle. The rule is arbitrary, but makes the limits of the law clear and was said by Lord Denning MR to be based on the policy ground that were such an action to be permitted, there would be no end of claims.

The vicarious liability issue

The discussion above assumes that Bob is personally responsible for his negligence, but if he is an employee acting in the course of his employment his employer may be vicariously liable for the torts committed by Bob.

Bob is normally employed by the County Council but has been 'lent' to Badman Batty, so who is Bob's employer? Relevant factors will include the terms of the contract between the Council and Badman Batty but the onus of proof lies on the permanent employer: *Mersey Docks & Harbour Board v Coggins & Griffith (Liverpool) Ltd* [1947] AC 1. In *Viasystems (Tyneside) Ltd v Thermal Transfer (Northern) Ltd* [2005] EWCA Civ 1151 and *Hawley v Luminar Leisure Ltd* [2006] EWCA Civ 18 it was held that it has to be ascertained which of the two employers was best positioned to prevent the tort from being committed and that there is a presumption that the lending employer still remains responsible (*Hawley*), but it can be displaced if the employee was so much under the control of the borrowing employer that he can prevent the employee from committing the tort (*Viasystems* at [16]). Assuming sufficient control has passed to Badman Batty, they may be the responsible employer, which appears to be reasonable if the Council has no obvious means of preventing any tort from being committed.

Bob acts on behalf of Badman Batty, but they will only be liable for his acts if he is an employee rather than an independent contractor. Although this rule departs from the fault principle, it is justified on the basis that employers rather than employees are best positioned to bear the loss through insurance (see *British Telecommunications plc v James Thomson & Sons (Engineers) Ltd* [1999] 1 WLR 9).

Traditionally, the test for determining who is an employee is based on the concept of control, so that an employee can be told by his employer what to do and how to do it (see *Collins v Hertfordshire County Council* [1947] **KB 598**), whereas an independent contractor is employed to do work but has a discretion as to the mode and time of doing the relevant work: *Honeywill v Stein & Larkin* [1934] **1 KB 191**. However, this test does not work well with professional employees, such as Bob, a surveyor, as his skill is such that the employer may have little knowledge of how the work is done. Nevertheless, the control test can be helpful but other factors such as the method of payment, the provision of equipment, the power of dismissal, and the 'employee's' personal investment may also be relevant.

Whether Bob is an employee will depend on the detailed wording of his contract with Badman Batty, which is not revealed in the question. But if Bob's work is done as an integral part of Badman Batty's business it would appear that he is likely to be regarded as an employee: *Stevenson, Jordan & Harrison Ltd v MacDonald* [1952] **1 TLR 101**.

Assuming Bob is an employee, Badman Batty, as employers, may be vicariously liable for Bob's torts committed in the course of employment. As a surveyor, he is unlikely to be employed to operate a surface stripping machine. On the other hand he may have been employed to supervise and give orders to those who do. The classic 'Salmond' test for determining when an employer is vicariously liable for an employee's tort was to ask if the employee had used a wrongful mode to carry out work he had been authorized to do or whether he had done some unauthorized act for which the employer would not be liable. This test produced a lot of difficult case law as courts attempted to massage the facts of a case into the 'wrongful mode' category in order to hold an employer vicariously liable.

Since the decision in *Lister v Hesley Hall* [2001] **UKHL 22**, particularly in cases where the employee's conduct amounts to a crime, the appropriate test to apply is whether the wrongful conduct is so closely connected with the acts the employee was authorized to do that the wrongful conduct may fairly and properly be regarded as done by the employee in the ordinary course of the employer's business. On this basis older case law involving dangerous acts that were closely connected to the work done by the employee but possibly difficult to explain as authorized, such as lighting a cigarette while delivering petrol to a garage, could be explained: *Northern Ireland Road Transport Board v Century Insurance* [1942] **AC 509**. Moreover, older cases indicating that even a prohibited act can be carried out in the course of employment if it is done in order to advance the employer's business can also be justified under the 'close connection' test: *Rose v Plenty* [1976] **1 WLR 141**. Here there is no evidence that Bob has been prohibited from operating the machine and it does appear that he is trying to further his employer's business.

Bob's act results in damage to the road and to a water main. In the unlikely event that this was done deliberately, this might constitute the criminal offence of causing criminal damage. This raises the question whether an overtly criminal act can be done in the course of employment. Generally, if the act is done with a view to furthering the employer's interests, it may still be regarded as an act done in the course of employment: *Poland v Parr* [1927] **1 KB 236**; *Vasey v Surrey Free Inns* [1996] **PIQR P373**. Similarly, if the wrongful act is a risk incidental to the purpose for which the employee is employed, there will be a sufficiently close connection: *Brinks Global Services v Igrox Ltd* [2010] **EWCA Civ 1207**. This would all seem to point towards an act by Bob that was done in the course of his employment.

Question 4

Constructors Ltd supplied and installed a compression system in a factory owned by Bodgit Ltd. A pipe attached to the compressor was damaged by an employee of Constructors Ltd, but the defect was not immediately noticeable as the piping was contained in a protective sleeve. Around seven years later Bodgit Ltd sold their factory and stock-in-trade to O'Bottle. At the time of sale, O'Bottle inspected the compressor and noticed cracking in a pipe leading from the equipment, but due to a failure to take care, the cause of the cracking was not identified.

Eleven years after installation of the compression system, there was an explosion caused by the rupture of the pipe in which cracking had been discovered at the time Bodgit Ltd sold their factory. The explosion totally destroyed the compressor and seriously damaged the rest of the factory. The cost of repairing the factory is assessed at £6 million, but the market value of a similar factory is considered to be £5 million.

At the time of the explosion, the compressor was being used to process a toxic gas, which escaped and severely burned Alice, a production line worker in O'Bottle's factory. Due to inexcusable delay on the part of Alice's solicitors, Doohey, Cheetham & Howe, an action is not commenced until more than three years after the date of the explosion, by which time the normal limitation period for personal injury actions has expired.

Advise Alice and O'Bottle of any remedies they may have in tort.

Commentary

This question is concerned with the liability of an installer for his defective workmanship, where this results in both economic loss and physical harm. The issue of limitation of actions also requires consideration, since the damage suffered by the claimant is only discovered some considerable time after the date on which it was, initially, caused.

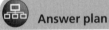

Answer plan

- Does the installation amount to a defective product under the **Consumer Protection Act 1987**?
- Can an installer be a producer for the purposes of the rule in ***Donoghue v Stevenson***?

- Is the damage actionable under the rule in **Donoghue v Stevenson**?
- How are damages in respect of harm to property to be assessed?
- How do the provisions of the **Limitation Act 1980** relating to discretionary extension of the limitation period affect the product liability action, the negligence action in respect of the events leading up to the explosion?

⇨ Suggested answer

Bodgit would have been able to sue Constructors for breach of contract, either for breach of an express term or the implied terms of satisfactory quality and fitness for purpose, but now that the business and stock-in-trade has been sold by Bodgit Ltd to O'Bottle the remedy must be found in the law of tort.

Under the **Consumer Protection Act 1987 (CPA)**, s. 2(1), the producer of a defective product is strictly liable for physical harm to the person or to property other than the defective product itself: **CPA 1987, s. 5(2)**. Under the Act, a mere supplier, such as Constructors Ltd, is not a producer unless they have failed to identify the producer upon request: **CPA 1987, s. 2(3)**. Moreover, the only physical harm occurs 11 years after the defective product was first put into circulation which will render any action time-barred: **Limitation Act 1980, s. 11A(3)**.

A manufacturer (including an installer, such as Constructors) owes a common law duty of care to the consumer of his product in respect of physical harm provided the product is in the same form as it left him and with no reasonable possibility of intermediate examination: *Donoghue v Stevenson* [1932] AC 562. O'Bottle's main difficulty in a negligence action will be to identify actionable damage, as the loss suffered comprises damage to the building itself which was classified as economic loss in *Murphy v Brentwood District Council* [1991] 1 AC 398; see also *D & F Estates Ltd v Church Commissioners for England* [1989] AC 177. The decision in *Murphy*, in particular, makes it clear that economic loss suffered as a result of the mere qualitative defectiveness of a product does not disclose a duty situation, since the claimant has a contract under which to sue or an insurance policy to claim from and that to extend the law of tort in such a way that it imposes liability for a transmissible warranty of quality would be to usurp the role of the law of contract: *Williams v Natural Life Health Foods* [1998] 2 All ER 577.

Eleven years after installation of the compression system, there is an explosion which damages the factory and the compressor owned by O'Bottle and injures Alice. If the compressor and the defective pipe are treated as a composite single product, the problem of economic loss considered above will arise, and O'Bottle will be unable to pursue Constructors Ltd in an action for negligence. However, exceptionally, if the pipe and the compressor are separate parts of a complex structure, damage to the structure caused by a component part may be regarded as property damage. The complex structure theory was developed in *D & F Estates Ltd v Church Commissioners for England* [1989] AC 177 as a possible explanation of the decision in *Anns v Merton LBC* [1978]

AC 728. In *Linklaters Business Services v Sir Robert McAlpine* [2010] EWHC 1145 (TCC) it was thought that the exception was more likely to be applicable where different contractors were responsible for the installation of different parts of the complex structure. The facts suggest that it was an employee of Constructors who damaged the pipe, which also suggests that Constructors were responsible for the installation of both the compressor and the pipe. Accordingly, the complex structure theory is unlikely to be of assistance to O'Bottle. The damage to the factory is actionable if Constructors failed to take reasonable care, subject to defences and time constraints. If the defect in the pipe is caused by the negligence of Constructors' employee, O'Bottle will be entitled to compensation for the damage to the factory. Damages for property damage can be assessed in two different ways. The claimant may be awarded the 'diminution in value measure' based on the reduced value of his property after the damage caused by the defendant or the 'cost of cure' measure based on repair costs. The first of these will normally apply where the claimant uses his land as an economic asset: *Taylor v Hepworths Ltd* [1977] 1 WLR 1262. However, if the land is required for commercial occupation, as appears to be the case here, the cost of repair or reinstatement is appropriate: *Harbutt's Plasticine Ltd v Wayne Tank & Pump Co Ltd* [1970] 1 QB 447.

Damages may be reduced under the **Law Reform (Contributory Negligence) Act 1945** if O'Bottle is considered to have been contributorily negligent in failing to identify the cause of the crack in the pipe attached to the compressor. Contributory negligence is a failure, by the claimant, to take reasonable care for his own safety and it is necessary to consider how far the claimant's failure to take care is a cause of the damage he has suffered: *Jones v Livox Quarries Ltd* [1952] 2 QB 608. O'Bottle's failure to take care may have been, in part, a cause of the accident as well as increasing the extent of harm suffered. In such cases, the courts have been prepared to make substantial reductions in the claimant's damages on the basis that his blameworthiness in relation to the harm suffered is substantial: see e.g. *Stapley v Gypsum Mines Ltd* [1953] AC 663 (80 per cent reduction).

O'Bottle's action may also be time barred under the **Limitation Act 1980, s. 2** if more than six years have elapsed since the date on which damage is caused. Since economic loss appears not to be actionable, no damage can be said to have been caused until the date of the explosion: *Nitrigin Eireann Teoranta v Inco Alloys Ltd* [1992] 1 All ER 854. This means that if an action is commenced within six years of the date of the explosion, it will be in time and it does not matter that O'Bottle failed to discover the cause of the crack as contributory negligence does not affect accrual of the cause of action: *Nitrigin Eireann Teoranta v Inco Alloys Ltd.*

Alice, an employee of O'Bottle, is injured by a gas leak resulting from the explosion. Her action for damages for personal injuries would lie against Constructors Ltd for their negligence or against O'Bottle under the **Employer's Liability (Defective Equipment) Act 1969**. If she were to proceed on the last basis, O'Bottle would be deemed liable for her injuries provided the defect in the equipment is attributable wholly or in part to the fault of a third party: **Employer's Liability (Defective Equipment) Act 1969, s. 1(1)**. Thus, it is still necessary to establish fault on the part of the producer or installer of the equipment.

In the case of personal injury actions, the relevant limitation period runs for three years from the date of accrual of the cause of action or for three years from the date when the claimant became aware of her injuries or could reasonably have done so: **Limitation Act 1980, s. 11(4)**. For these purposes, knowledge does not mean that the claimant must know with absolute certainty that she has been injured (*Halford v Brookes* [1991] 3 All ER 559; *Collins v Tesco plc* [2003] EWCA Civ 1308), but Alice is likely to realize that an explosion resulting in burns is likely to have been caused by the fault of the person who controls the thing that has exploded. Alice must also be aware that the injury is attributable to the fault of the defendant (**Limitation Act 1980, s. 14(1) (b)**) and be aware of the identity of the defendant (**Limitation Act 1980, s. 14(1)**(c)), both of which appear to be the case. It seems likely that the date of the explosion will be the starting date under the two alternative limitation periods. Although the normal three-year period has expired, the court has a discretion to allow an action for damages for personal injury to be commenced out of time where it is equitable to do so: **Limitation Act 1980, s. 33**. Relevant factors in exercising this discretion are the degree of prejudice to the claimant and the defendant should the discretion be exercised or not, the length of and reasons for the delay, the cogency of the evidence in the light of the delay, and the promptness, and reasonableness, of the claimant's action after becoming aware of the cause of action. If the delay is only a matter of days or weeks rather than years, the court may exercise its discretion in Alice's favour (see *Hartley v Birmingham City District Council* [1992] 2 All ER 213—one day late). This is particularly important since the later the action is commenced, the greater will be the prejudice to the defendant in having to face a stale claim which might be difficult to defend (*Donovan v Gwentoys Ltd* [1990] 1 All ER 1018).

The prejudice issue works both ways, since if the court exercises its discretion to allow the action to proceed out of time, there is inevitable prejudice to the defendant since he will be denied a 'windfall' limitation defence (*Buckler v Finnegan* [2004] EWCA Civ 920). But there is also prejudice to the claimant where he is told that he may not proceed with his action because he is out of time. Factors which may be relevant here are the length of the delay (*KR v Bryn Alyn Community (Holdings) Ltd* [2003] EWCA Civ 85), whether it is proportionate to allow the claim to proceed (*McGhie v British Telecommunications plc* [2005] EWCA Civ 920), the strength or weakness of the claimant's case, the size of any possible award of damages, and whether the claimant has an alternative defendant to sue, which is, for Alice, a relevant factor as she may have an action for professional negligence against her legal adviser. Requiring the claimant to sue her solicitor can prejudice her if the professional negligence case is not cast iron: *Conry v Simpson* [1983] 3 All ER 369. Moreover, if the claimant is required to sue her solicitor, regard should be had to the fact that she is being forced to give up an action against a tortfeasor who may know little of the weaker aspects of her case, to bring an action against a person who knows all the finer details of that case by virtue of having represented the claimant: *Hartley v Birmingham City District Council* [1992] 2 All ER 213. All of this may suggest that the court might be inclined to exercise its discretion in order to allow Alice to sue out of time, so that she does not have to pursue her solicitors, Doohey, Cheetham & Howe.

Question 5

Punter, a partly qualified accountant, has recently been left a substantial sum of money by his late aunt, which he now wishes to invest. He is told by Spiv, a stockbroker client of his employers, that Flybinight plc is currently enjoying considerable success and that since the company's shares are underpriced Punter should buy now. He offers to undertake the purchase for Punter when given the go-ahead by him. Punter meets Hackett, an old friend of his, for a drink in a pub. Hackett has recently been appointed under-manager at Eastminster Bank and Punter asks him about the wisdom of buying the shares. Hackett says that although he does not have much experience in financial advising as yet, he is interested in business matters and always reads the relevant papers. He says that *Whizz Weekly*, one of the more respected financial papers, predicts that Flybinight is undervalued since the company seems poised to declare record profits. Hackett therefore concludes that on the basis of this report and his general overview of business affairs, Punter should go ahead and buy.

Following the advice he received, Punter invests heavily in the company. After two months the company is put into liquidation by its creditors and Punter loses his investment.

Advise Punter as to whether he has any legal redress to recover his losses against Spiv, Hackett, and *Whizz Weekly*.

Commentary

Generally, the tort of negligence is more attuned to dealing with actions that result in physical harm to the person or to property. However, in limited circumstances it may also be used to deal with financial losses, particularly those caused by negligently prepared or communicated statements. Generally, physical harm tends to 'lie where it falls' so that the range of possible claimants will be limited. Words or advice present different problems since words can be heard and acted on by a much wider range of individuals.

This question requires consideration of the rules governing economic loss caused by negligent statements. In particular an examination of the principles governing the imposition of a duty of care is required.

Answer plan

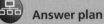

- Why is the advice both prepared and communicated: **Caparo plc v Dickman**?
- Is advice given on a social occasion actionable: **Choudhry v Prabhakar**?
- Have any of the advisers voluntarily assumed a responsibility to Punter for the advice they give: **Henderson v Merrett Syndicates**?
- Is there a distinction between those who merely transmit information and those who produce it?

⇨ Suggested answer

The *Donoghue v Stevenson* [1932] AC 562 'neighbour principle' alone is not sufficient to address the issue of economic loss caused by a carelessly made statement with the result that the courts have developed more restrictive tests importing policy reasoning to avoid the possibility of indeterminate liability to an indeterminate class of claimants. Unlike careless acts that result in physical harm where losses tend to rest where they fall, advice can be relied upon by any number of people who come into contact with it. In formulating the rules governing liability, the courts have long been mindful of the so-called 'floodgates' argument, encapsulated in Cardozo CJ's warning against the possibility of 'liability in an indeterminate amount for an indeterminate time to an indeterminate class' (*Ultramares Corp v Touche* (1931) 174 NE 441).

Whether Spiv owes Punter a duty of care in respect of his advice to purchase the shares will depend on one of three different tests identified in *Customs & Excise Commissioners v Barclays Bank plc* [2006] UKHL 28. One test asks whether the defendant has voluntarily assumed responsibility for what he said and did. Alternatively, there is a threefold test of reasonable foresight of loss; whether the relationship between the parties is sufficiently proximate; and whether it is fair, just, and reasonable to impose liability (*Caparo Industries v Dickman* [1990] 2 AC 549). Thirdly, there is the incremental test (*Sutherland Shire Council v Heyman* (1985) 157 CLR 424, 481 *per* Brennan J) which indicates that new duty situations should be developed only incrementally and by analogy with existing cases, rather than by massive leaps into new areas.

These alternative tests assist in identifying whether the relationship between the parties can be described as a 'special relationship' under the rule in *Hedley Byrne & Co v Heller & Partners Ltd* [1964] AC 465. For these purposes the relationship between representor and representee must be such that the latter reasonably relies on the advice given by the former and that the representor is, or ought to be aware of this. Furthermore, in advice cases where the defendant gives information to X on behalf of Y, it needs to be asked whether the defendant has assumed responsibility to X or whether he was merely discharging his responsibility towards Y (*Williams v Natural Life Health Foods Ltd* [1998] 2 All ER 577). The assumption of responsibility test has been noted to be particularly useful in determining whether a defendant owes a duty of care in respect of advice given by him to the claimant (*Customs & Excise Commissioners v Barclays Bank plc* [2006] UKHL 28 at [35] *per* Lord Hoffmann). Likewise, it is relevant to consider whether the defendant has assumed responsibility for advice given for one purpose, when the claimant relies on that advice for another, different purpose (*Caparo Industries v Dickman* [1990] 2 AC 605). In determining whether there is a voluntary assumption of responsibility, it is important to apply the test objectively and it is not to be answered by reference to what the defendant thought or intended (*Henderson v Merrett Syndicates Ltd* [1994] 2 AC 145). Thus, as was observed by Lord Griffiths in *Smith v Eric S Bush* [1990] 1 AC 831, 862, the phrase 'assumption of responsibility' can only have any real meaning if it is understood as referring to the circumstances in which the law will deem the defendant to have assumed responsibility to the claimant (see also *White v Jones* [1995] 2 AC 207).

Generally, the decision in *Caparo Industries v Dickman* makes four factors relevant to the question whether a duty of care is owed, namely:

(a) Was the representor fully aware of the nature of the transaction which the claimant had in contemplation?

(b) Did the representor know that the information would be communicated to the claimant, either directly or indirectly?

(c) Did the representor know that it was very likely that the claimant would rely on the information when deciding whether or not to engage in the transaction in question?

(d) Was the purpose for which the claimant relied on the information one that is connected with interests which it is proper to expect the representor to protect?

In applying the rules laid down in *Hedley Byrne* (as interpreted by the House of Lords in *Caparo v Dickman* and *Customs & Excise Commissioners v Barclays Bank plc*) to Spiv, it is suggested that there may be a 'special relationship' between Punter and Spiv as a stockbroker ought to know that the advice, 'buy now', was directly communicated and was likely to be relied upon for investment purposes. As a professional, Spiv obviously has skill and it is reasonable and proper to expect Spiv to have due regard to the interests of those who receive his advice and information. The meaning of 'special skill' has been held to include special knowledge (*Henderson v Merrett Syndicates Ltd* [1995] 2 AC 145, *per* Lord Goff). Further, as a stockbroker, Spiv may be held to be in a fiduciary relationship with Punter, in which case there is no need for the claimant to prove foreseeable reliance if a fiduciary duty is owed: *White v Jones* [1995] 2 AC 207. Lord Browne-Wilkinson observed that in the case of a fiduciary, it was sufficient that the defendant was aware that the claimant's financial welfare was dependent upon the exercise of proper care by him and, as such, a 'special relationship' arises.

The advice given by Hackett to Punter requires consideration of the circumstances in which the advice was given and the nature of the relationship between him and Punter. In *Hedley Byrne* Lord Reid observed that opinions expressed on social occasions may be given without the care that would normally be accorded if asked for professionally. Hackett's status as an under-manager may suggest a lack of specific expertise on his part. Despite all of this it was held in *Choudhry v Prabhakar* [1988] 3 All ER 718 that a duty of care may still be owed where advice was given in a social context by a friend with no special skill. However, it is pertinent to note that the decision was based on a concession by counsel that a duty of care was owed and later case law might make it more difficult to establish the existence of a duty of care, bearing in mind that the imposition of a duty in such circumstances might make 'social regulations [*sic*] and responsibilities between friends unnecessarily hazardous' (ibid. at 275, *per* May LJ).

Since Hackett had informed Punter that he lacked relevant experience and did not profess to be an expert, coupled with the fact that the advice appears to be tendered on a social occasion, the court is unlikely to impose a duty of care in these circumstances. Further, in *Royal Bank Trust (Trinidad) v Pampellonne* [1987] 1 Lloyd's Rep 218, the Privy Council distinguished between those who merely transmit information and those who produce it who are more likely to owe a duty of care. Hackett appears to be a transmitter of information and therefore less likely to owe a duty of care.

The imposition of a duty of care on *Whizz Weekly* is also unlikely, since in *Hedley Byrne* the House of Lords recognized the danger of formulating rules which could result in the maker of a careless *statement* being liable to a wide, indeterminate class of claimants. For this reason, Lord Bridge in *Caparo* emphasized the need for 'proximity' between the claimant and defendant and warned against the dangers of holding a defendant liable 'to all and sundry' for any purpose for which they may choose to rely on it. The statement that the shares of Flybinight are 'undervalued' does not amount to an unequivocal recommendation that the company's shares should be bought. Moreover, there does not appear to have been any direct or indirect contact between *Whizz Weekly* and the claimant such as to give rise to an inference that there has been a voluntary assumption of responsibility for the advice contained in the paper (*Williams v Natural Life Health Foods* [1998] 2 All ER 577).

(4) Omissions

? Question 6

Hayley lives in a block of flats owned by Crumbridge City Council and the Council has recently served an eviction notice on Reggie, Hayley's neighbour, alleging that he has engaged in anti-social behaviour towards Hayley and other residents in the block of flats. Crumbridge City Council has not warned Hayley of these events.

David, a painter and decorator who lives opposite the block of flats, knows that Hayley is keen to have her flat decorated and he offers to do the job for her at the weekend saying that if he ever needed a return favour he would know where to come.

On the Saturday when David paints the flat, Hayley spends the afternoon sunbathing on her balcony. In view of the weather and in order to let the premises 'air' David leaves the front door open.

While David is painting the kitchen window, Reggie, who believes Hayley to be responsible for reporting him to the City Council, enters the flat, steals Hayley's valuable antiques and causes serious criminal damage to the living room. In addition Reggie takes the opportunity of being inside the main door to the block of flats to break into and burgle Pam's third-floor apartment, knowing that she is on holiday in Greece.

Reggie has absconded and has not been caught.

Advise David, Hayley, Pam, and Crumbridge City Council as to their respective rights and duties.

Commentary

This question requires consideration of the general rule that tortious liability is not ordinarily imposed for the failure to act to prevent harm (nonfeasance), in the absence of any voluntary assumption of responsibility on the part of the defendant.

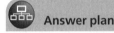

Answer plan

- Consider the nature of David's undertaking to Hayley.
- Does a public authority owe a duty of care to protect a person against the possible actions of a third party?
- Consider the limited circumstances in which occupiers of property may be placed under a duty to take reasonable precautions against the wrongdoing of third parties to determine whether Hayley owes a duty of care to Pam.

Suggested answer

The central issue is whether either David or Hayley can be held responsible for failing to prevent the infliction of damage by the act of a third party. It is also necessary to consider whether the City Council owes a duty of care to Hayley when it fails to warn her that it intends to serve an eviction notice on Reggie.

The general rule is that there is no duty, at common law, to prevent persons harming others by their deliberate wrongdoing, however foreseeable such harm may be, since the law of torts does not generally impose liability for pure omissions. Thus in *Smith v Littlewoods Organisation Ltd* [1987] AC 241, the House of Lords held that the defendants, who were unaware that vandalism was a problem, were not liable for damage caused to neighbouring property by vandals who had broken into the defendant's premises. Of primary concern to their Lordships was that if a duty of care were to be imposed on occupiers of property in such circumstances, it could not be discharged short of placing an intolerable burden on the occupiers to mount a 24-hour guard on empty premises. In *Stovin v Wise* [1996] AC 923 Lord Hoffmann justified the restrictive approach to liability for omissions on political, moral, and economic grounds. Politically, it would be an invasion of a person's freedom to impose liability for doing nothing. Moreover, if there are others who could also have acted why is it right for the law to pick on the defendant. Finally, the law does not reward a person for voluntarily conferring a benefit on a third party, so why should someone who fails to confer a benefit on a third party be made to pay for his omission?

In examining David's duty to Hayley, it is important to determine the nature of the undertaking he makes since an affirmative duty to prevent harm may arise depending on what was said and understood by both parties. If there is a contractual relationship between them, liability for the theft of the antiques may arise out of an implied term in the contract for services: **Supply of Goods and Services Act 1982, s. 13**. Similarly, a decorator will owe a duty of care in respect of property stolen by a thief, if he has been given specific instructions to lock the door of the premises he is decorating if he should decide to go out: *Stansbie v Troman* [1948] 2 KB 48.

There may be other circumstances in which a defendant is liable for an omission if he is in control of the person or thing that causes harm to a third party: see *Home Office v Dorset Yacht Co Ltd* [1970] AC 1004. As Lord Diplock observed, control imports responsibility but that responsibility was restricted to the harm caused in the course of an escape from a correction centre to those in close physical proximity.

Applying these authorities to the facts of the problem, it seems unlikely that David will be considered to owe a duty of care to Hayley. Carrying out the job on the loose understanding that if he 'ever needed a return favour he would know where to come' does not of itself suggest a contract between them from which a term can be implied to keep the door locked. Moreover, as Hayley is sunbathing on the balcony, it is likely that she will still be in control of the premises rather than David.

Pam is in an analogous position to the neighbouring property owners in *Smith v Littlewoods Organisation Ltd*. In considering the situation where a thief gains access to property through the failure of an adjacent neighbour to keep his property lockfast, Lord Goff opined that liability cannot be imposed on the neighbour for the burglary since every occupier must take such steps as he thinks fit for the protection of his own property. His Lordship stated that when considering what precautions should be taken, an occupier should take into account the fact that, from time to time, his neighbours may leave their properties unlocked. Such a proposition follows from the rule that there is no general duty to prevent third parties causing damage to others. As Lord Keith observed in *Yuen Kun Yeu v Attorney-General of Hong Kong* [1988] AC 175, a person who sees another about to walk over a cliff is not guilty of negligence if he fails to warn that other of the danger. Lord Goff went on to explain that exceptionally liability for the activities of others may arise in two situations. First, where a landowner has knowledge, or the means of knowledge, that trespassers have created a risk of fire on his property, and then fails to abate that risk. It is clear that the given facts do not fall within this exception. Secondly, where a landowner creates, or allows to be created, an unusual source of danger on his land and it is reasonably foreseeable that a third party may interfere with it thereby causing damage to another (*Haynes v Harwood* [1935] 1 KB 146). Lord Goff stressed that liability under this principle should only be imposed where a defendant has negligently caused or permitted a source of danger and it is foreseeable that a third party may 'spark it off'. If the act of the third party is deliberate or reckless, it will normally sever the chain of causation if that act is no more than a mere possibility. To render the defendant liable, the third-party action must be more probable than a 'mere possibility': *Chubb Fire Ltd v Vicar of Spalding* [2010] EWCA Civ 981. Hayley's failure to ensure that her decorator keeps the apartment block locked is not of itself likely to result in theft to a resident, and therefore cannot be described as creating a source of danger which was foreseeably 'sparked off' by Reggie.

In *P Perl (Exporters) Ltd v Camden LBC* [1984] QB 342 a local authority was not liable for a burglary in the claimant's flat when it failed to secure an unoccupied, basement flat in the same block of flats. The relationship of neighbouring property owners was not sufficient to impose on one owner the duty to guard the other against the foreseeable risk of burglary through unsecured property. In *Smith v Littlewoods* Lord Goff thought that *Perl* was correctly decided and pointed out that the law has to accommodate 'the untidy complexity of life' and therefore there are situations where considerations of practical justice will pre-empt the imposition of a duty of care. See also *Topp v London Country Bus Ltd* [1993] 1 WLR 976. Applying the language of *Caparo Industries plc v Dickman* [1990] 2 AC 605, it would not be 'fair, just, and reasonable' to recognize a duty of care on the facts since any affirmative duty to prevent deliberate wrongdoing by third parties, if recognized by English law, is likely to be strictly limited. Accordingly, it is submitted that Pam is not owed a duty of care by Hayley to prevent Reggie gaining access to the building by her failure to ensure that her decorator kept the building lockfast during the repainting. Given that this factual situation does not fall within the exceptional circumstances outlined by Lord Goff, it would not be just and reasonable to subject Hayley to such a duty. As such, the facts fall squarely within the principle formulated by Lord Sumner in *Weld-Blundell v Stephens* [1920] AC 956, that in general, 'even though A is at fault, he is not responsible for injury to C which B, a stranger to him, deliberately chose to do'.

Hayley may try to argue that Crumbridge City Council should have warned her of its intention to serve an eviction notice on Reggie; however, this too raises the issue of liability for an omission. A similar issue arose in *Mitchell v Glasgow City Council* [2009] UKHL 11 when the Council served notice on one of its tenants that he would be evicted. The tenant became verbally abusive, returned to the flats in which he lived, and killed his neighbour with an iron bar. The family of the deceased argued that the Council should have warned the deceased as soon as the meeting with the violent neighbour was over. However, the House of Lords held that foreseeability of harm alone is insufficient to establish the existence of a duty of care. Liability will only arise if the Council had assumed responsibility to advise the deceased of the steps it was about to take. On the facts, there was nothing to suggest to the Council that the violent neighbour might kill the deceased. Accordingly, no duty of care was owed. On similar lines of reasoning, it seems unlikely that Crumbridge City Council will be liable for the actions of Reggie in stealing Hayley's antiques and causing criminal damage to her flat.

Further reading

Cane, P., *Tort Law and Economic Interests*, 2nd edn (Oxford: Clarendon Press, 1996).

Gilliker, P., 'Revisiting Pure Economic Loss' (2005) 25 LS 49.

Hepple, B., 'The Search for Coherence' (1997) 50 CLP 69.

McBride, N., 'Duties of Care—Do They Really Exist?' (2004) 24(3) OJLS 417.

Murphy, J., 'Expectation Losses, Negligent Omissions and the Tortious Duty of Care' (1996) 55 CLJ 43.

Norris, W., 'The Duty of Care to Prevent Personal Injury' (2009) 2 JPIL 114.

Rogers, W. V. H., *Winfield and Jolowicz on Tort*, 18th edn (London: Sweet and Maxwell, 2010).

Stapleton, J., 'Duty of Care and Economic Loss: A Wider Agenda' (1991) 107 LQR 249.

Stapleton, J., 'Duty of Care: Peripheral Parties and Alternative Opportunities for Deterrence' (1995) 111 LQR 301.

Whittaker, S., 'The Application of the Broad Principle of Hedley Byrne as between Parties to a Contract' (1997) 17 LS 169.

Witting, C., 'Distinguishing between Property Damage and Economic Loss in Negligence: A Personality Thesis' (2001) 21 LS 481.

Witting, C., 'Duty of Care: An Analytical Approach' (2005) 25(1) OJLS 33.

Witting, C., 'Justifying Liability to Third Parties for Negligent Misstatements' (2000) 20 OJLS 615.

Negligence II: breach of duty

Introduction

Breach of duty involves an objective consideration of what a reasonable person in the same position as the defendant would have done. Thus it is necessary to ask if the defendant has reached the standards set by a reasonable person, or the 'man on the Clapham omnibus'. Expressed in this way, the test sounds perfectly straightforward and designed to achieve certainty (and therefore justice) in the law since it appears to eliminate any consideration of the personal characteristics of individual defendants. In reality, of course, other factors may be taken into account, and the law is prepared in some circumstances to accept a lower standard, for example from children, and may expect a higher standard from, for example, a skilled professional. Policy issues are again relevant, so for example the courts' approach to the standard applicable to medical negligence has been tailored in such a way as to avoid any detrimental effect on the development of new techniques and procedures.

Once a suitable description of the appropriate standard has been identified, in any problem, there remains the question, 'What steps would such a person be required to take?' This will involve an analysis of the factors that might raise or lower the level of precautions needed. Such factors include: an assessment of the degree of risk, by reference to the likelihood of harm occurring together with the potential severity of the harm, should it occur; the social utility of the defendant's activity; and the practicability of any precautions that might be needed.

☆ Examiner's tip

It should be remembered that in negligence one is expected to act reasonably *in all the circumstances*, and that an answer that fails to go through the full reasoning process is incomplete. Also, examiners are looking for evidence of a thorough knowledge of the relevant *legal* principles, so you must be especially careful to avoid reading the question as a story and responding with a common-sense, rather than a legal, answer.

? Question 1

'In general the relevant circumstances [occasioning variations in the standard of care] will be the physical conditions in which the act takes place…and should exclude those factors which describe the actor rather than the act.'

(Kidner, *Casebook on Torts*)

To what extent is this, and should it be, the case?

Commentary

This question requires consideration of the factors which, in English law, are relevant to the process of determining whether the defendant is in breach of a duty of care in a negligence action. In particular, it is inviting the student to question the suggestion that individual characteristics of the defendant are always to be disregarded, and to consider the justice of any such variation.

Answer plan

- Special characteristics of the tortfeasor/defendant (the 'actor' in the quote).
- The circumstances in which the alleged negligence took place.
- The question also requires an intelligent critique of whether factors which are specific to the actor should ever be relevant to the setting of a standard of care which purports to be objective in nature.

Suggested answer

For the most part, it is true to say that the idiosyncrasies of the tortfeasor are irrelevant to ascertaining the requisite standard of care in a negligence action. This is because, according to received wisdom, the standard of care is an objective one. In *Blyth v Birmingham Waterworks* (1856) 11 Ex 781 Alderson B described the standard as being determined by reference to the 'prudent and reasonable man'. Lord Macmillan, in

Glasgow Corp v Muir [1943] 2 All ER 44 endorsed this, saying such an approach, 'eliminates the personal equation and is independent of the idiosyncracies of the particular person whose conduct is in question'. His Lordship also noted that the determination of legal standard is a question of law to be determined by the courts, and there is therefore (at least potentially) scope for some diversity as judges themselves will vary in their perceptions of risk.

So, generally the standard will be judged according to risks connected with the activity undertaken, rather than by reference to the individual performing it. Even so, as will be explained, there are factors which relate to the defendant as *a member of a particular class* of persons which can equally affect the level of care that must be shown in order to avoid liability in negligence. It is not, however, all classes of person which seem to attract 'special treatment' under the law. This fact no doubt forms the basis of the generalization comprising the essay title. But it remains, nonetheless, a generalization. As such, it is necessarily destined to be least helpful where specificity and precision are most needed.

A sophisticated analysis of the law relating to the standard of care might seek to argue that the (seeming) inconsistency in the decided case law stems from the several, sometimes conflicting, objectives which the law of tort strives to achieve. Thus, briefly to supply an example (which will be further considered below), the desire to ensure that a 'worthy' claimant receives compensation might conflict, for example, with the aim of the tort system to do justice. Accordingly, in *Nettleship v Weston* [1971] 2 QB 691, the price of compensating the injured party was holding a learner driver liable for failure to meet the driving standard one would expect of a qualified driver. This, on one conception of justice, might seem unreasonable and mightily unfair on the learner driver, but equally it would seem unduly hard on a victim to deprive him of compensation simply because his injuries happened to be caused by a learner. Of course, a desire to do justice was not the only factor, and another significant part of the reasoning in *Nettleship* was the need for clarity in the law; a standard that varied with the relative competence of the learner would leave both drivers and their potential victims uncertain as to the scope of the law.

For present purposes, appropriate scrutiny of the hypothesis put forward in the title entails a two-step approach. First, it is necessary to assess whether the standard of care is indeed more responsive to changes in the physical conditions in which the act takes place than the particular characteristics of the defendant. Secondly, it is necessary to explain why the law should take this approach.

To begin with, it is clear that the standard of care is fixed with the circumstances in which the accident takes place very much in mind. No more stark example of this may be supplied than the case of *Watt v Hertfordshire CC* [1954] 2 All ER 368. There, because of an accident, a woman found herself trapped under a lorry. In a hurry to release her, a truck ill-suited to transporting a heavy jack was used for just that purpose. When the driver was obliged to brake suddenly on his way to releasing the trapped woman, the jack was propelled forwards injuring the claimant, one of the firemen. In finding the defendants not negligent, Denning LJ stated that:

> If this accident had occurred in a commercial enterprise without any emergency, there
> can be no doubt that the servant would succeed. But the commercial end to make
> profit is very different from the human end to save life or limb. The saving of life or
> limb justifies considerable risk.

It is also clear that other circumstantial factors may affect the level of care demanded of the defendant, such as the relative cost of precautionary measures (*Latimer v AEC Ltd* [1953] AC 653); the likelihood of harm occurring (*Bolton v Stone* [1951] AC 850); the severity of harm should it occur (*Paris v Stepney BC* [1951] AC 367); and the social utility of the defendant's conduct (*Daborn v Bath Tramways* [1946] 2 All ER 333). In short, in respect of the first limb of Kidner's proposition, it would be incorrect to assert that the scenario in which the accident occurs is unimportant. But that is, in truth, only part of the matter. There are equally as many factors which relate to the characteristics of the defendant (albeit as a member of an identifiable class) that affect the level of care expected at law. The significance of 'class' being that the standard of care is varied (objectively) for the class as a whole, not (subjectively) for the individual member.

The first factor which the courts take into account in ascertaining the appropriate standard of care is the youth of the defendant. In *McHale v Watson* (1965) 111 CLR 384, for example, a decision of the High Court of Australia, the fact of the defendant's age (he was a 12-year-old boy) was held relevant to the standard of care issue. This approach has more recently been adopted in England by the Court of Appeal in *Mullin v Richards* [1998] 1 All ER 920, reflecting a similar attitude to the level of care to be looked for from children in relation to the defence of contributory negligence, where it had been held at Court of Appeal level that age is a relevant criterion when the court assesses the degree of care that that child can be expected to take for his own safety (*Gough v Thorne* [1966] 3 All ER 398). Clearly, therefore, English law does take account of youth in setting the standard of care.

A second factor which the courts may take into account is the degree of skill or professionalism that can be expected of the particular defendant. Thus, in *Philips v William Whiteley Ltd* [1938] 1 All ER 566, for example, it was held that a jeweller performing an ear-piercing was not expected to meet the same standards of hygiene as a surgeon performing a comparable 'operation'. But the point must be stressed that the standard of care expected of the jeweller in that case is the standard which *all* ear-piercing jewellers should meet. The standard was set by reference to the jeweller, not as an individual, but as a member of a particular class. It is clear that there will not be variations of the standard of care within a class. Thus, a junior and overworked houseman is expected to demonstrate the same standard of care as a more experienced doctor occupying the same post (*Wilsher v Essex AHA* [1987] QB 730). To allow a lower standard would be to:

> subordinate the legitimate expectation of the patient that he will receive from each
> person concerned with his care a degree of skill appropriate to the task that [the
> doctor] undertakes to an understandable wish to minimize the psychological and
> financial pressures on hard pressed young doctors.

A final factor that describes the actor more than the act, and which is again relevant to setting the standard of care, is the fact that the defendant was, at the time of the accident, engaged in a sporting pursuit. Here the standard of care will be lowered to take account of the fact that the sporting arena is one which naturally gives rise to the need to take spur-of-the-moment decisions (*Wooldridge v Sumner* [1963] 2 QB 43). But even here, outright recklessness on the part of a sportsperson will not be tolerated (*Condon v Basi* [1985] 2 All ER 453; *Caldwell v Maguire and Fitzgerald* [2001] EWCA Civ 1054).

So, it may be seen that English law takes account of many factors in setting the relevant standard of care. Some such factors do relate to the characteristics of the defendant, perhaps more than Kidner's suggestion that this is not generally the case would imply. However, those factors which describe the actor, and which are relevant in this context, do so *only* so far as they take account of the defendant as a member of a defined class of persons. But one should still ask whether such factors ought to be relevant in the first place. Simply to identify that certain characteristics of the defendant are taken into account by the courts is not also to justify them.

It can certainly be argued that no variations in the standard of care should properly be founded on the idiosyncrasies of the defendant. To do so would be to drive a sledgehammer through the principle that the standard of care is an objective one, intended to promote certainty both as to when a defendant will be held negligent and as to the level of safety a claimant may legitimately expect. The same objection—i.e. the loss of objectivity—arises when the standard is set with a class of persons in mind as it is ultimately the judiciary who decide when class status is made out. This is important since the standard of care may only be adjusted if such class status (and where its boundaries lie) is recognized. Such determinations may be policy driven: for example, in cases where an insurance company ultimately bears the loss rather than an individual citizen, the standard may be kept artificially high by a failure to recognize class status. Thus, learner drivers, potentially a distinct class of road users, are simply bracketed with qualified drivers and the fact of compulsory insurance means that anyone injured by a mishap will receive compensation (*Nettleship v Weston* [1971] 2 QB 691). Equally, policy might be said to underpin the approach taken in *Wilsher* where Mustill J was clearly of the view that patients must be able to have confidence in the quality of their health care regardless of the absence of seniority in the doctor in attendance. Arguably flexibility promotes justice, whilst rigid objectivity promotes certainty. While these may, at first sight, appear to be two different aims there are many who would argue they are no more than two sides of the same coin—certainty is justice, and justice certainty. Ultimately, taking characteristics of the defendant into account militates against the principle that the standard of care is an objective one. This can promote justice. But if the courts' approach to the matter of identifying a class of persons that deserve individual treatment lacks consistency, as seems to be the case in English law, then, it may be argued, neither justice nor certainty are achieved and, particularly in relation to some areas of potential liability, the law may have the appearance of being both inconsistent and flawed.

Question 2

Consider the issues of standard of care and breach of duty in negligence raised by the following facts:

Clarence, who was walking along the street, was hit by a milk bottle which fell from one of the upper windows of the local primary school. The local education authority claims that there were no children in the school at the time because lessons had ended 45 minutes earlier and all the children had gone home. Clarence wishes to sue the local education authority in negligence.

Omolade was cut when, on hearing an explosion in the street outside, Liz, her manicurist, momentarily took her eyes off Omolade's hand. At the time, Liz simply gave her a sticking plaster for the cut, but since then the cut has turned septic causing Omolade considerable pain. Omolade seeks your advice as regards suing Liz in negligence.

Pierre was injured when he was rescued by the air-sea rescue team after bad weather capsized his boat. The rescue team used only a rope, instead of the padded harness usually employed by rescue teams, to hoist him into a helicopter. Pierre received several cracked ribs in the process. He seeks your advice in relation to a potential negligence action against his rescuers.

Commentary

This question raises three different, but related, kinds of problems associated with breach of duty in the tort of negligence. It calls for a detailed consideration of the factors defining the appropriate standard, and of the elements of the balancing process a defendant must engage in so as to meet foreseeable risks with reasonable precautions.

Answer plan

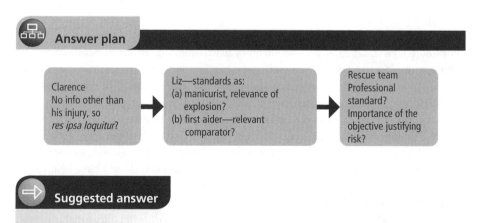

Clarence
No info other than his injury, so
res ipsa loquitur?

Liz—standards as:
(a) manicurist, relevance of explosion?
(b) first aider—relevant comparator?

Rescue team
Professional standard?
Importance of the objective justifying risk?

Suggested answer

Since Clarence was unaware of the milk bottles above him, and because there is no obvious explanation as to why the milk bottles should have fallen, Clarence faces a problem of proving negligence on the part of the local education authority. However, as the accident is of a kind that does not normally occur in everyday life, Clarence may invoke the doctrine of *res ipsa loquitur* (let the thing speak for itself). Although it is sometimes said that this raises a rebuttable presumption of negligence on the part of the defendant it has more recently been said to be no more than an inference of negligence drawn from the facts. Put another way, the doctrine does not shift the burden of proof from the claimant, it is simply offered, by the claimant, as evidence of negligence. In a recent application of this principle, the Privy Council in *George v Eagle Air Services Ltd* [2009] UKPC 21 held that aeroplanes do not normally crash without negligence. In order to invoke the doctrine, Clarence must, on the authority of Erle CJ in *Scott v London and St Katherine Docks Co* (1865) 33 H & C 596, show three things. He must show first that the accident was of a kind that does not normally occur in the absence of a want of care. Secondly, he must show that the defendant had exclusive control over the thing which has caused him harm and he must show, finally, that the defendant has no plausible alternative (innocent) explanation of how the accident might have occurred.

In respect of the first of these, there is ample authority to suggest that falling objects are within the class of things that do not normally occur without negligence (*Byrne v Boadle* (1863) 2 H & C 722, barrels of flour from a warehouse; *Scott v London and St Katherine Docks Co*, bags of sugar from a hoist).

In respect of the second limb, it is clear that bottles fell from the premises of the defendants and were thus under their exclusive control since the school had closed some 45 minutes earlier and the bottles, like the underwear in *Grant v Australian Knitting Mills* [1936] AC 85, could not have been interfered with by an intermediary. In relation to the third hurdle, the local education authority, on the facts that we are given, does not appear able to supply evidence of a plausible alternative explanation of how the bottles fell, which would be enough to dislodge the inference of negligence. For example, in *Ng Chun Pui v Lee Chuen Tat* [1988] RTR 298, in which a bus had crossed the central reservation, the defendant was able to defeat the doctrine by stating he had been obliged to swerve to avoid another vehicle, thus leaving the claimant to prove breach in the ordinary way.

With respect to Omolade's injury, several potential instances of negligence need to be considered. First, whether Liz's momentary inattention due to the explosion could be characterized as negligence; secondly, whether her subsequent treatment of the cut could amount to negligent conduct; and, thirdly, whether it could be established that any lack of hygiene in relation to her manicuring tools was negligent.

As regards the infliction of the cut, the starting point is to note that the law of negligence distinguishes between (actionable) negligence and (non-actionable) errors. The law of negligence does not demand that a defendant should act to the highest standard humanly possible. Instead, it requires only that the defendant should have behaved in a manner consistent with the actions of a reasonable person (*Blyth v Birmingham Waterworks Co* (1856) 11 Exch 781; *Glasgow Corp v Muir* [1943] AC 448), i.e. doing what a reasonable person would have done or omitting to do what a reasonable person would not have done. This is an objective standard, related chiefly to the nature of the activity undertaken, thus in *Blyth v Birmingham* it was the standard of the reasonable operator of waterworks and pipes, and in *Glasgow Corp v Muir* it was the standard of the reasonable café manager who, as Lord Macmillan noted, should be neither too fearful of something happening nor over-confident that accidents will not occur. The standard, in the case of some activities, may be determined by reference to any profession or other calling the defendant engaged in; so, for example, it would be expected that a doctor's conduct would be tested against the standard of a reasonably competent medical practitioner rather than the reasonable person. In our case, it is arguably material that Liz's slip stemmed from the 'heat of the moment' in which the explosion took place. In *Marshall v Osmond* [1983] QB 1034, it was held that errors of judgement in the heat of the moment should be regarded as errors that the reasonable man might make and, therefore, not actionable.

In relation to the second point—the application of a sticking plaster to Omolade's injury—there can be little doubt that Liz owed a duty to Omolade on the basis of her assumption of responsibility towards Omolade (*Barrett v Ministry of Defence* [1995] 3 All ER 87). Next, it is relevant to ask whether her 'treatment' of Liz was negligent. Here, it is to be noted that the standard demanded of Liz will not, on the authority of *Philips v William Whitely* [1938] 1 All ER 566, be the same as that demanded of a doctor, had a doctor been summoned to treat Omolade. In the *Philips* case a jeweller was held not liable in respect of an infection in the claimant's neck caused (allegedly) by the jeweller's ear-piercing. The court in that case held that the standard required in respect of hygiene etc. was that of a jeweller doing such work, not that of a doctor. There is no direct analogy here, since ear-piercing was part of the service offered by the jeweller, whereas Liz holds herself out simply as a manicurist. However, it is clear she will not be judged by the standard of the reasonable doctor but as someone offering basic first aid. Arguably, she has met this standard in supplying her client with a sticking plaster.

In light of the fact that Omolade's cut has turned septic, she may seek to argue that Liz has been negligent in failing to keep her manicuring tools in a suitably hygienic state. Since there are many possible ways in which a cut may become infected, the doctrine of *res ipsa loquitur* will not assist Omolade and she would need evidence of the actual cleanliness of Liz's tools. Whatever the outcome of this enquiry, the standard Liz has reached will be judged according to what is reasonable in all the circumstances. Relevant information could be gained from the hygiene practices customary amongst competent manicurists, though this will not be legally definitive and so the standard will also be measured by a balancing of reasonably practicable precautions against reasonably foreseeable risk. So, the likelihood of breaking the skin during a manicure may be judged from the frequency with which it occurs—in *Bolton v Stone* [1951] AC 850 the fact that very few cricket balls had escaped over a period of decades was evidence of low statistical probability; and the potential severity of any infection should also be taken into account as a factor increasing overall risk—in *Paris v Stepney BC* [1951] AC 367 the House of Lords held more protection was needed against potential injury to an employee with only one eye.

So far as Pierre is concerned, the standard of care demanded of the rescue team is that of any organization offering such a service and possessed of the skills required to do the same job, namely 'the standard of an ordinary skilled man exercising and professing to have that special skill' (*Bolam v Friern Hospital* [1957] 1 WLR 582, *per* McNair J). The fact that we are told of other air-sea rescue teams using different, safer equipment begs the question whether this team was negligent in merely using a rope. The answer to this lies in two stages. First, and by analogy with the law's approach to medical practitioners, it could be argued that so long as a significant body of professional opinion, gleaned from other rescue teams, supports the use of a rope alone that, prima facie, will exculpate the team in our case. As Lord Scarman put it in *Maynard v West Midlands RHA* [1984] 1 WLR 634: '[A] judge's preference for one body of distinguished professional opinion to another also professionally distinguished is not sufficient to establish negligence.' However, the policy reasoning in favour of greater flexibility for medical practitioners (so that advances in medical science are not stifled by fear of litigation) rather lacks conviction when applied to air-sea rescue. Should it apply, however, if the decision to use a rope alone could be shown to be so unreasonable a choice that no reasonable rescue team could have made it, an action for negligence might still lie (*Bolitho v City and Hackney Health Authority* [1997] 4 All ER 771). As regards the reasonableness of using a cheap rope rather than an expensive harness, the court would be entitled to consider whether the cost of preventing an injury outweighed the risk of the injury (both in terms of the magnitude and likelihood of that injury occurring: *Bolton v Stone* [1951] AC 850; *Latimer v AEC Ltd* [1953] AC 643).

Even if all other rescue teams would not use merely a rope it remains to be asked whether the rescue team may nonetheless escape liability on other grounds. The rescue team might argue that, had they had more time they could have procured a harness to use in the operation but, since it was a life and death situation they were forced to act swiftly with whatever (non-ideal) tools they had to hand. Such an argument would clearly be premised on the analogous case of *Watt v Hertfordshire CC* [1954] 1 All ER 835 where the emergency services used an inappropriate lorry to transport a jack desperately needed to rescue a casualty and a fireman was injured when steadying the jack on the lorry. The employer was held not liable because the risk inherent in the decision to proceed using this lorry was not unreasonable in light of the importance of the objective to be achieved—the genuine need to save a life. This analysis does not offer automatic immunity from liability and there have been cases where emergency vehicles going to an emergency have been driven carelessly causing harm and liability has been found, e.g. *Ward v London County Council* [1938] 2 All ER 341. It is clear that all the circumstances must be weighed in the balance, so on the facts of the scenario there may be no liability if the risk to the claimant in not doing anything to rescue him was apparent and this outweighed the risk in using the rope.

Further reading

Kidner, R. A., *Casebook on Torts*, 12th edn (Oxford: Oxford Univertisy Press, 2012).

Witting, C., 'Res Ipsa Loquitur: Some Last Words?' (2001) 117 LQR 392.

6 Negligence III: causation and remoteness of damage

Introduction

The defendant who has failed to reach the standard of the reasonable man is not necessarily liable for harm suffered by the claimant since his breach of duty must also have caused that harm, both factually and legally.

Factual causation is established in most cases initially, but not exclusively, by reference to the 'but for' test, which asks whether it is true to say that the harm would not have occurred to the claimant 'but for' the defendant's negligence. In most circumstances this works well as a first filter for eliminating those defendants whose negligent acts were *not* the cause of the claimant's loss or damage. Often, though, a defendant's negligence is only the first step in a chain of events. Some of the claimant's own acts, and those of third parties who become involved, are so connected with the negligence that they may be regarded, in law, as the responsibility of the defendant. Other events that impact on the claimant's loss or damage may be wholly independent and therefore are said to break the chain of causation. Problem questions on this area call for a systematic and carefully reasoned analysis of all the relevant factors, and a student needs to be especially careful when dealing with questions in which there are competing causes, whether concurrent or consecutive.

Even damage that has been factually caused by the defendant may be regarded as legally too remote if it is of a kind that could not reasonably have been foreseen. Another deceptively simple test since judges, as the determinants of reasonable foreseeability, will necessarily be influenced by their own views, and what may seem to one judge an obvious consequence may be regarded by another as quite improbable. A finding that the damage in question was too remote may also reflect a policy-based decision that the claimant *ought* not to be compensated.

Examiner's tip

You need to be very systematic: concentrate on the relevant legal principles, rather than allowing yourself to be drawn into the story. Also, don't allow the fact you can see a defendant's argument (*novus actus*, or defence, perhaps) that might defeat the claim to prevent you from dealing fully with legal arguments the claimant would raise.

Question 1

Adeel is crossing the road at a pedestrian crossing when he is struck by a car driven by Beatrice. Adeel is knocked to the ground and staggers to his feet, but is concussed and temporarily blinded by blood from a head wound. He is then hit by a car driven by Cassandra, who was texting on her mobile at the time, and knocked to the ground again, unconscious. Beatrice and Cassandra have both been breath-tested by the police, and Beatrice has been found to be significantly affected by alcohol.

Adeel has serious injuries which will make it impossible for him to work again, but his doctors are not able to say which car caused which specific injuries. Adeel's laptop computer was also damaged, causing information to be destroyed which led to loss of business for his employers, FatCat Ltd.

Advise Adeel and FatCat Ltd whether they have any remedy against Beatrice and/or Cassandra.

Commentary

The question is about the tort of negligence. For a full answer, issues of duty and breach must be looked at but will, on these facts, readily be answered. The main issues to be considered concern factual and legal causation, and the problems raised when the damage is associated with two rapidly consecutive events.

Answer plan

- Beatrice and Cassandra are joint tortfeasors.
- Does the law of negligence require particular damage to be ascribed to particular defendants?
- Does the criminal act of a third party amount to a *novus actus interveniens*?
- Does a motorist owe a duty of care to persons not present at the scene of an accident, particularly if they only suffer economic loss?

Suggested answer

Assuming Adeel's injuries have been caused by the traffic collision, it is necessary to consider the liability of Cassandra and Beatrice. *Nettleship v Weston* [1971] 2 QB 691 is one of numerous cases recognizing the long-established duty of care owed by motorists to other road users, so there will be no dispute about the duty Beatrice and Cassandra owe to Adeel. Under **s. 11 of the Civil Evidence Act 1968**, if either driver is convicted of a criminal offence relating to her driving, or her fitness to drive, the conviction will be admissible evidence against her in any relevant civil proceedings brought by Adeel.

There is little to choose between Beatrice and Cassandra so far as their breach of duty is concerned. Nevertheless, it is possible that Cassandra may argue, in terms of causation, that she was not to blame (or not solely to blame) for the second collision with Adeel because he stumbled unpredictably into her path. This would involve focusing the whole of the allegation of negligence against Beatrice on the basis that Adeel was still suffering from the effects of the first collision at the time.

Using this approach, and applying the 'but for' test from *Barnett v Chelsea and Kensington Hospital Management Committee* [1969] 1 QB 428, it would have to be shown that Adeel would not have suffered any injury but for Cassandra's negligence. At first sight, this reasoning looks quite promising, but Cassandra will argue that Beatrice's negligence constitutes a *novus actus interveniens*—an intervening act which breaks the chain of causation and frees her from liability in respect of the second batch of injuries. The test identified in *Knightley v Johns* [1982] 1 All ER 851 states that third party acts will break the chain unless they were a natural and probable consequence of the defendant's negligence. Several aspects of the question will make the application of this test problematic, not least the fact that it is impossible to attribute individual injuries to either car.

Although it would appear that the second collision caused worse injuries than the first, this case is not to be likened to *Baker v Willoughby* [1967] AC 467, in which there was a pre-existing disability caused by one tortfeasor and a subsequent worsening of that disability by another tortfeasor. In *Baker* there was no connection between the two tortfeasors or between the two incidents giving rise to the successive disabilities. Moreover, there were also important policy considerations since the later injury was caused by a criminal who shot the claimant in the leg, causing that leg to be amputated. This later act was held not to affect the claimant's existing claim for damages against the first defendant for injuries caused to the same leg in a road traffic accident. Ignoring the 'but for' test, the first defendant (the negligent driver) was held liable for the loss resulting from the original accident but the additional damage caused by the criminal was discounted. Had the claimant sought to bring an action in respect of the later injuries caused by the criminal, it was considered that the pre-existing injuries to the leg would have to be taken into account, thereby reducing the claimant's quantum of damages. However, since the criminal would not have been insured in respect of the damage he had caused there was probably little likelihood of the criminal being able to pay the damages even if the claimant had chosen to sue him.

As an alternative to the *Baker v Willoughby* approach, it was held in *Jobling v Associated Dairies Ltd* [1982] AC 794 that a court should take account of the vicissitudes of life, such as (in that case) the subsequent development of a disease, which reduced the claimant's projected working lifespan and hence his overall claim for damages against the defendant in respect of a negligently caused work injury. However, it may be argued that the second road accident in the problem is not a 'vicissitude of life' but a separate tortious act, and therefore rather more like *Baker*. In any case, in both *Baker* and *Jobling* the supervening event—whether tortious or natural—occurred well after the original negligence, whereas here the events occurred in very close proximity.

The present case should also be distinguished from the situation which arises when the claimant *must* have been injured by one of two defendants, but it cannot be determined which of the two is responsible. This type of scenario has come under recent scrutiny in *Fairchild v Glenhaven Funeral Services Ltd* [2002] UKHL 22 in the context of mesothelioma caused by exposure to asbestos, where the damage must have been caused by one of a series of negligent defendants. Ordinarily, a claim would fail wherever the claimant was unable to satisfy the 'but for' test and prove that a specific defendant had caused the injury. In *Fairchild*, however, the House of Lords, in recognition of the injustice that would result were the test to be applied too rigidly, agreed the circumstances called for an alternative approach. This was a scenario better dealt with by an application of the approach previously applied in *McGhee v NCB* [1973] 1 WLR 1, namely that if the defendant had negligently exposed the claimant to a material risk of injury and the injury actually suffered fell within the foreseeable range, causation is made out.

The House of Lords has held that, in cases where damage might have been caused by one tortfeasor or by natural causes, the tortfeasor cannot be held responsible unless it can be shown that the tortfeasor's negligence is, on the balance of probabilities, the most likely cause of the damage (*Wilsher v Essex AHA* [1988] AC 1074). When there is doubt as to whether a particular defendant caused certain damage to the claimant, or whether it was caused by a *novus actus interveniens*, English law seems to dictate that there is no substitute for proof, except in certain very narrow circumstances when public policy and notions of justice might promote a modified approach.

In practice, it is most likely that Beatrice and Cassandra will both be regarded as causes of the harm suffered by Adeel as in *Fitzgerald v Lane* [1989] AC 328, where a careless pedestrian was hit by two cars at a pelican crossing. If this is the case, the issue of contribution between joint tortfeasors will arise. Such argument is permissible under **s. 1 of the Civil Liability (Contribution) Act 1978**. Section 2(1) provides:

> …in any proceedings for contribution under section 1 above the amount of the contribution recoverable from any person shall be such as may be found by the court to be just and equitable having regard to the extent of that person's responsibility for the damage in question.

So far as this Act is concerned, it will make no difference whether Beatrice acted deliberately and Cassandra only negligently, since they will both be regarded as joint tortfeasors. Both may be required to make a contribution under the terms of the Act, and it will not be a defence for the merely negligent to argue that the degree of fault of the other tortfeasor was greater. However, the greater degree of fault of one joint tortfeasor will clearly be a relevant consideration in determining what share of responsibility should be allocated to each defendant.

Finally, the question arises whether FatCat Ltd can successfully sue Beatrice or Cassandra for the loss of business that was due to the destruction of data on Adeel's computer. Such a claim would face two possible problems. First, a negligent motorist may not owe a duty of care to the employers of a pedestrian who is injured as a result of the motorist's negligent driving, since, arguably, they would not meet the *Caparo* requirements of foreseeability, proximity, and fair, just, and reasonableness. Secondly, the employers have suffered pure economic loss, at least against Beatrice and Cassandra, since their loss of business is not connected with any physical damage to FatCat's property caused by the two defendants.

? Question 2

Graham, a professional cricketer, had been driving along the motorway when he noticed that a lorry, owned and operated by Speedy Ltd, had stopped in the middle lane ahead of him, having run out of fuel. Graham slowed but was struck by a car driven by Tom, which had crossed the central reservation from the other side of the motorway. Tom's attention had been drawn to the stationary lorry on Graham's side of the road and he had crashed through the central reservation.

Graham's leg was badly injured in the collision and, while he was awaiting medical treatment at the roadside, Nick, a thief, stole his wallet and made off with it.

At the hospital Graham was treated for his injuries by Dr Botch who, tired after working 20 hours with few breaks, failed to take proper notes of his medical history. The drug she mistakenly prescribed because of this failure caused a severe allergic reaction. As a result, Graham was left with permanent damage to the sight in one eye, and the emergency resuscitation procedure delayed treatment for his leg injuries.

It soon became clear that Graham would never play cricket again and that he would lose earnings of £60,000 per year for the next two years.

Advise Speedy Ltd, Tom, and the doctor as to their respective potential liabilities in tort.

 Commentary

Once again, the issues relating to duty of care and to breach are quite clear-cut, but the question of liability and on whom it should fall will require a detailed consideration of both factual and legal causation.

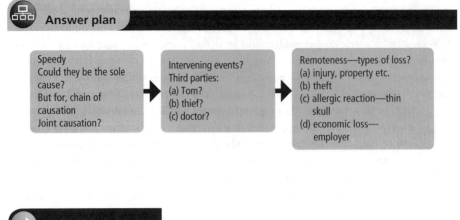

Answer plan

Speedy
Could they be the sole cause?
But for, chain of causation
Joint causation?

→

Intervening events?
Third parties:
(a) Tom?
(b) thief?
(c) doctor?

→

Remoteness—types of loss?
(a) injury, property etc.
(b) theft
(c) allergic reaction—thin skull
(d) economic loss—employer

Suggested answer

The first problem facing Graham is that of identifying whom to sue in respect of the injuries sustained in the car crash. There is prima facie evidence of negligence on the part both of Speedy Ltd (in their failure to ensure that the lorry was fit for motorway driving) and of Tom (who failed to drive with sufficient attention). This, however, does not resolve the difficult causation question of who, for the purposes of the tort of negligence, may be held responsible for the several losses that have been suffered by Graham. For the purposes of clarity of analysis, it is best to treat each head of loss separately.

In respect of the initial injuries occasioned by the crash between Tom and Graham, it is clear that the usual determinant of causation—the 'but for' test propounded in *Barnett v Chelsea and Kensington Hospital Management Committee* [1969] 1 QB 428—is of limited use, as this applies only to situations in which there is clearly only one factor that has caused the claimant's loss, though it may result in the elimination of a competing cause. In the present situation there are the two possible causes. The relevant law in this context is contained in *Rouse v Squires* [1973] QB 889, where Cairns LJ said:

> If a driver so negligently manages his vehicle as to cause it to obstruct the highway and constitute a danger to other road users, including those who are driving too fast, or not keeping a proper look-out, but not those who deliberately or recklessly drive into the obstruction, then the first driver's negligence may be held to have contributed to the causation of an accident of which the immediate cause was the negligent driving of the vehicle which because of the presence of the obstruction collides with it or with some other vehicle or some other person.

In applying that speech to the present facts it is apparent that if Tom's driving was merely negligent, then both he and Speedy would be liable for the injuries suffered by Graham. If, however, Tom's driving was reckless—and the fact that he was apparently oblivious to what was happening in his own carriageway suggests this—then Tom's act will constitute a *novus actus interveniens* rendering him solely liable for the injuries suffered by Graham as held in *Wright v Lodge* **[1994] 4 All ER 299**.

Since there is no evidence to suggest any contributory negligence on Graham's part it can be stated with some measure of confidence that (at least) Tom (if not Tom and Speedy jointly) may be held liable for the full extent of those losses flowing from the original accident. The key question thus becomes: which of the losses may be treated, in law, as having been caused by the original accident? The theft of Graham's wallet, as an act by a third party, may break the chain of causation. In *Knightley v Johns* **[1982] 1 All ER 851** the Court of Appeal held that a third party act will break the chain unless it was a 'natural and probable consequence' of the negligence. It is likely a court would take the view that the intervention of an opportunistic thief was too unforeseeable an event to be regarded as flowing from the initial accident. Accordingly, it would mark a break in the chain of causation and hence be something for which neither Tom nor Speedy could be held liable.

The allergic reaction to medical treatment could, by virtue of a chain of causation, be attributed to the negligent driver(s) in that it would not have occurred but for the negligent collision. Clearly, the medical treatment will be raised as a third party *novus actus* so the question is, in what circumstances will medical treatment break a chain of causation? *Knightley* is authority that negligent acts are more likely than mere errors of judgement to constitute a *novus actus*, and on the facts given it would appear that Dr Botch was negligent. However, in this area negligence mirrors the position in criminal law. *Hogan v Bentinck West Hartley Collieries (Owners) Ltd* **[1949] 1 All ER 588** is authority that courts are most unwilling to allow even negligent medical treatment to absolve a negligent defendant. More recently, in *Webb v Barclays Bank plc* **[2001] EWCA Civ 1141**, this was confirmed as applicable even in circumstances where the medical intervention is such as would give rise to liability in negligence on the part of the doctor.

A further question arises in respect of any impact the delay has had on Graham's leg injuries. Even if the medical negligence is capable, in law, of constituting a *novus actus*, it must still be established that it has *caused* his long-term disability, in the sense of shifting his prospects from one who would (statistically, at least) have recovered, into someone who will not. In other words, it would need to be shown that Dr Botch's negligence has deprived him of a better than 50 per cent chance of recovery. Otherwise, liability will remain with the negligent driver(s).

In *Hotson v East Berkshire AHA* **[1987] 3 WLR 232**, a schoolboy who had injured his hip by falling from a tree was initially misdiagnosed. By the time his condition was properly identified it was too late for the injury to be corrected and he was left with a permanent disability. Medical evidence indicated that, statistically, he had always had no better than a 25 per cent chance of recovery even with a prompt and proper diagnosis. That the lower courts accordingly awarded him 25 per cent of the damages was a just outcome. The House of Lords, however, allowed the defendant's appeal on the basis that the claimant had not met the burden of proving *on the balance of probabilities* that the negligence caused his injury. More recently, in *Gregg v Scott* **[2005]**

UKHL 2, the House of Lords was again invited to consider damages for a claimant whose prospects of a positive medical outcome had been reduced from 42 per cent to 25 per cent by his doctor's negligent delay in diagnosis. While acknowledging that 'lost chance' claims were available in some areas of negligence, the majority were emphatic that in medical negligence cases the claimant must meet the balance of probabilities standard or lose his case.

So far as remoteness of damage is concerned, Graham's leg injuries fall within the *Wagon Mound* test of 'damage of a kind that was reasonably foreseeable': *Wagon Mound (No. 1)* [1961] AC 388. As for the loss of sight, this, although arguably unforeseeable as a result of the original crash, occurred due to Graham's idiosyncratic reaction to the drug he was misprescribed, and therefore falls within the 'egg-shell skull rule', as first identified in *Dulieu v White* [1901] 2 KB 669, which states that defendants must take their victims as they find them. The principle was questioned following the decision in *Wagon Mound (No. 1)*, but it was subsequently confirmed by the House of Lords in *Smith v Leech Brain & Co Ltd* [1961] 3 All ER 1159 that the new approach to remoteness had no impact on the principle. So Graham's loss of sight is not too remote.

Overall, it is best not to assume that Graham's loss of a professional cricketing career is attributable to any unitary cause and the likelihood is, given the complex facts, that Graham would sue them all as joint defendants. This would be advisable since it would help to ensure the recovery of compensation by way of damages. Assuming that a remedy could be awarded, damages would not be calculated on the usual multiplier basis because of the short-term nature of sports careers. We are told that Graham only had a very limited number of years to go and this would figure in the assessment of damages.

? Question 3

Will, a student, invited a couple of mates from university, Qing and Emma, to stay at his family's farmhouse during the vacation. One day, keen to impress his friends, Will proposed taking shotguns up into the fields to see what they could shoot. Neither Qing nor Emma had ever handled a shotgun before, but Will announced that there were enough guns to go round and that he would show them what to do. When Will opened the gun cabinet he noticed that his shotgun licence had expired several months previously, but as he did not want to look silly in front of his friends he gave each a gun and some cartridges from the store. Although they had been intending to shoot in a field across the road from the farmhouse, the sight of a road sign proved too much temptation for them and all three fired at it at once. Pat, the village postwoman who had just cycled into range, was struck in the eye by a single pellet, while Will suffered a number of injuries from pellets ricocheting off the sign. Both casualties were rushed to hospital, where the shotgun pellets were removed but there was nothing to indicate from whose gun any of the pellets had been fired.

Consider the potential liability of the parties in negligence. You may assume that issues relating to duty of care and breach have already been resolved.

Commentary

The question is about the tort of negligence, and focuses on the issue of causation—in particular the courts' approach when there are competing causes, only one of which can actually be responsible for the damage. It will be necessary to consider the standard test for causation, as well as the circumstances in which, for policy reasons, this might be adapted.

Examiner's tip

A good answer will also examine the rationale expressed in cases that have departed from the orthodox approach, and question its application to certain facts in this problem.

Answer plan

- Standard 'but for' approach to causation.
- Applicability of joint tortfeasors.
- Development through case law of a modified approach.
- Application to facts.
- Defences?

Suggested answer

This is a complex situation, in which the two claimants are Pat, the injured postwoman, and Will, who is also a potential defendant along with his two friends, Qing and Emma. In the interests of clarity, each claimant will be considered separately. Although many of the principles will apply to both, one's instinctive reaction is that their claims are not equally valid (at least in moral terms) and it will be necessary to explore the ways in which the law can respond to perceived notions of justice.

Since the issues of duty and breach are said in the question to have been resolved, the starting point is with causation. Taking Pat as the first claimant, the orthodox approach would be to apply the 'but for' test (*Barnett v Chelsea and Kensington Hospital Management Committee* [1968] 1 All ER 1068, in which a doctor's negligence in failing to see a patient was eliminated as a factual cause because the victim was already beyond saving prior to the time of the negligence), and ask whether, but for the negligence of the defendant(s) she would not have been injured. Clearly, if the defendants were to be considered as a single unit this would be true, but the law calls for claimants to prove their case against defendants as individuals. In the right circumstances, it may be possible to establish that more than one defendant contributed to the overall damage without being able to attribute each separate element (as in *Fitzgerald v Lane* [1989] AC 328, where a careless pedestrian suffered multiple injuries from being struck by two negligently driven vehicles). On the facts in the problem, however, Pat has been injured by a single pellet so only one of the defendants is responsible, and the burden of proof lies on Pat to show, on the balance of probabilities, which one. This will be an insuperable problem, since statistically the likelihood of any one of the defendants having been the guilty party is, in the absence of any further evidence (*Wilsher v Essex AHA* [1988] AC 1074) one in three, or 33 per cent. The facts state that there is nothing to distinguish between any of the individual pellets so the orthodox approach will not assist Pat.

In certain circumstances, the House of Lords has adopted, in order to meet what it has seen as the justice of the case, a modified approach to the test for causation. The majority of these cases involve the workplace, and employees who have suffered injury or illness through exposure to a single substance, but in circumstances where they cannot prove as a fact (a) in some of the cases that it was the negligent (as opposed to another, innocent) exposure by their employer that caused the harm; or (b) in other cases that it was a specific employer out of a number of equally negligent candidates who bore the responsibility. So, in *Wardlaw v Bonnington Castings* [1956] 1 All ER 615 and *McGhee v NCB* [1972] 3 All ER 1008, the claimants suffered, respectively, from pneumoconiosis and dermatitis from exposure to dust. In *Wardlaw's* case, the claimant worked in an environment in which negligent mica dust was mingled with dust that could not reasonably have been avoided and which was therefore classed as 'innocent'. McGhee worked in a hot sweaty environment where brick dust became (unavoidably) stuck to his body, but the negligent failure of his employer to provide showers prolonged the contact since he was obliged to travel home in the same condition. Neither claimant was in a position to prove scientifically that it was the 'guilty' or negligent dust that had caused the damage, as opposed to the innocent.

In *Wardlaw*, the House of Lords concluded that it was sufficient for the claimant in circumstances such as these to prove on the balance of probabilities that the negligent dust had 'materially contributed to the disease' (*per* Lord Reid). A similar approach was applied in *McGhee*, and although it was noted that while it could be shown that pieces of brick dust had contributed to McGhee's condition (by contrast with *Wardlaw's* case in which every particle of dust could be shown to have played its part in causing the disease), Lord Reid observed that, '[f]rom a broad and practical viewpoint I can see no substantial difference between saying that what the respondents did materially increased the risk of injury to the appellant and saying that what the respondents did made a material contribution to his injury'.

While it is true that this distinction between contribution to the *damage* and contribution to the *risk* of damage may be of little significance in cases in which an accumulation of some substance (through prolonged exposure to it) lies at the root of the damage, it becomes crucial when the form of damage suffered stems from a single exposure amongst many different exposures experienced by the claimant, as was the case in *Fairchild v Glenhaven Funeral Services Ltd* [2002] UKHL 22. These appeals concerned sufferers from mesothelioma, a cancer caused by exposure to asbestos but, so far as is best understood at this time, which may be triggered by inhalation of a single fibre, rather than by an accumulation of asbestos. Logically, therefore, any individual who had been negligently exposed to asbestos during periods of work for different employers could never prove scientifically that any individual employer had caused the disease, nor could he prove that any individual had materially contributed to it. This was a situation in which the law is left with a stark choice between two potential injustices: apply a strict test for causation—proof of causation of the *damage* or, at least, of material contribution to it—and the rights of the gravely injured employees must go unprotected; or apply a modified approach—material contribution to the *risk* of damage—and a defendant may be obliged to shoulder liability without factually having been responsible. The House of Lords was unanimous in adopting the modified approach. Building, amongst other things, upon the reasoning in *McGhee* that to allow the current shortcomings of medical science to thwart the claims of injured employees would be to empty the employer's duty of any legal content, Lord Hoffmann, in *Fairchild*, observed, 'the purpose of the causal requirement rules is to produce a just result by delimiting the scope of liability in a way which relates to the reasons why liability for the conduct in question exists in the first place' and that the law must reflect the fact that, 'the just solution to different kinds of case may require different causal requirement rules'.

Lord Bingham, in *Fairchild*, considered cases from a range of jurisdictions, each involving negligent shootings (*Litzinger v Kintzler* Cass civ 2e, 5 June 1957, D 1957 Jur 493; *Summers v Tice* (1948) 199 P 2d 1; *Oliver v Miles* (1926) 50 ALR 357; *Cook v Lewis* [1951] SCR 830) and which involved findings of joint and several liability on the part of each defendant who had fired. In each case, this outcome had been held preferable to the prospect of leaving a negligently injured claimant uncompensated. Turning back to the problem, this line of reasoning could undoubtedly assist Pat, since it would relieve her of the burden of proving causation on the 'but for' test. Each of the three defendants has, by discharging their gun, materially contributed to the risk of Pat's injury so causation is made out. Remoteness of damage is readily established, and there are no applicable defences.

No doubt Will would be pleased to adopt the same argument regarding causation. Although he has suffered a number of injuries, there is still nothing to indicate from whose gun the pellets were fired, and it is even possible they all came from his own weapon. His position (being also one of the defendants in the case) is, on the face of it, somewhat analogous to that of one of the mesothelioma victims in *Barker v Corus* [2006] UKHL 20, who had also been exposed to asbestos during a period of self-employment. The House of Lords, in *Barker*, reconsidered the justice of holding each defendant jointly and severally liable and adopted a new approach, quantifying the liability of each according to his contribution to the overall exposure. This approach was, arguably, unsatisfactory as being just to neither party and any prospective effect of the ruling was nullified by Parliament, at least in asbestos cases, by the passing of the **Compensation Act 2006.**

So, it would appear that Will can establish causation. On the other hand, what might seem to be very clearly the justice of the case in respect of the negligently injured Pat feels instinctively far less acceptable in respect of Will, who was the instigator of the whole incident. A court wishing to avoid compensating Will would have two options open to it: (a) revisit the test for causation in his case; or (b) use other principles to deny him a remedy. Option (a) would be a problem, because it risks bringing the *Fairchild* principle into disrepute, both by undermining its relative certainty and by giving the appearance that rules may be made and broken at whim so as to allow courts to administer rough justice. However, other principles may well offer a 'just' solution. It could be argued either that the principle of *volenti* applies, since Will was in a position to understand the nature of the risk involved in this joint enterprise and yet went ahead, thereby voluntarily assuming the very risk that materialized. Alternatively, it could be argued that the principle *ex turpi causa non oritur actio* (also known as the illegality defence) would act as a bar to an action (*Ashton v Turner* **[1980] 3 All ER 870;** *Pitts v Hunt* **[1990] 3 All ER 344**). On one analysis, this requires that the activity engaged in by the claimant at the time of the negligent injury was not only unlawful but so wrong as to make it morally unacceptable for the court to assist him in seeking compensation. Arguably, the mere expiry of his shotgun licence would not on its own be enough to trigger the defence, but proceeding to encourage and participate in the discharge of shotguns on the highway, especially in light of Pat's injury, might well suffice. Will is therefore unlikely to succeed in his claim.

Further reading

Bailey, S. H., 'Causation in Negligence: What Is a Material Contribution?' (2010) 30 LS 167.

Burrows, A., 'Uncertainty about Uncertainty: Damages for Loss of a Chance' [2008] JPIL 31.

Cox, N., 'Civil Liability for Foul Play in Sport' (2003) 54 NILQ 351.

Khoury, L., 'Causation and Risk in the Highest Courts of Canada, England and France' (2008) 124 LQR 103.

McGregor, H., 'Loss of Chance: Where Has It Come From and Where Is It Going?' (2008) 24(1) PN 2.

Stapleton, J., 'Cause in Fact and the Scope of Liability for Consequences' (2003) 119 LQR 388.

Employers' liability

Introduction

There is a personal, non-delegable duty of care owed by an employer to his employees, so it cannot be discharged by delegating responsibility to a third party. This is a fault-based duty and can be discharged by the exercise of reasonable care. Where the duty applies, it is to take reasonable care to provide a competent staff, a safe place of work, and a safe system of work.

An employer may also be liable for the breach of a statutory duty giving rise to a civil cause of action in damages, such as the duties created by industrial safety legislation which creates penalties for a failure to keep a safe place of work. It must be decided whether the statutory provision also confers an action in tort and that is dependent upon what the court determines to be the intention of Parliament, but this may not always be easy since what Parliament intended may not be immediately apparent and if Parliament has not expressed an intention, it may be that the legislators gave no thought to the possibility of tortious liability. Having established that a cause of action exists, it then has to be determined whether the duty is owed to the claimant, whether it has been broken and whether the breach is the cause of the harm complained of by the claimant. In other words the process normally encountered in negligence cases applies equally here.

Question 1

The (fictional) Safety at Work (Miscellaneous Provisions) Regulations 1994 state:

(i) Employers shall ensure, so far as is reasonably practicable, that all abrasive wheels are safe to use.

(ii) It shall be the responsibility of both employer and employee to ensure that safety harnesses are worn when work is carried out more than six metres from ground level.

(iii) Where inflammable materials are stored in the workplace, it shall be the responsibility of the employer to ensure that for the protection of employees and the community at large all fire appliances are adequately maintained.

The regulations state that breach of the provisions is a criminal offence punishable by the payment of a fine. No provision is made for civil law remedies.

Eric and Roland are employed to clean the windows in a factory operated by Plasticraft Ltd. Neither is wearing a safety harness. Roland is working five metres from ground level and Eric is working seven metres from ground level. Eric slips and falls on to Roland. Both are injured. The noise causes Norman to look away while he is sharpening a chisel on an abrasive wheel. Norman's finger is badly injured when it touches the rotating wheel. Evidence shows that a device could have been fitted to the wheel which would cause it to stop as soon as a chisel ceases to make contact. Plasticraft Ltd claim not to have the resources to be able to fit such a device. During the incident, a spark created by moving parts ignites some rags on the floor. Because fire extinguishers have not been properly maintained, the fire spreads and damages a car owned by Percy, a visitor to the factory.

Advise Plasticraft Ltd of their tortious liability for breach of the Regulations.

Commentary

The question assumes the application of settled general principles governing the common law tort of breach of statutory duty, and does not require or call for any detailed knowledge of specialist legislation, although cases on such legislation may illuminate the answer if relevant. The question is best addressed by describing the nature of the tort and the general principles underpinning it. It calls for knowledge of a wide range of cases and their legal outcomes. These principles can then be applied to the facts of the problem.

Answer plan

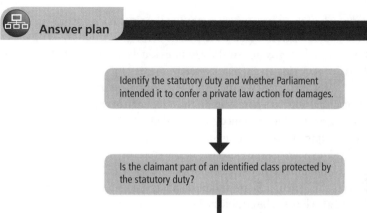

Identify the statutory duty and whether Parliament intended it to confer a private law action for damages.

Is the claimant part of an identified class protected by the statutory duty?

Is the harm suffered within the language of the statutory provision?

Assuming a statutory duty is owed, does it impose strict or fault-based liability and is there a breach of the duty?

Has the breach of duty caused the harm complained of?

Suggested answer

Two principal issues arise when it comes to be decided whether the breach of a statutory regulation gives rise to an action for damages. First, it must be asked whether the regulation confers an action in tort and, second, whether there is an actionable tort.

Whether or not a statutory provision creates a civil cause of action (known as an action for breach of statutory duty *simpliciter* by Lord Browne-Wilkinson in *X (minors) v Bedfordshire County Council* [1995] 3 WLR 152) turns on an interpretation of the intention of Parliament (*Hague v Deputy Governor of Parkhurst Prison* [1991] 3 All ER 733), although Lord Denning thought (in *Ex parte Island Records* [1978] Ch 122) that you might as well toss a coin to decide the point. There is a primary assumption that where a statute creates an obligation and provides for its enforcement in a particular manner, it does not confer a civil cause of action unless it is intended to protect an identified class of persons (*Lonrho Ltd v Shell Petroleum Ltd* [1981] 2 All ER 456).

The penalty for breach of these regulations might suggest that this is the only intended consequence of breach: see e.g. *Atkinson v Newcastle Waterworks Co* (1877) 2 Ex D 441 (water authority owed no private law duty to individual customers). Indeed, if the statutory provision does provide an adequate remedy, there is a presumption that there will be no civil action for damages (*Wentworth v Wiltshire County Council* [1993] 2 WLR 175). However, the emphasis here is upon the adequacy of the statutory remedy. Thus there may be cases in which a remedy is provided which a civil court may not regard as adequate recompense for an injured claimant: see e.g. *Read v Croydon Corp* [1938] 4 All ER 631. Furthermore the existence of the statutory duty does not prevent a claimant from pursuing an alternative cause of action, such as one for negligence if the evidence supports this. Even if the presumption against a civil cause of action were not to apply, it would also have to be established by the various potential claimants that they formed part of an identifiable class of persons Parliament intended to protect. Importantly, employees are, generally, treated as a sufficiently identifiable class to warrant protection (*Groves v Lord Wimborne* [1898] 2 QB 402). Moreover, a visitor to unsafe premises may sue for breach of fire safety regulations: *Solomons v Gertzenstein Ltd* [1954] 2 QB 243. However persons forming part of a very wide class such as highway users (*Phillips v Britannia Laundry Ltd* [1923] 2 KB 832) or water consumers (*Atkinson v Newcastle Waterworks Co*) are unlikely to be owed a duty. These rules might be taken to indicate that regulations (i) and (ii) which are intended for the benefit of employees will confer an action in tort, but that regulation (iii) may be construed so as not to give rise to an action in tort.

Even if the claimant falls within a protected class, the wording of the duty must be such that the harm suffered is of a type intended to be protected against by the statute. For example a statutory provision requiring an employer to keep protective boots in good repair has been interpreted to extend only to protecting an employee's feet from falling heavy objects rather than from frostbite in cold weather: *Fytche v Wincanton Logistics plc* [2004] UKHL 31. Along similar lines, fire safety regulations are likely to be aimed at the protection of individuals rather than their property. This would seem to suggest that Percy may have no cause of action under the 1994 Regulations in respect of the damage to his car.

Norman is likely to bring an action for damages based on the breach of regulation (i) which clearly places a duty on employers to ensure, so far as is practicable, that all abrasive wheels are safe to use. The phrase 'so far as practicable' might suggest a standard of reasonable care on the part of the employer, although it has been held to impose a stricter standard (*Edwards v National Coal Board* [1949] 1 All ER 743) and its presence in a statutory provision may place the burden of proving the practicability of precautions on the employer: *Larner v British Steel plc* [1993] 4 All ER 102. The employee would still have to prove that the lack of safety was the cause of his injury. (See also *Nimmo v Alexander Cowan & Sons Ltd* [1968] AC 107.) Moreover, it is for the defendant to plead and prove that it was not reasonably practicable to keep the workplace safe, which will involve an assessment of the degree of risk and the time and cost involved in averting the risk (*Mains v Uniroyal Engelbert Tyres Ltd* (1995) *The Times*, 29 September).

Assuming the safety device that could have been fitted is not exorbitantly expensive, Plasticraft may not have taken reasonably practicable precautions, in which case they may be liable for Norman's injury.

Paragraph (ii) of the Regulations places joint responsibility on the employer and his employees to ensure that safety harnesses are used when work is carried out at a height greater than six metres from ground level. The wording of regulation (ii) is so specific that it seems unlikely that anyone working at a height lower than six metres will be owed a duty (*Chipchase v British Titan Products Ltd* [1956] 1 QB 545). On this basis, Rowland will have no remedy under regulation (ii) since he is working only five metres from ground level, but Eric's position is different. It must be considered whether Plasticraft's alleged breach of the duty is the cause of the harm suffered by Eric, but the problem is that Eric is also in breach of the duty which rests on him to ensure that a safety harness is used. The answer to this problem may turn on whether there were further precautions which could have been taken by the employer to ensure compliance with the safety regulation as in *Ginty v Belmont Building Supplies Ltd* [1959] 1 All ER 414, where the employer could not have done more than he had to explain to employees the importance of using crawling boards when working on an unsafe roof, so that the employee's actions were the cause of the harm suffered. However, in *Boyle v Kodak Ltd* [1969] 2 All ER 439, the employer could have better explained how to use a ladder with the result that his breach of duty was the cause of injury. It follows that if Plasticraft Ltd could have done more, their failure to ensure that a safety harness is used by Eric is the cause of the injury.

? Question 2

Sanjay is a petrol tanker driver for British Diesel Fuels Ltd (BDF); he is an employee employed under a contract of service.

Sanjay has been told not to offer lifts to anyone. In breach of this instruction, he takes his 17-year-old son, Nilesh, on a delivery round. They take a brief detour so that Sanjay can collect some winnings from a betting shop. Sanjay negligently fails to apply the brake to his tanker while he goes into the betting shop. While he is away, he asks Nilesh to look after the vehicle. The tanker rolls forward and strikes a petrol pump owned by Petrol Dispensers Ltd, causing a fire in which Nilesh is badly burned.

Subsequently, when Sanjay is collecting his new tanker from the depot he spots Alphonse, another employee of BDF, who had been responsible for a particularly cruel joke on Sanjay. Still enraged by this earlier incident Sanjay remonstrates with Alphonse and when no apology is forthcoming he strikes him on the nose causing very serious injury for which he is prosecuted.

Advise British Diesel Fuels Ltd whether they are vicariously liable for these incidents.

Examiner's tip

You are told that Sanjay is employed under a contract of service, so there is no need to discuss whether he is 'an employee'. If you do you will get no credit.

Commentary

Vicarious liability is a legal device to achieve a fair result between two innocent parties and has been the subject of considerable analysis by the House of Lords in *Lister v Hesley Hall* **[2001] UKHL 22** and *Dubai Aluminium v Salaam* **[2002] UKHL 48**, which should be referred to whenever appropriate with the caveat that the earlier cases may well have been decided differently had the test in *Lister* been applied. Most questions will deal with negligence where it is relatively easy to use the 'course of employment' or 'Salmond' test, but where the tort is one that requires proof of intention, the *Lister* test is more helpful.

Answer plan

- Describe the principle of vicarious liability and the underlying policy.
- Identify briefly the torts Sanjay may have committed.
- Explain the test(s) for concluding whether Sanjay has acted in the course of his employment.
- Apply these tests to the facts and use illustrative cases.

Suggested answer

Vicarious liability applies to torts committed by an employee in the course of his employment. Vicarious liability may be contrasted with the personal or primary liability of the employer, e.g. the duty to provide a safe system of work. This liability is fault-based in contrast to the strictness of vicarious liability.

In *Lister v Hesley Hall*, Lord Millett described vicarious liability as a 'species of strict liability' which 'is not premised on any culpable act or omission on the part of the employer' so it is a loss distribution device that reflects judicial ideas as to social or economic policy. It is thought broadly to reflect the enterprise risk model to the effect that fairness requires a person who employs others in pursuit of economic gain to be made liable for losses incurred during the course of the enterprise.

The facts of the problem reveal two torts, namely Sanjay's failure to apply correctly the brake to his vehicle which, arguably, amounts to negligence as a driver owes a duty of care to other road users and in not applying his brakes, Sanjay falls below the standard expected of a reasonable driver. Secondly, Sanjay's deliberate blow is a battery and also a criminal offence.

The existence of vicarious liability does not relieve the employee of personal liability and each of them remain as tortfeasors who may well be joined in the action. This is important, because there is an employer's indemnity which permits employers to recover their outlay from the employee: *Lister v Romford Ice & Cold Storage Co* [1957] AC 555. The central issue is whether or not Sanjay's torts were committed in the course of his employment. There is no problem where the action is authorized expressly or by implication but vicarious liability goes wider than this and, according to the test in *Salmond and Heuston on the Law of Torts* Heuston and Buckley, 1996), encompasses liability for acts the employer has not authorized 'provided that they are so connected with acts which he has authorized that they may be regarded as modes—although improper modes—of doing them'. The test involves imposing liability for the way in which an employee does an authorized act.

This test was useful for torts involving carelessness but was not so convenient for torts involving intention, particularly where there was an element of personal greed or self-interest that was not closely linked to the interests of the employer, e.g. theft or battery in some circumstances. The law did not impose a requirement that the conduct had to be in the interests of the employer: see *Lloyd v Grace Smith* [1912] AC 716; *Morris v Martin* [1965] 2 All ER 725. However, in *Lister v Hesley Hall* [2001] UKHL 22 the House of Lords accepted that policy demanded that the test should not be whether there was a tort that was an unauthorized mode of doing an authorized act, but whether there was a close connection between the tort and the employment. Thus, although an act involving sexual abuse could never be regarded as an authorized act, it could be closely connected to the employment, if committed by an employee so as to warrant the imposition of vicarious liability.

Generally, an employer will be vicariously liable if an employee carelessly performs a function he is employed to carry out: *Century Insurance Ltd v Northern Ireland Road Transport Board* [1942] AC 509 (lighting a cigarette whilst unloading a petrol tanker), but will not be liable if the employee is engaged on a 'frolic of his own': *Joel v Morrison* (1834) 6 C & P 501.

Apart from the problem of prohibited acts, Sanjay has detoured to a betting shop at the time the accident occurs, which might be regarded as a frolic of his own, as was the case when an employee took a meal during working hours: *Crook v Derbyshire Stone* [1956] 1 WLR 432 and *Hilton v Thomas Burton (Rhodes) Ltd* [1961] 1 WLR 705. However, the case law in this area is contradictory, so that in *Harvey v O'Dell* [1958] 2 QB 78 a detour to buy tools and get lunch was an act done in the course of employment. The issue may resolve into a question of degree. Sanjay has detoured briefly and is still in charge of his vehicle and he may therefore still be acting in the course of his employment.

The failure to apply the handbrake was a careless way of performing his usual driving tasks. This is almost self-evident and BDF will be liable vicariously to Petrol Dispensers Ltd. The second point is that the courts will ask whether or not the giving of a lift to Nilesh, in breach of the express prohibition, will take Sanjay outside the scope of his employment. The mere fact that there has been an express prohibition does not necessarily mean that the forbidden act is not done in the course of employment. For example, in *Limpus v General Omnibus Co* (1862) 1 H & C 526, the defendant's bus driver was forbidden to race competitors to bus stops. When an accident occurred the defendant was held liable despite the driver having been racing. In *Twine v Bean's Express* (1946) 62 TLR 458, a prohibition on giving lifts to others was held to exclude the possibility of vicarious liability where a hitch-hiker was injured in a collision caused by the employee's negligence. However, in *Rose v Plenty* [1976] 1 WLR 141, regard was had to the purpose for which the prohibited act was done. It followed that an express prohibition against giving lifts to others had no effect where a milkman had asked the plaintiff to help him on his milk round. The prohibited act had been done for the purposes of the employer.

These two cases are very difficult, if not impossible, to reconcile. *Rose v Plenty* is a more sympathetic approach and is consistent with the approach in *Lister v Hesley Hall* which gave tacit approval to the conclusion reached in *Rose v Plenty*. The issue resolves into one difficult factual question: was the prohibition concerned with the mode of doing a job he was employed to do, or did it relate to the scope of what he was required to do, i.e. the sphere of his employment? The conclusion must be that the carelessness of Sanjay did not serve to take him outside the scope of his employment but was an improper mode of doing an authorized act and accordingly BDF will be liable vicariously to Nilesh.

More difficulties arise in connection with the attack on Alphonse. The issues raised are close to those identified in *Lister v Hesley Hall*: what is the appropriate test for determining whether or not employers will be responsible for the deliberate torts of their employee? In *Lister's* case the defendants were held vicariously liable for deliberate acts of sexual abuse by a warden on boys resident at their hostel as there was a sufficient closeness of connection between the nature of the employment and the particular wrongdoing as the warden had been employed in order to discharge the defendants' undertaking to care for the boys. The House of Lords said that the tort did not have to be committed for the benefit of the employer.

Some earlier decisions supported the imposition of vicarious liability for intentional torts—indeed in two of the most difficult cases (*Lloyd v Grace Smith* [1912] AC 716 and *Morris v Martin* [1965] 2 All ER 725) the House of Lords had accepted that there could be vicarious liability where the criminal acts had been committed without any furtherance to the employer's business interests. The earlier cases on personal violence against customers may well have to be reconsidered in the light of what was said in *Lister v Hesley Hall*, but application of the test is not always easy as is illustrated in *Mattis v Pollock* [2003] EWCA Civ 887 where an employer was held vicariously liable for an exceptionally serious battery committed by a nightclub bouncer as, although the attack had taken place some time after the original dispute and was motivated by revenge, he was doing the job he was employed to do. In *Dyer v Munday* [1895] 1 QBD 742 an employer was held vicariously liable for a criminal assault committed by his employee while attempting to repossess his employer's property, while in *Warren v*

Henlys Ltd [1948] 2 All ER 935 there was no liability for an assault by a petrol pump attendant on a customer during a dispute over payment. According to *Lister*, *Warren* can be explained since it was no part of the duties of the pump attendant to keep order.

These principles were applied in *Brown v Robinson* [2004] UKPC 56 where the Privy Council adopted the *Lister* approach that the key question was the closeness of the connection between the job description and the tortious behaviour, and to ask if the connection was so close that it would be just and reasonable to hold the employer liable. In this case, the shooting by a security guard of a person trying to gain entry to a football match fell within this and was a tort motivated by revenge or retaliation.

Accordingly in this case since there was no close connection between what Sanjay had done and the terms of his employment duties, there would be no basis under the *Lister* approach to require the imposition of vicarious liability for the battery.

Further reading

Buckley, R. A., 'Liability in Tort for Breach of Statutory Duty' (1984) 100 LQR 204.

Giliker, P., 'Rough Justice in an Unjust World' (2002) 65 MLR 269.

Giliker, P., 'The Ongoing March of Vicarious Liability' (2006) 65 CLJ 489.

Heuston, R. F. V., Buckley, R. A., *Salmond and Heuston on the Law of Torts*, 21st edn (London: Sweet and Maxwell, 1996).

Levinson, J., 'Vicarious Liability for Intentional Torts' [2005] JPIL 304.

McBride, N. J., 'Vicarious Liability in England and Australia' (2003) 62 CLJ 255.

McKendrick, E., 'Vicarious Liability and Independent Contractors—A Re-examination' (1980) 53 MLR 770.

Newark, F. H., 'Twine v Bean's Express Ltd' (1954) 17 MLR 102.

Stanton, K. M., *Breach of Statutory Duty in Tort (Modern Legal Studies)* (London: Sweet & Maxwell, 1986).

Stanton, K. M., 'New Forms of the Tort of Breach of Statutory Duty' (2004) 120 LQR 324.

Williams, G. L., 'The Effect of Penal Legislation in the Law of Tort' (1960) 23 MLR 233.

Williams, G. L., 'Vicarious Liability: Tort of the Master or of the Servant' (1956) 72 LQR 522.

8

Occupiers' liability

Introduction

Although the **Occupiers' Liability Acts (OLA) of 1957** and **1984** are based on the previous common law rules which they replaced, they are a self-contained code for imposing a duty of reasonable care on an occupier in favour of either a visitor or a non-visitor. Trespassers are the commonest form of non-visitor but that category will mask the potentially very wide range of potential unlawful entrants, from the burglar to the wandering child. The duty, where one exists, is based on reasonable care under all the circumstances and questions of breach will tend to attract similar issues as breach of the ordinary common law duty in negligence. Issues of causation and remoteness are as likely to occur in connection with the liability of an occupier as with any other action in negligence. Commonly, an occupier will attempt to warn of a particular danger or to exclude liability for any potential liability. In respect of the latter, but not the former, the provisions of the **Unfair Contract Terms Act 1977** may become relevant.

? Question 1

Multimillion plc owns a building and contracts with Shambles Ltd to demolish it. Shambles Ltd is responsible for the security of the site and it leaves it unattended on Sundays when work is not in progress. The site is protected by a perimeter fence topped with razor wire.

During working hours, Sven, an electrician from another company, has been called to the site to repair a defective generator. He is told by a security guard that he must report to the site office in order to be provided with protective headgear to guard against the risks present on a demolition site, especially the possibility of debris falling from overhead operations which are in progress.

Sven sees the defective generator and decides to make a preliminary inspection before reporting to the site office. As he approaches the generator, Sven stumbles over a drainage pipe left on the ground and as he limps to the site office he is struck by a brick which falls off a wall.

As a result of these incidents Sven suffers head and leg injuries. Some time after the event, Shambles Ltd put up a notice near the site office which states clearly that visitors should keep their eyes on the ground to avoid tripping over articles left temporarily on the site.

On Sunday, Fabio, aged 20, decides to enter the site to take scrap metal to exchange for cash. He climbs over the tall fence but falls off because the top strand of wire is loose, and breaks an arm. As he tries to recover a handful of brass fittings he slips into a deep trench and is injured.

Advise Multimillion plc and Shambles Ltd as to their potential liability under the **OLA 1957** and the **OLA 1984**.

Commentary

This question raises the narrow issue of occupiers' liability under the legislation and does not require an account of potential liability under other possible causes of action such as negligence or breach of statutory duty. The **OLA 1957** refers to 'visitors' and it is advisable to employ this term in the answer even though occasionally even the judges refer to 'lawful visitors' as if to suggest that there may be 'unlawful visitors'. The **OLA 1984** refers to 'non-visitors'. Trespassers are the most frequently encountered category of non-visitor and that term may be used provided the point is made clear at the outset that this is for convenience. In an examination, unless the statute is provided, there will be a temptation to use a short version of each of the sections since 100 per cent recollection and reproduction verbatim is unlikely. Concentrate on encapsulating accurately within your version of each section the important aspects, e.g. in **s. 2(4)(a)** the warning must be sufficient to enable the visitor to be *reasonably safe*, not to be *safe*. Answers should contain reference to those cases which address broad issues of principle.

Answer plan

- Identify who is the occupier, and there may be more than one.
- Identify what duty is owed and to whom.
- Consider when an occupier is able to discharge (perform) their duty by using an independent contractor.
- In order to effectively discharge the common duty of care, identify what a warning must do.
- Consider who is a non-visitor and the nature of the duty owed to a non-visitor.
- State in what circumstances that duty is broken.

⇨ **Suggested answer**

Both the **OLA 1957** and the **OLA 1984** deal with harm arising from dangers due to the state of the premises rather than activities on the premises: see *Fairchild v Glenhaven Funeral Services Ltd* [2002] UKHL 22. Under the 1957 Act an occupier who employs a subcontractor will only be liable for damage caused by the contractor if it affects the state of the premises.

Both the **OLA 1957** and the **OLA 1984** require a danger arising from 'the state of the premises', which was said to signify something unusual and dangerous for that type of premises in *Tomlinson v Congleton Borough Council* [2003] UKHL 47 with the result that it was held that no such risk was posed by a lake if it was just like any other lake, i.e. shallow at the margin with muddy water and uneven depth. But if the lake possesses some unusual feature it may pose such a risk: *Rhind v Astbury Water Park* [2004] EWCA Civ 756. Here, a building site could be regarded as no different to any other building site with no additional risks, but the fence had a loose strand of wire which suggests that it is defective which could pose additional risk.

Another issue common to the injured parties is that the duty of care, if owed, is owed by the occupier of the premises that pose the risk and that is the person in control of those premises: *Wheat v Lacon & Co* [1966] AC 552. Under the **OLA 1957** a duty is automatically owed by an occupier to visitors, but under the **OLA 1984** the duty may be owed to non-visitors only provided certain pre-conditions are satisfied. In *Wheat v Lacon & Co* it was held that it is possible for there to be more than one occupier of premises as different people may control different parts of the same premises. For example, in *Collier v Anglian Water* (1983) *The Times*, 26 March, a local authority and a water company were considered to be in joint control of a sea wall, but because the water company controlled the physical integrity of the sea wall it was the responsible occupier when the uneven surface caused the claimant to trip, but had the accident been caused by a banana skin left lying around, the local authority would have been responsible. Here it is likely that both Multimillion plc and Shambles Ltd will be occupiers and that each will owe a duty dependent upon their degree of control and its nature.

Once it is decided that both parties may be occupiers then under the **OLA 1957** the common duty of care will be owed towards visitors, but is Sven a visitor? He has been told to report to the site office but as he does not do so a condition of entry has not been complied with which may make him a non-visitor outside the scope of the **OLA 1957** (see below). Thus it is important that an implied licensee does only those activities the implied licence extends to otherwise the occupier will owe no duty of care: see *Harvey v Plymouth City Council* [2010] EWCA Civ 860 (normal recreational activity consented to, but not reckless acts). If Sven is a visitor, he is owed the common duty of care, under s. 2(1). Under s. 2(2), this is a duty to take such care as is necessary to see that the visitor is reasonably safe in using the premises for the purposes for which he is invited by the occupier to be there.

Multimillion plc is not answerable for damage caused by any work of construction, maintenance, or repair by an independent contractor if, in the circumstances of the case, it was reasonable to entrust the work to an independent contractor and if such steps as are reasonable have been taken to ascertain that the contractor was competent and the work was properly done: **OLA 1957, s. 2(4)(b)**. In *Ferguson v Welsh* [1987] 3 All ER 777, it was held that demolition fell within the scope of **s. 2(4)(b)** so it will be reasonable to entrust demolition to an expert and Multimillion plc will have to show that they had exercised reasonable care in selecting the independent contractor. If the contractor does technical work which the occupier cannot be expected to check, the occupier can be expected to do no more than check that the contractor is competent: see *Haseldine v Daw & Sons Ltd* [1941] 2 KB 343. However, very complex work, such as a major building project, may require specialist supervision: *AMF International Ltd v Magnet Bowling Ltd* [1968] 2 All ER 789. Accordingly it is suggested that Multimillion have discharged their duty of care since it would not be reasonable to expect them to employ another contractor, such as an architect, to supervise the work.

Since Shambles Ltd, as demolition contractors, have responsibility for the security of the site, it is assumed that they have control of the premises and are occupiers: *AMF International Ltd v Magnet Bowling Ltd*, and *Collier v Anglian Water*.

The duty under the **OLA 1957, s. 2(2)** is to take steps to ensure that the visitor is *reasonably* safe for the purposes for which he is invited or permitted to be there. A visitor can be made safe by means of a warning that a risk exists, but the warning must be such as would enable the visitor to be reasonably safe: **s. 2(4)(a)**. The warning given to Sven by Shambles regarding the risk of tripping over a pipe is non-specific. If Sven had gone to the site office, he would have been provided with a hat, which might have protected him from falling rubble, but it would have little effect in relation to the risk of harm resulting from tripping over a pipe. By contrast in *Roles v Nathan* [1963] 2 All ER 908 the chimney sweeps were clearly told that entering a particular alcove with the sweep-hole in the flue open and with the fire lit would place them in peril. They proceeded despite this warning and died as a result. It was held that the warning was sufficient under the circumstances to allow them to be safe as they knew what to avoid. The risk of tripping over a pipe might be regarded as obvious and there is case law to suggest that there is no need to warn of such: *Staples v West Dorset District Council* (1995) 93 LGR 536 (algae on sea wall); *Cotton v Derbyshire Dales* (1994) *The Times*, 20 June (steep cliff). Sven might also argue that the subsequent erection of a notice warning of the danger which has resulted in his injury is some admission of liability. Certain visitors such as children or the visually handicapped may pose special risks and specialist contractors may have the skill to guard against risks ordinarily incident to the job he does: **s. 2(3)(b)**.

In *Roles v Nathan* the chimney sweeps were expert and the risk of entering the sweep-hole was one which was incidental to their calling. In Sven's case, the pipe and the brick might be regarded as a general risk rather than one specific to the calling of an electrician.

If Sven is a trespasser he will be in the same position as Fabio as a non-visitor outside the scope of the **OLA 1957**. Under the **OLA 1984, s. 1(3)** there are three criteria to be satisfied before a duty of care will be owed by an occupier to a non-visitor. First Shambles Ltd must be aware of the danger or have reasonable grounds for believing that it exists: **s. 1(3)(a)**. Here the danger due to the state of the premises has already been identified (see *Tomlinson v Congleton Borough Council* [2003] **UKHL 47** and *Rhind v Astbury Water Park* [2004] **EWCA Civ 756**). In Sven's case an occupier would be aware of the dangers inherent in a building site such as the falling brick and the pipe, whereas in *Rhind*, as a matter of objective fact, the occupier could not have been expected to be aware of the danger hidden at the bottom of the murky lake.

Secondly, Shambles Ltd must have known or must have had reasonable grounds to believe that the particular non-visitor is in or may come into, the vicinity of the danger: **OLA 1984, s. 1(3)(b)**. They know that Sven is on site and must be aware that he is or may come into the vicinity of the danger. On the other hand, there would have to be evidence that a trespasser such as Fabio would have been anticipated at that time. In *Higgs v Foster* [2004] **EWCA Civ 843** it was not anticipated that a trespassing police officer would enter a bus depot and come into the vicinity of an uncovered inspection chamber into which he fell. The provision of a fence should not normally be taken as an acceptance that trespassers are likely (see *White v St Albans City and District Council* (1990) *The Times,* **12 March**) and there would have to be sufficient evidence that there had been previous trespasses or attempts.

The third requirement is that Shambles Ltd must be aware that the risk is one against which they could reasonably be expected to offer the particular non-visitor some protection: **s. 1(3)(c)**. This may require consideration of the practicality of taking greater precautions, the utility of the defendant's behaviour, and the nature of the claimant's behaviour: *Tomlinson v Congleton Borough Council*. In *Tomlinson* diving into a lake was regarded as normal activity so that an occupier would not be expected to take special precautions for the benefit of visitors. It would seem to follow that the same should also be the case for non-visitors.

Where a duty is owed, it must also be shown that there has been a breach and under the **OLA 1984, s. 1(4)** Shambles Ltd must take reasonable care to ensure that the non-visitors do not suffer personal injury or death due to the danger arising out of the state of the premises. Factors such as the magnitude of risk, precautions necessary to guard against that risk and the cost of taking such precautions, the objective to be attained by Shambles Ltd, the age of the trespassers, and the nature of the premises will require consideration. For the purposes of lawful visitors, obvious risks, such as the presence of razor wire, do not need to be warned of, so the same ought to be the case for non-visitors.

Shambles Ltd may argue that under the **OLA 1984, s. 1(5)** they have discharged their duty by taking sufficient steps to discourage Fabio from taking the risk in the first place.

They have erected a fence which is topped with razor wire. They may also suggest that in respect of Sven they warned of the risk, and the earlier discussion applies to this point.

Causation may also be an issue to the extent that Fabio may have been so intent on theft that he would not have been deterred even if the fence had not been faulty. Finally, it could be argued that Fabio and Sven are contributorily negligent, having failed to take reasonable precautions for their own safety and having been in part a cause of the harm they suffer: *Jones v Livox Quarries* [1952] 2 QB 608.

Question 2

Pleasureland Ltd own and operate Thrill Towers, an entertainment park. At the entrance to the park there is a prominent notice that 'Pleasureland Ltd and Kidikicks Ltd can accept no liability for any injury suffered'. One of the attractions, the Serpent, has been leased from Pleasureland Ltd by Kidikicks Ltd; the lease provides for Kidikicks to maintain the ride. The Serpent is a notoriously frightening car ride which for part of its route travels underground. At the entrance to the Serpent ride there is a notice which states:

> All possible precautions are taken in the interests of safety. This tunnel for this ride has a low ceiling. People taller than 6 feet 3 inches are not permitted on this ride.

Adam, aged 21, is 6 feet 4 inches tall but decides that this cannot matter and bends his knees as he passes under the height checking device provided by Kidikicks Ltd. During the ride, the Serpent dips sharply into an underground cavern and Adam, who is sitting high up in his seat, suffers a glancing blow to the head from a low light used in emergencies but which has come free from its support. Sitting behind Adam is Bronwen who is also struck by the light; she is 5 feet 3 inches tall. The light has recently been maintained by Sparky, an independent contractor. Both Adam and Bronwen are seriously injured.

Advise on the potential liability of Pleasureland Ltd and Kidikicks Ltd under the **Occupiers' Liability Acts**.

Commentary

This question is concerned with the liability of an occupier to a visitor. The first thing to notice is that the rubric asks the student to focus on the legislation and not common law negligence. The rubric identifies the **Occupiers' Liability Acts**, which is a hint that there may be a trespassing non-visitor to consider.

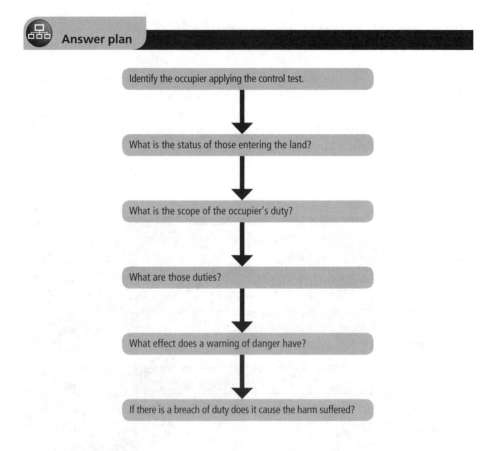

Answer plan

- Identify the occupier applying the control test.
- What is the status of those entering the land?
- What is the scope of the occupier's duty?
- What are those duties?
- What effect does a warning of danger have?
- If there is a breach of duty does it cause the harm suffered?

Suggested answer

The duty under the **OLA 1957** and the **OLA 1984** is placed on the occupier, who is a person who has control of that part of the premises on which the accident occurs: *Wheat v Lacon Ltd* [1966] AC 552. *Wheat* also shows that there can be more than one occupier but that the nature and content of the duty owed by each occupier will depend upon the nature of their control, so that in *Wheat* the pub manager was liable for the state of the furnishings, but the brewery that owned the pub could be liable for the state of the electrical system (see also *Collier v Anglian Water* (1983) *The Times*, 26 March). In the problem much will depend on the arrangements in place between Kidikicks Ltd and Pleasureland. It seems likely that both will be treated as occupiers under the **OLA 1957** on the basis that they have control over the state of the premises but any liability for the light would depend on who had responsibility for it.

For the purposes of the **OLA 1957**, the common duty of care is owed to any person who would have been treated as an invitee or a licensee at common law (**s. 1(2)**), which includes contractual visitors such as Adam, assuming he has paid to enter Thrill Towers. The duty owed to Adam will be the same whether he sues in contract or under the Act (OLA 1957, s. 5(1)). As regards Adam and Kidikicks the position is more complex, since Adam's deception may vitiate the implied consent to enter the land so that he becomes a trespasser and the only duty owed to him will arise under the OLA 1984. If the deception does not vitiate the consent then Adam will be a visitor under the OLA 1957. In *Tomlinson v Congleton Borough Council* [2003] UKHL 47 the claimant was treated as a trespasser from the time he ran into the water with a view to diving. In *Keown v Coventry Healthcare NHS Trust* [2006] EWCA Civ 39 an 11-year-old who climbed a fire escape on the underside was a trespasser on the basis of the dictum of Scrutton LJ in *The Carlgarth* [1927] P 93, 110 that: 'When you invite a person into your house to use the staircase, you do not invite him to slide down the banisters, you invite him to use the staircase in the ordinary way in which it is used.'

If either Act is to apply, the danger complained of must arise from the state of the premises in the sense that there must be something in the nature of a defect in the premises. In *Tomlinson* a muddy lake with shallow water and variable depth was not defective as it was typical of other lakes, but in *Rhind v Astbury Water Park* [2004] EWCA Civ 756 a lake with a hard object buried in the silt was unusual and so defective. The light-fitting hanging down is clearly a defect in the state of the premises and gives rise to a danger, since both Bronwen and Adam make contact with it.

Assuming Bronwen and Adam are visitors, the OLA 1957 will apply and the duty will be the same whether they would have been invitees or licensees at common law. Section 2(2) requires the occupier 'to take such care as in all the circumstances of the case is reasonable to see that the visitor is reasonably safe in using the premises for the purposes for which he is invited or permitted by the occupier to be there.' The test for determining whether there has been a breach of that duty is the same as at common law, taking account of the degree of risk and the cost of taking precautions. Kidikicks will argue that they have discharged their duty of care by using an independent contractor to do the work within s. 2(4)(b). They will have to show that they had acted reasonably in delegating responsibility by demonstrating that they had ascertained the competence of the contractor and had checked that the work had been properly done. The facts say little about the competence of Sparky but it is reasonable to obtain the services of an independent contractor for these purposes. Arguably the more complex the job the greater the need for supervision (as in *AMF v Magnet Bowling* [1968] 2 All ER 789 where the complex structure being built demanded that there should be architect supervision of the contractors). Here perhaps a visual check would suffice. If s. 2(4) has been satisfied then Kidikicks will have performed their duty and no liability on their part will arise. Any potential liability of Sparky would be considered under negligence principles.

It might be argued that by entering the ride, Adam has consented to the risk of injury under the OLA 1957, s. 2(5), however all Adam is aware of is a low ceiling, and he is injured by a low-hanging light fitting, so it is unlikely that he will be taken to have consented.

Kidikicks Ltd may argue that the warning notice at the entrance to the ride discharges their duty under the Act. However s. 2(4)(a) requires a warning to enable a visitor to be reasonably safe taking account of all the circumstances of the case. In *Roles v Nathan* [1963] 2 All ER 908, two industrial chimney sweeps ignored a warning that they should not work on certain boiler flues if the fire in the boiler was lit, and were overcome by carbon monoxide fumes, a danger to which they had been alerted. The warning was held to have discharged the occupier's duty of care. Kidikick's warning does not indicate how a user of the ride can remain safe so that it is unlikely to discharge the duty.

The defence of contributory negligence may be available: OLA 1957, s. 2(3). This allows a court to consider 'the degree of care, and want of care, which would ordinarily be looked for in such a visitor'. Adam, as an adult, may have failed to take reasonable care for his own safety and may be guilty of contributory negligence, so that any damages awarded may be reduced under the provisions of the **Law Reform (Contributory Negligence) Act 1945**. The defence will operate to reduce his damages only if the injury was due to, or was made worse by, his being too tall for the ride. However, as Bronwen, who is only 5 feet 3 inches tall, was also injured by the low-hanging light, it may be that Adam's height is not the root cause of the problem.

If Adam is treated as a trespasser, he is a non-visitor who is owed the duty identified in the **OLA 1984**. This Act requires the non-visitor to establish that a duty is owed. Under s. 1(3) three conditions must be satisfied, namely that (i) the occupier knows or has reasonable grounds to believe that the danger exists, (ii) the occupier knows or has reasonable grounds to believe that the non-visitor is or will come into the vicinity of the danger, (iii) the risk is one against which in all the circumstances it is reasonable to offer the other some protection. Arguably, in respect of a simple maintenance matter, the occupier ought to have been aware of this danger.

Adam has found it relatively easy to gain access to the danger by practising his deception, but simple ease of access does not mean that the occupier ought to have been aware of his presence on the ride: see e.g. *Higgs v WH Foster* [2004] EWCA Civ 843. Moreover, a simple prohibition of an activity does not, of itself, show that the occupier is aware of the presence of a trespasser: see *White v St Albans City and District Council* (1990) *The Times*, 12 March.

The more difficult question is whether the non-visitor should reasonably be offered some protection as there is a difference between a merely careless trespasser and a deliberate trespasser such as a burglar. The occupier may be expected to tolerate the former to a greater extent than the latter and as Adam is merely careless it may be reasonable for him to be afforded some protection.

Exclusion notices are permitted by the **OLA 1957** in relation to visitors, subject to the **Unfair Contract Terms Act 1977, s. 2(1)** which renders such notices ineffective in relation to death or bodily injury caused by negligence, if displayed by a person acting in the course of a business. However, the **OLA 1984** is silent on the matter of exclusion or modification of the duty which might suggest that exclusion of liability is not permissible. If this is so then possibly this will place the non-visitor to whom a duty is owed (which is going to be very rare) in a better position than a visitor to business premises.

? Question 3

The Grotbag Trust, a charitable organization, owns a 50-acre estate consisting of gardens and country walks, which are open to the public on the payment of a small charge to defray the expenses of the charity. Day-to-day management of the estate, including all aspects of care and maintenance of the garden, is entrusted to Dastardly Ltd, which charges the Grotbag Trust a management fee.

At the public entrance to the estate, there is a prominently displayed notice which states:

> Dastardly Ltd and the Grotbag Trust ask you to take care on these premises. Children must be accompanied and supervised by responsible adults. No responsibility can be accepted for injury or damage suffered while on these premises.

Tadeusz and his wife Harriet take their child, Marta, aged six, for a day trip to the Grotbag estate. Tadeusz and Harriet are keen gardeners but Marta becomes bored and wanders off. She comes upon a bush bearing bright red berries. In front of the tree there is a notice which states that the berries are poisonous and should not be eaten. The notice carries a symbol of a skull and crossbones to indicate poison. There is also a small fence around the bush which Marta is able to step over. Marta eats some of the berries and is taken very ill.

Tadeusz is walking in the grounds when a tree-branch hanging over the path falls onto his head. The branch had been left carelessly suspended over the path by Rhoda Dendron, an independent tree surgeon employed by Dastardly.

Despite a sign which says 'No paddling', Harriet decides to cool off in the pond which she sees is murky. She uses a stick to test the depth of water but does so only in an area where there is, unknown to her, a planting ledge. Her testing suggests that the water is very shallow and therefore safe. As she steps from the planting ledge she falls into a deep hole and suffers serious injury.

Advise the Grotbag Trust Ltd and Dastardly Ltd as to their potential liability under the **OLA 1957** and **OLA 1984**.

Commentary

This question raises the narrow issue of occupiers' liability under the legislation and does not require an account of potential liability under other possible causes of action such as negligence. Use the terms 'visitors' and 'non-visitors', although since trespassers are the commonest category of non-visitor 'trespasser' may be used provided the point is made clear at the outset that this is for convenience. Again, avoid the temptation to use an overly simplistic shorthand version of each of the sections. Concentrate on encapsulating within your version the important aspects. Answers should contain reference to the recent cases which address broad issues of principle.

The question concerns the liability of an occupier of premises to both visitors and non-visitors. It differs from the previous question in that the issue of exclusion of liability is raised as well as the issue of the duty owed in the case of children. As regards the matter of exclusion, the question is a tort question and detailed analysis of when an organization becomes a business for the purposes of the **Unfair Contract Terms Act 1977** would be beyond the scope of the answer; simply identify the issue that turns upon this point and then move on.

Answer plan

- Identify who is an occupier and what duty may be owed.
- Identify who is a visitor and who a non-visitor.
- Consider what duty is owed to young children.
- Consider whether a warning notice will suffice.
- Identify the principle that applies to obvious dangers.
- State whether and how the duty may be discharged by the use of an independent contractor.
- Deal with the structure and impact of the **OLA 1984**.
- Consider whether exclusions or restrictions on liability are permitted and in what circumstances the **Unfair Contract terms Act 1977** comes into play.

Suggested answer

A duty of care is owed by the occupier of premises to a visitor under the **OLA 1957** and to a non-visitor under the **OLA 1984**. For both Acts, the occupier is a person with control over the premises that pose a risk of injury and there may be more than one person with the required degree of control: see *Wheat v Lacon & Co* [1966] AC 552 and *Collier v Anglian Water* (1983) *The Times*, 26 March. Here it is likely that each of Grotbag Trust and Dastardly Ltd will be occupiers and that the content of the duty each owes will be dependent upon the relative degree and the nature of the control. Since day-to-day management of the estate has been entrusted to Dastardly Ltd, this would seem to suggest that they have primary control of the premises and it could be that the Grotbag Trust has little relevant control.

The **OLA 1957, s. 2(2)** provides that the occupier owes a common duty of care to all visitors, namely a duty to take such care as in all the circumstances of the case is reasonable to see that the visitor is reasonably safe in using the premises for the purposes for which he is invited or permitted by the occupier to be there.

Tadeusz is a visitor who is owed the common duty of care and as Dastardly Ltd, rather than the Grotbag Trust, are responsible for the day-to-day maintenance of the gardens their duty extends to the branch that presents a danger. The House of Lords in *Tomlinson v Congleton Borough Council* [2003] UKHL 47 emphasized that the state of the premises must present an identifiable risk, which was not the case on the facts, as there was nothing extraordinary about the lake, having the same general features as any other lake. According to the facts of the problem, there is a risk of injury due to the state of the premises as the tree has been left in a dangerous state.

It must also be decided if the Grotbag Trust has discharged its duty of care towards Tadeusz. The **OLA 1957, s. 2(4)(b)** provides that an occupier is not to be treated as answerable for damage caused by any work of construction, maintenance, or repair by an independent contractor if, in the circumstances of the case, it was reasonable to entrust the work to an independent contractor and that such steps as are reasonable have been taken to ascertain that the contractor was competent and the work was properly done.

The task of lopping branches from a tree involves a certain degree of skill, so that it is probably reasonable to entrust that work to a specialist, so that the first limb of **s. 2(4)(b)** appears to have been satisfied. However, in order to satisfy the second limb of **s. 2(4)(b)** it must be shown that reasonable care has been taken in the selection of the independent contractor. If the work done by the contractor is technical, which the occupier cannot be expected to check, it may be sufficient that the occupier has ascertained that the contractor is competent before employing him: *Haseldine v Daw & Sons Ltd* [1941] 2 KB 343, but in *AMF International Ltd v Magnet Bowling Ltd* [1968] 2 All ER 789, it was suggested that the more complex the project then the more complex had to be the supervision. It is suggested that Grotbag Trust has discharged its duty of care provided that it has perhaps reviewed the work done by the contractor. Tadeusz's remedy would then lie against Rhoda Dendron in negligence. If either Dastardly or Grotbag Trust were to be found liable then the issue of the exclusion clause would become relevant (see below).

It may be questioned whether the risk to Marta arises from danger due to the state of the premises as there is nothing defective about the bush, and *Tomlinson v Congleton* suggests that a bush that is no different to any other bush will not be regarded as defective. However, the positioning of the bush with knowledge that people, including children, may pass in close proximity could amount to a danger due to the state of the premises, as it did in *Glasgow Corp v Taylor* [1922] 1 AC 44, decided before the 1957 Act was passed.

The fact that Marta is six years old is a relevant consideration since the **1957 Act, s. 2(3)(a)** provides that in deciding what is reasonable, an occupier must expect children to be less careful than adults. In the cases of premises generally where dangers may not be obvious this rule is sound, but both the nature of the premises and the role and duty of parents or carers should also be considered.

Because the nature of the premises is relevant to the content of the specific duty, there is an essential difference between the problem and the position in *Glasgow Corp v Taylor* where a child ate poisonous berries from a tree in a public park and died. A relevant factor was that children were expected to go to the park unaccompanied and unsupervised, but in the problem set there is an expectation that young children will be supervised and the essence of the garden is viewing the plants and grounds and nothing else. In the *Glasgow Corp* case it was emphasized that both the parents and the occupier had to act reasonably; in that case the parents had acted reasonably but the corporation had not because it had left in such a place a poisonous bush. The expectation of parental oversight of young children was specifically relied on by the court in *Phipps v Rochester Corp* [1955] 1 QB 540 where the parents were expected to do more than leave a five-year-old child in the care of an older sibling when they crossed open land forming part of a building site where the younger child fell into a trench. Since Marta's parents have allowed her to wander off on her own, it may be that they do not regard the estate to be a dangerous place, in which case, the occupiers may also be able to argue that the estate is not dangerous (*Simkiss v Rhondda Borough Council* (1983) 81 LGR 460). It must be emphasized that what is required of the occupier is that he should take reasonable care, rather than all possible care. (See also *Bourne Leisure Ltd v Marsden* [2009] EWCA Civ 671).

If it is decided that the occupier has acted unreasonably, a warning may become relevant if it satisfies the requirement in the **OLA 1957, s. 2(4)(a)** that it should enable the visitor to be reasonably safe. Lord Denning in *Roles v Nathan* [1963] 2 All ER 908 gave the example of a warning which indicated that a particular bridge was dangerous and that there was a safe alternative. Here the notice may not be sufficient to discharge the duty owed to a child visitor, since it is possible that a six-year-old child cannot appreciate the message or may take no notice of the warning. The warning would not be such as to enable her to be reasonably safe.

Harriet has disobeyed the sign and has probably become a trespasser, like the claimant in *Tomlinson v Congleton* when he ran into the water prior to diving forwards. (See also *Keown v Coventry Healthcare NHS Trust* [2006] EWCA Civ 39.) As Scrutton LJ in *The Calgarth* [1927] P 93, 110 observed: 'When you invite a person into your house to use the staircase, you do not invite him to slide down the banisters, you invite him to use the staircase in the ordinary way in which it is used.' Accordingly Harriet is a non-visitor and any duty of care owed to her will arise under the **OLA 1984**. In contrast to the **OLA 1957** the existence of a duty of care is not automatic. **The OLA 1984, s. 1(3)** provides that a duty of care is owed to a non-visitor if (i) the occupier is aware of the danger or has reasonable grounds to believe that it exists; and (ii) he knows or has reasonable grounds to believe that the other person is in the vicinity of the danger or may come into that vicinity; and (iii) the risk is one against which the occupier may reasonably be expected to offer some protection. The House of Lords in the *Tomlinson* case explored the criteria for the creation of a duty in great detail in speeches which emphasized the balance which has to be drawn between the behaviour of the claimant on the one hand and over-onerous duties on the other. It came down in favour of not imposing onerous duties on occupiers where the harm was in reality brought on the claimant of full competency by his own high-spirited behaviour.

But the starting point in *Tomlinson* was the analysis of risk of injury by reason of a danger due to the state of the premises. It was held that the lake, in that case, was an ordinary lake without hidden dangers or obstacles. Accordingly, there was no danger due to the state of the premises such as would give rise to a duty of care. Here the position is broadly similar. The pond is murky and of uneven depth, but so are many ponds. Accordingly Harriet's case would fall at this very early hurdle.

Under **s. 1(3)(b)**, even if there was a danger within the meaning of the Act then it would have to be shown that Dastardly Ltd were aware or had reasonable grounds to believe that it existed and that the other person would come into the vicinity of the danger. Finally, under **s. 1(3)(c)**, it would have to be shown that the risk was one against which the occupier may reasonably be expected to offer the other some protection. The members of the House of Lords in the *Tomlinson* case pointed out that even if the trespassing swimmer in that case had been a visitor then no duty to warn of a danger would have been owed because the risks of diving in a lake were obvious (see also *Staples v West Dorset* (1995) 93 LGR 536; *Cotton v Derbyshire Dales District Council* (1994) *The Times*, 20 June and *Darby v National Trust* [2001] EWCA Civ 189). If nothing more could be expected of an occupier in respect of a visitor then there was no reason why a trespasser should be placed in a better position.

Furthermore there had to be a balance drawn which took into account not only the likelihood that someone may be injured and the seriousness of the injury, but also the social value of the activity which gives rise to the risk and the cost of preventative measures. In *Tomlinson*, the social value was of major concern to the House of Lords who felt that it would be unfair to restrict the ordinary lakeside activities of visitors in order to protect trespassing divers. The balance in the problem may not be as clear cut since measures such as appropriate planting could be sympathetically carried out so as not to destroy the attraction of the pond to other visitors. But, Harriet would have great difficulty in maintaining that she should have been warned of the uneven bottom given the obviousness of the dangers in paddling in a pond.

Even if a duty is owed under **s. 1(3)**, it has to be considered whether there is a breach of that duty. In this respect, **s. 1(4)** provides that the occupier must take such care as is reasonable in all the circumstances of the case, although the approach in *Tomlinson* comes close to deciding the standard issue since the relevant failure has been considered when asking the key question whether the risk was one in respect of which some protection ought to have been offered. This creates an objective standard which will require consideration of, *inter alia*, the magnitude of risk, and the precautions which could have been taken to guard against the risk. It is likely that a similar conclusion would be reached as under **s. 1(3)(c)**.

The duty owed to visitors may be restricted, modified, or excluded by agreement or otherwise, so far as this is permitted by law: **OLA 1957, s. 2(1)**. The words 'or otherwise' will be sufficient to cover a general notice modifying the common duty of care (**Ashdown v Samuel Williams & Sons Ltd [1957] 1 QB 409**). The notice will also be subject to the provisions of the **Unfair Contract Terms Act 1977**, provided the occupiers fall within the intended scope of that Act. For the **1977 Act** to apply, the premises must be occupied in a business capacity (**s. 1(3)**), but Grotbag Trust makes a charge for entry in order to defray its expenses as a charity. However, a charity can also be a business as is the case with the National Trust or Eton College. If a purely charitable organization is not a business, the result is that the Trust will not be affected by the provisions of the **1977 Act**. In contrast, Dastardly Ltd charge a management fee, which suggests that they are in business with a view to profit, in which case, the provisions of the **1977 Act** will affect their ability to exclude or limit their liability to lawful visitors.

By virtue of the **Unfair Contract Terms Act 1977, s. 2(1)**, any attempt to exclude or limit liability for death or bodily injury caused by negligence (including the common duty of care under the **OLA 1957**), is void. Accordingly, Dastardly Ltd will not be able to exclude liability for the injury caused to Tadeusz (assuming that they are otherwise liable).

Even if Grotbag Trust does owe a relevant duty and is somehow in breach of it, on the assumption that it does not act in the course of a business, the provisions of the **1977 Act** will have no application to its operations, and it would seem that the exclusion, insofar as it relates to its liability, will be operative as regards visitors.

On the other hand, there is nothing in the **OLA 1984** which sanctions (or prohibits) the use of exclusion notices. As a matter of policy, if the duty imposed by the **OLA 1984** is akin to the duty of common humanity created in *British Railways Board v Herrington* **[1972] AC 877**, this might suggest that it is a basic level of protection which cannot be excluded by way of a notice or a disclaimer of liability. Accordingly, if Harriet is a trespasser then the exclusion of liability will have no effect in relation to any duty which may be found, even if the finding of such a duty and subsequent breach is most unlikely.

Further reading

Buckley, R., 'Occupiers' Liability in England and Canada' (2006) 35 *Common Law World Review* 197.

Jones, M., 'The Occupiers' Liability Act 1984' (1984) 47 MLR 359.

Law Commission Report No. 75, Cmnd 6428, 1976.

9

Product liability

Introduction

This chapter contains questions relating to liability for harm caused by defective products. The regime imposed by the **Consumer Protection Act 1987** is a form of strict liability the rationale for which has been extensively explored in both the standard legal journals and the cases. Students should be aware of this theoretical underpinning which helps explain the interpretation of the legislation.

At common law a manufacturer who produces a defective product is liable in damages only if it can be proved by the claimant that there has been a failure to exercise reasonable care: see *Donoghue v Stevenson* [1932] AC 562. However, the European Community required Member States to impose a form of strict liability based on consumer expectations of safety. The **1987 Act** did not displace the fault-based form of liability in negligence under the narrow principle emerging from *Donoghue v Stevenson*. It is therefore necessary to identify in any question which form of liability the answer is required to deal with: frequently it will be both.

? Question 1

Albert is a fruit and vegetable farmer who grows apples, some of which he processes into cider, others he supplies to local retailers. Jane purchases five bottles of Albert's cider and 10 pounds of Albert's apples from George, a local retailer who has since gone out of business. Jane eats one of the apples, but becomes ill due to the presence of insecticide traces on the skin.

The bottles of cider all bear the warning that it has a very high alcohol content and that no more than two litres should be consumed in any period of 24 hours. Albert is also aware that he has used an additive in the cider which possesses hallucinogenic qualities.

Jane arrives home for her evening meal. After the meal, a curry, Jane opens a bottle of cider, but as she does so, a plastic plug flies off the bottle top and part of the contents of the bottle splash into the face of Susan, Jane's sister. Susan licks the cider and suffers from a delusion that she can walk on water. She then jumps into Jane's swimming pool and drowns. Jane consumes three litres of the cider as a means of coping with Susan's death. Subsequently she feels sick. It transpires that her sickness is due partly to a chemical reaction between the contents of the cider and traces of curry she had recently eaten and partly due to excessive alcohol consumption. An article in the little heard of *Journal of Apple Science* has recently identified the possibility of a chemical reaction between certain varieties of curry and strong cider.

Advise Albert of his potential liability.

Commentary

This question concerns the liability of a manufacturer of a product for the physical harm suffered by a consumer of his product and requires consideration of the different approach to defective products according to whether the action is based in the tort of negligence or under the strict liability regime created by the **Consumer Protection Act 1987**. The former focuses on the conduct of the manufacturer whereas the latter has as its central focus consumer expectations as to the safety of the end product.

Answer plan

- What is the narrow rule in **Donoghue v Stevenson**?
- How is fault established?
- Is the manufacturer the cause of the harm suffered?
- What is a defective product under the **Consumer Protection Act 1987**?
- What defences to liability are available?

Suggested answer

The 'narrow' rule in *Donoghue v Stevenson* [1932] AC 562 states that a manufacturer of products, which he sells in such a form as to show that he intends them to reach the ultimate consumer in the form in which they left him with no reasonable possibility of intermediate examination, and with the knowledge that the absence of reasonable care in the preparation or putting up of the product will result in an injury to the consumer's life or property, owes a duty to the consumer to take reasonable care.

The narrow rule creates a form of fault-based liability that focuses on the wrongful conduct of the manufacturer. Although the rule refers to 'manufacturers' it is better to think in terms of a person who has put a product into circulation, so that anyone in the chain of distribution is capable of owing the duty of care, including a farmer such as Albert, if he is at fault.

Fault (or breach of the duty) on the part of a manufacturer may be found in a breakdown in the production process whereby there is one or more 'rogue' products capable of causing harm to the consumer. Thus a failure to remove impurities from the fabric used to manufacture clothing (*Grant v Australian Knitting Mills* [1936] AC 85) or the production of ginger beer containing a snail (*Donoghue v Stevenson*) are examples of such fault. By analogy, the failure by Albert to wash his apples so as to rid them of traces of insecticide before putting them into circulation may amount to a breach of his duty to take care, especially if he ought reasonably to have foreseen that the presence of traces of the insecticide would be harmful to a consumer of the apples. Moreover, the use of inadequate materials in the product or its packaging is also capable of constituting a breach of duty. (See *Fisher v Harrods Ltd* [1966] 1 Lloyd's Rep 500; *Hill v James Crowe (Cases) Ltd* [1978] 1 All ER 812.)

A further possible breach of duty arises where the manufacturer fails to give an adequate warning of a known risk. The question informs us that Albert has warned of the danger of over-consumption, but he has not warned of the possible hallucinogenic qualities of his cider. It is clear that a warning can be inadequate for what it does *not* say: see *Vacwell Engineering Ltd v BDH Chemicals Ltd* [1971] QB 88 (warning of fumes, but no warning of a violent reaction to water). It may follow from this that the failure to warn of the hallucinogenic effect of the preservative used by Albert constitutes a breach of duty, especially since this indirectly results in Susan's death.

There may also be a breach of duty where a range of products suffers from a design fault, such as the cider in the question that chemically reacts with certain varieties of curry so as to cause illness. Since this possibility has only been referred to in an obscure scientific journal, this may not be a fact of which Albert can reasonably have been aware. It is important that in a fault-based enquiry the defendant is only judged by reference to information available to him at the time of the alleged breach of duty (*Roe v Minister of Health* [1954] QB 66).

The mere fact that there is a potential breach of duty does not settle the matter since it must also be shown that the breach of duty is the cause of the harm suffered by the claimant. Jane may be affected by the possibility of intermediate examination and by her own misuse of the cider. If the manufacturer can reasonably expect another person to inspect or do something to the product before it reaches the ultimate consumer, this possibility of intermediate examination may exonerate the manufacturer on the basis that his fault is no longer the cause of the harm suffered. In *Grant v Australian Knitting Mills*, it was unsuccessfully argued that the consumer ought to have washed the underwear he had purchased. This shows that the mere opportunity for intermediate examination is not sufficient to point to a cause other than defective manufacture and that the manufacturer must reasonably expect someone else to take up the opportunity to examine the goods. There may be a reasonable expectation that the product will be tested before use and this is more likely where the manufacturer has issued an appropriately worded warning (*Kubach v Hollands* [1937] 3 All ER 907). Here there appears to be no warning given by Albert which requires any sort of examination, but there is a warning pertaining to consumer misuse as it is stated that no more than two litres of the cider should be consumed in a period of 24 hours. Jane fails to heed this warning and becomes ill in which case Albert may not be the cause of that illness: *Farr v Butters Bros Ltd* [1932] 2 KB 606.

Jane and Susan's estate must prove that there is a causal link between Albert's breach of duty and the illness/ death. Jane will have to prove that it is the chemical reaction rather than her own misuse of the cider which is the cause of the harm she has suffered otherwise her action will fail: *Evans v Triplex Safety Glass Ltd* [1936] 1 All ER 283. A possible difficulty in the action by Susan's estate is that while only a very small amount of the cider has resulted in the delusion that leads to Susan's death, Jane has consumed a considerably greater quantity of the same cider without suffering the same reaction, suggesting that Susan is unusually prone to suffer from this type of delusion. However, in a negligence action, the 'egg-shell skull' rule indicates that where a claimant is unusually prone to a particular type of harm, the defendant must 'take his victim as he finds him': *Smith v Leech Brain & Co Ltd* [1962] 2 QB 405. Jane and Susan's estate may have an action under **Part I of the Consumer Protection Act (CPA) 1987** which purports to create strict liability in respect of defective products that cause physical harm to the person or to property (**CPA 1987, s. 2(1)**). As a producer of a processed product (the cider) Albert will be subject to the Act (**CPA 1987, s. 1(2)(a)**) and as the grower of the apples, he will also be a producer.

The **CPA 1987, s. 3(1)** provides that a product is defective if it is not as safe as persons generally are entitled to expect. In determining what persons generally are entitled to expect **s. 3(2)** requires the court to consider (a) the manner in which and the purposes for which the product has been marketed, (b) what might reasonably be expected to be done with the product, and (c) the time of supply. In *A v National Blood Authority* [2001] 3 All ER 289, Burton J drew a distinction between standard and non-standard products and held that the Hepatitis-infected blood supplied by the defendants was non-standard as it differed from the norm that the producer intended for use by the public. In concluding that the blood was defective, Burton J dismissed the defendant's argument that the presence of the defect was unavoidable as this raised issues concerning the conduct of the producer. This might suggest that products containing an abnormal defect will always be regarded as non-standard and therefore defective. However, in *Tesco Stores Ltd v Pollard* [2006] EWCA Civ 393 the defendants were not liable for injury suffered by a child who opened a 'child-proof' safety cap on a dishwasher detergent container as all the public could expect was that the cap would make it more difficult for a child to open the container, which purpose it did serve.

Here, the apple eaten by Jane is a natural product that is contaminated by traces of insecticide and is likely to be a non-standard product that is abnormally dangerous. Albert probably intended such contamination to be eliminated before his apples were put into circulation. The public would also probably expect better, unlike the apparently low expectations of the safety cap in *Tesco v Pollard* so it seems likely that Albert will be liable for Jane's illness.

The bottles of cider would appear to raise different considerations, due to their intended target market. Being an alcoholic drink prepared for human consumption, persons generally would expect it to be consumed only by those over the age of 18. Although Jane's age is not stated, it would be reasonable to assume that she is an adult as she appears to own her own house. However, the question remains whether the cider put into circulation by Albert achieves the desired level of safety in the light of its alleged defects. The **CPA 1987, s. 3(2)(b)** allows the court to consider what can reasonably be expected to be done with the product, which may raise the issue of consumer misuse in the light of the warning printed on the bottles of cider. A danger that is adequately warned against may cease to be a danger at all. In the present case, Jane has consumed three litres of the cider when the printed warning advises against consumption of more than two litres in a 24-hour period. This might make it difficult for Jane to establish the causal link between the alleged defect in the cider and the harm she has suffered. A court might be persuaded that Jane's failure to heed the warning is the cause of the harm she has suffered. Alternatively, it is also clear from the **CPA 1987, s. 6(4)** that the defence of contributory negligence provided for in the **Law Reform (Contributory Negligence) Act 1945** will apply to an action in respect of a defective product, so that the claimant's damages may be reduced in accordance with her degree of blameworthiness.

The death of Susan raises different considerations if it can be assumed that the cider is a standard product since Albert is aware of the hallucinogenic qualities of the additive he has used. There is no warning about this danger and Susan has not deliberately consumed the cider with a view to experiencing its hallucinogenic effects, so the question is what would persons generally expect in terms of safety of a cider possessing these qualities? The cider has been marketed as a product intended for human consumption and if such a small amount as a splash on the lips is capable of producing such extreme consequences as the delusion from which Susan suffers, this might suggest that the cider has fallen below the standard of safety that might generally be expected. However, Jane has also consumed a much larger quantity of cider than did Susan without suffering the same consequences, which may suggest something unusual about Susan. In this last event, a court might be able to conclude that the cider is not unsafe in the light of general expectations. Conversely, if the effect upon Susan is one that is likely to be repeated in other consumers, it would seem to follow that the cider is not as safe as persons generally are entitled to expect. In this case, perhaps the only means of rendering the product safe will be to have it withdrawn from the market altogether.

Jane suffers as a result of a chemical reaction between strong cider and curry but this phenomenon is little known to the scientific world. The **CPA 1987** provides for a development risks defence under **s. 4(1)(e)** so that a producer can avoid liability where the state of scientific and technological knowledge was not such that a producer of products of the same description as the product in question might be expected to have discovered if the defect had existed in his products while they were under his control. This complex wording differs from that used in the **European Product Liability Directive (Dir. 85/374/EEC)**, which asks simply what was the state of scientific and technical knowledge at the time the product was put into circulation. **Section 4(1)(e)** appears to import a subjective test based on factors relevant to the producer, whereas the **Product Liability Directive** sets an objective test of knowledge. The alleged difference was considered by the European Court of Justice in *EC Commission v United Kingdom (Re the Product Liability Directive)* (Case C-300/951) [1997] 3 CMLR 923 but it was held that s. 4(1)(e) did not set a subjective standard, as at the time there was no evidence that UK courts were misinterpreting the defence. In *A v National Blood Authority* [2001] 3 All ER 289, Burton J considered the position under **art. 7(e)** of the **Directive** (CPA 1987, s. 4(1)(e)) to be that the state of scientific knowledge is the most advanced available to anyone, although this does require an enquiry into what is discoverable evidence. **Article 7** is not concerned with the conduct of the individual producer, but is concerned with the expected conduct of producers, generally, in the light of what was objectively discoverable, but this does not require consideration of standard industry practice. The relevant question, therefore, appears to be whether Albert should have taken account of the article published in the *Journal of Apple Science*. If the article was published after the cider was put into circulation by Albert, this will raise an issue of defectiveness, since the **CPA 1987, s. 3(2)(c)** directs the court to consider the time when a product was put into circulation in determining whether it is defective and if that was before the date on which the article was published there is a presumption that the product is not defective, unless the claimant can prove otherwise: *Piper v JRI Manufacturing Ltd* [2007] EWCA Civ 1344.

If the relevant copy of the *Journal of Apple Science* was in existence before the cider was put into circulation the question is whether this is information Albert should have had regard to before marketing his cider. In *EC Commission v United Kingdom (Re the Product Liability Directive)*, Tessauro A-G gave the example of a piece of scientific evidence published in Chinese in a Manchurian scientific journal, compared with an article published in a major scientific publication widely available to the English-speaking world. While the latter would normally be objectively discoverable by a UK producer, the former might not. In the present case, it would be necessary to have regard to the obscurity of the relevant journal and whether other cider producers, generally, might have taken account of it, especially in the light of the fact that there is only a possibility of the identified chemical reaction and that the reaction only occurs with some, but not all, varieties of curry.

? Question 2

Koffman Latrash plc manufacture a pharmaceutical product called 'Offenden' which is marketed as a cure for morning sickness suffered by pregnant women, subject to a warning that the drug should not be used by people who suffer from high blood pressure. Extensive trials have failed to reveal any other defect in the drug despite the fact that an article published in a New Zealand medical journal has established that the principal ingredient in 'Offenden' may be capable of causing severe foetal limb abnormalities in rats in 1 per cent of cases in which the drug is used.

Neelam, who knows herself to be pregnant, attends the surgery of Dr Vijay who recommends the use of 'Offenden'. Neelam has high blood pressure, a fact of which she is aware but which is not known to Dr Vijay since he failed to make appropriate enquiries.

Neelam suffers a heart attack in the course of giving birth to her son, Sanjay, but she survives. The heart attack is shown to have been caused by high blood pressure exacerbated by ingredients in 'Offenden'. Sanjay is born with shortened arms and severe sight defects. Two months after the birth of Sanjay, a major scientific journal establishes incontrovertibly that one of the ingredients in 'Offenden' is likely, in more than 50 per cent of cases of use, to cause sight defects in newborn children.

Advise Neelam and Sanjay.

Commentary

This question requires consideration of the liability of a pharmaceuticals manufacturer for injuries caused to the immediate consumer of a drug and the effect of such consumption on an unborn child.

Answer plan

- Is there a breach of duty to exercise reasonable care and how does the issue of a warning affect liability?
- Is the doctor in breach of a duty of care?
- Does the **CPA 1987** apply to the drug and, if so, is it defective and what defences are available?
- Is the unborn child protected by the **Congenital Disabilities (Civil Liability) Act 1976**?

Suggested answer

As a consumer of the drug 'Offenden' Neelam is owed a duty of care by the manufacturer, Koffman Latrash plc, under the narrow rule in *Donoghue v Stevenson* [1932] AC **562**. This states that a manufacturer of products which he sells in such a form as to show that he intends them to reach the ultimate consumer in the form in which they left him with no reasonable possibility of intermediate examination, and with the knowledge that the absence of reasonable care in the preparation or putting up of the product will result in an injury to the consumer's life or property, owes a duty to the consumer to take reasonable care. On these facts, the drug suffers from a design defect, in which case the burden of proof on the claimant is difficult, but not impossible, to discharge.

Koffman Latrash plc have warned that the drug should not be used by persons with high blood pressure and warnings are an effective way of discharging the duty of care owed by a manufacturer: *Kubach v Hollands* [1937] 3 All ER 907. A warning may also raise a reasonable expectation that someone else, e.g. a doctor, will check that the instructions are complied with: see e.g. *Holmes v Ashford* [1950] 2 All ER 76 (hairdresser expected to patch test hair dye), in which case the intermediary may be in breach of duty. (See also *Perrett v Collins* [1998] 2 Lloyd's Rep 255). Neelam is unlikely to succeed in an action against Koffman Latrash plc, since there is a specific warning against the use of 'Offenden' by patients with high blood pressure, but Dr Vijay may have failed to act as would a reasonable medical practitioner in making appropriate enquiries, having regard to the warning supplied with the product: *Bolam v Friern Hospital Management Committee* [1957] 2 All ER 118.

Despite being unborn at the time damage was caused, Sanjay is owed a duty of care (*Burton v Islington Health Authority* [1992] 3 All ER 833, and see now the **Congenital Disabilities (Civil Liability) Act 1976** which supplants the common law). Under the **1976 Act, s. 1(1)** if a child is born disabled as a result of an occurrence before its birth, including events affecting the mother during pregnancy, and a person other than the child's mother is answerable for those disabilities, then the child may sue for the wrongful damage, but only if he is or would have been liable in tort to the parents had actionable damage been sustained (**1976 Act, s. 1(3)**). This may be problematic as the propensity of 'Offenden' to cause sight defects is only discovered after the drug is put into circulation, so that there may not be a breach of duty: see *Roe v Minister of Health* [1954] QB 66. A defendant can only be judged by information available at the time of the alleged negligent act, so Koffman Latrash may not be liable in this respect. But there is evidence to show that the drug has caused foetal abnormalities in rats. If this converts into a similar percentage risk in relation to human beings it may be evidence of negligence on the part of Koffman Latrash plc, but the information must have been reasonably available to the manufacturer and since the relevant research is contained in an obscure journal, it may not amount to a failure to exercise *reasonable* care not to have been aware of it.

Both Neelam and Sanjay may sue under the **CPA 1987**. The **CPA 1987** implements the **European Product Liability Directive**, the wording and interpretation of which prevails over the Act: **A v National Blood Authority** [2001] 3 All ER 289.

Koffman Latrash plc are producers of the drug by virtue of the **CPA 1987, s. 1(2)(a)**. Drugs, being substances which are not otherwise excluded from the scope of the Act, are products (**CPA 1987, s. 45(1)**), but the central issues are whether the drug is defective within the meaning of the **CPA 1987, s. 3** and if defectiveness is the cause of the harm suffered by the claimant, which must be proved by the claimant (*Foster v Biosil* (2001) 59 BMLR 178).

A product is defective if it is not as safe as persons generally are entitled to expect (CPA 1987, s. 3(1)). In *A v National Blood Authority*, it was held that factors such as the fault of the defendant, whether the defendant could have taken steps to make the product safer, and whether the product is a socially useful utility are irrelevant under s. 3, except to the extent that persons generally may accept a risk of harm because of the benefit the product confers. For example, everyone knows a knife is sharp but if marketed as a kitchen knife it will not be defective. Factors that Burton J in *A v National Blood Authority* did consider to be relevant were whether or not the harmful characteristic in the product caused the injury complained of and whether the product was a standard or non-standard product. A standard product is one that has been produced as intended by the producer, whereas a non-standard product is one that fails to reach the normal standard set by the producer. The drug 'Offenden' was produced as designed and as such would be a standard product, but the nature of the design defect will need to be considered as it may render the product unsafe, unless a defence can be pleaded.

What persons generally expect by way of safety has to be considered in the light of the manner and purposes for which the product is marketed and any instructions or warnings as to use. Thus a product may be defective if it is aimed at child consumers, even if the product would not be harmful to an adult (*A v National Blood Authority* [2001] 3 All ER 289, at [22]). 'Offenden' is targeted at pregnant women, but it will also be relevant that the drug is likely to be available only on prescription and under the supervision of a qualified medical practitioner, which is relevant as the CPA 1987, s. 3(2)(b) allows the court to consider what can reasonably be expected to be done with the product. If the producer can expect supervision by a medical practitioner, taken in conjunction with the warning that the drug should not be used by those suffering from high blood pressure, it may be argued that the drug is not defective, insofar as it has resulted in Neelam suffering a heart attack. Under the CPA 1987, s. 3(2)(c) regard should be had to the time at which the product was put into circulation, but the facts tell us that the defects in 'Offenden' existed at the time the product was put into circulation. However, this is not the case for Sanjay, as the only evidence that 'Offenden' may cause foetal abnormality is to be found in an 'obscure' scientific journal article. There is also incontrovertible scientific evidence regarding sight defects, but this comes to light two months after 'Offenden' is first put into circulation, so that the drug will not be defective in relation to Sanjay's vision.

Koffman Latrash plc may be liable for the foetal abnormality which results in Sanjay's shortened arms, as the facts suggest that the producer may have been aware of the propensity of the drug for causing this variety of harm, due to the existence of obscure scientific evidence of the defectiveness of the drug at the time it was put into circulation. Although the CPA 1987 is said to impose strict liability, it also provides a development risks defence in s. 4(1)(e), that gives a defence where the state of scientific and technical knowledge was not such that a producer of products of the same description as the product in question might be expected to have discovered if the defect had existed in his products while they were under his control. The wording of **s. 4(1)(e)** appears to import subjective factors relevant to the individual producer and differs from the purely objective wording of the **Product Liability Directive, art. 7(e)**. However the European Court of Justice has ruled in *EC Commission v United Kingdom (Re the Product Liability Directive)* (Case C-300/951) [1997] 3 CMLR 923 that there is nothing wrong in the wording used in the **CPA 1987**. In *A v National Blood Authority* [2001] 3 All ER 289, Burton J thought that the relevant state of knowledge is the most advanced available to anyone, not just the defendants, although this does require an enquiry into what is discoverable evidence. In determining what is objectively discoverable, Burton J considered that standard industry practice could be discounted. The relevant question, therefore, appears to be whether Koffman Latrash plc have failed to take the necessary precautions to guard against the defectiveness of their product by not considering the article published in the New Zealand medical journal. In *EC Commission v United Kingdom (Re the Product Liability Directive)*, Tessauro A-G gave the example of a piece of scientific evidence published in Chinese in a Manchurian scientific journal, compared with an article published in a major scientific publication widely available to the English-speaking world. While the latter would normally be objectively discoverable by a UK producer, the former might not. In the present case, it would be necessary to have regard to the obscurity of the relevant journal and whether other drug producers, generally, might have taken account of it, especially in the light of the fact that the article is less than conclusive on the matter of foetal limb abnormalities in human beings. Possibly, it might be a piece of evidence that, objectively, Koffman Latrash plc could have chosen not to take into account.

Further reading

Howells, G., et al., *Product Liability*, 3rd edn (London: Butterworths, 2011).

Howells, G., and Mildred, M., 'Infected Blood: Defect and Discoverability: A First Exposition of the EC Product Liability Directive' (2002) 65 MLR 95.

Newdick, C., 'The Future of the Development Risks Defence—The Role of Negligence in Product Liability Actions' (1987) 103 LQR 288.

Newdick, C., 'The Development Risks Defence and the Consumer Protection Act 1987' (1988) 47 CLJ 455.

Torts relating to land

Introduction

This chapter is concerned with the competing interests of landowners and other miscellaneous matters concerned with land ownership. Public and private nuisance may both offer remedies in tort, although the former is primarily a crime. Public nuisance can take many forms but for present purposes we are concerned with unreasonable interferences which affect a class of Her Majesty's subjects and which, generally, must have a wide-ranging effect. Where there is a sufficiently widespread public nuisance then the local authority will have power to take steps to obtain an injunction, or the Attorney-General can bring an action in the name of those affected to obtain an injunction. Private nuisance is concerned with private property rights and is based on the unreasonableness of the defendant's interference with the claimant's use or enjoyment of land. The principal underlying theme is one of give and take. Landowners must expect to put up with some level of inconvenience from their neighbours, but not to an unreasonable extent. For the purposes of private nuisance it is not generally the actions of the defendant which matter (except, perhaps, where malice is a factor) but the effects of an activity or state of affairs which has been allowed to continue. While damages may be an appropriate remedy, nuisance may frequently attract the remedy of an injunction, since the nature of many nuisances is that they are liable to continue.

The rule in *Rylands v Fletcher* (1868) LR 3 HL 330 is traditionally seen as a rule of strict liability based on the notion of escape. However, as a rule of strict liability it has not survived well, because of the judicial hostility which seems to exist towards the imposition of liability in the absence of fault. It now appears that the rule in *Rylands v Fletcher* is little more than a special application of the rule of nuisance in the context of an isolated escape, thus reducing any impact the rule may have had in terms of environmental protection. This is especially so in the light of the defences to liability under the rule and the interpretation of the concept of non-natural user in *Cambridge Water Co v Eastern Counties Leather plc* [1994] 1 All ER 53.

The third of the 'land torts' is trespass to land, which is concerned with intentional interferences with the claimant's right to possession of property. Frequently this action will be used to decide on matters such as boundary disputes, though in other instances claimants have attempted to use it in defence of their privacy. The questions which follow are designed to show how each of these land-related torts operates and how they can overlap.

? Question 1

Atif buys a farmhouse and the surrounding farm buildings in Toddington. He plans to convert the house into a 50-bed private hospital, retaining an apartment for his private use. Planning permission to convert the land from agricultural use has been granted by Toddington District Council.

During the building works, Desmond, a neighbouring landowner, complains that dust produced by Bashitt Ltd, the building contractors employed by Atif to convert the farm buildings, has clogged up the engine of his, Desmond's, car. When the hospital opens, Desmond objects to the increased traffic to the premises and retaliates by frequently firing guns, day and night, on his own land. Desmond claims this is necessary in order to control the rabbit population and to frighten off birds.

Some weeks after Atif's private hospital received its first patients, Desmond let some of his outbuildings to John, who organizes a 'rave' on one night only. Many of the patients at the hospital are unable to sleep and one of the patients, Mary, suffers a broken arm when she falls down some stairs on her way to complain to Atif about the noise. Many of the patients ask to be transferred elsewhere, resulting in loss of income to Atif.

Advise Atif, Bashitt Ltd, Desmond, and John of their liability in tort and how, if at all, Atif can prevent raves from taking place in future.

Commentary

This question deals with the problem of disputes between neighbouring landowners and requires consideration of both public and private nuisance. It is important to bear in mind that the characteristics of the different forms of action, in terms of legal standing, type of damage covered, and remedy sought, must be considered in relation to their suitability for each of the claimants.

☆ Examiner's tip

Nuisance questions can seem quite complex, so it is important to impose your own structure on the legal content and apply the principles as appropriate. If you rely on the problem itself to set your structure you are likely to fall into pointless repetition.

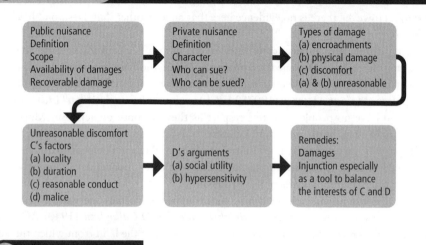

Answer plan

Public nuisance	Private nuisance	Types of damage
Definition	Definition	(a) encroachments
Scope	Character	(b) physical damage
Availability of damages	Who can sue?	(c) discomfort
Recoverable damage	Who can be sued?	(a) & (b) unreasonable

Unreasonable discomfort	D's arguments	Remedies:
C's factors	(a) social utility	Damages
(a) locality	(b) hypersensitivity	Injunction especially
(b) duration		as a tool to balance
(c) reasonable conduct		the interests of C and D
(d) malice		

Suggested answer

Public nuisance is generally a crime, which is actionable as a tort on proof of special damage and is defined as an act or omission which materially affects the reasonable comfort and convenience of life of a class of Her Majesty's subjects (*Attorney-General v PYA Quarries Ltd* [1957] 2 QB 169). It is concerned with 'public rights', which are not clearly defined, although interferences with public health appear to be covered. A class of people has to be affected, and although this usually refers to a neighbourhood, the 50 patients and Atif may well be a sufficiently large group. Private rights are irrelevant, so there is no need for a claimant to have an interest in land in order to be able to claim damages for a public nuisance. This will be important to Mary, in particular.

For a person to succeed in a private action arising out of a public nuisance, it must be shown that the claimant has suffered special damage, i.e. damage over and above that suffered by others. It is unclear whether the special damage must be a different kind to that suffered by others, or whether a difference in terms of extent will suffice. Here the inconvenience caused by the noise is suffered by everyone, but there are items of damage specific to particular individuals, for example, Mary's broken arm and the loss of income to Atif caused by the departure of patients. According to *Walsh v Ervin* [1952] VLR 361, the damage must be substantial, direct, and not consequential, although it may include general damage. Although personal injury has previously been held to be recoverable in public nuisance (*Castle v St Augustine's Links* (1922) 38 TLR 615), this now seems unlikely since the House of Lords' decision in *Hunter v Canary Wharf Ltd* [1997] 2 All ER 426 which suggested personal injury claims should no longer be considered within any form of nuisance but instead under the 'now fully developed law of negligence'. In any event, given the circumstances in which Mary's arm was broken, the injury should arguably be regarded as consequential rather than direct damage. Financial loss such as loss of income is also recognized as special damage (*Benjamin v Storr*

(1874) **LR 9 CP 400**). The dust produced by Atif's contractors may also give rise to public nuisance liability, if the damage is sufficiently widespread (***Hunter v Canary Wharf***). However, there is no evidence here that anyone other than Desmond has been affected.

Private nuisance is unreasonable interference with a person's use or enjoyment of land. In order to be able to sue for a private nuisance, the claimant must have a proprietary interest in the land affected, e.g. as owner, tenant, or having an exclusive right of occupation (***Malone v Laskey*** [1907] 2 KB 141; ***Hunter v Canary Wharf Ltd***). Atif and Desmond have no problems in this respect as they are both owners. But Mary, as a patient, is likely to be no more than a contractual visitor. In addition, her claim is solely for personal injury and there is no English authority which recognizes this as a recoverable head of damage in private nuisance, since the tort is concerned exclusively with land interests (***Hunter v Canary Wharf Ltd***).

An action for private nuisance may be brought against anyone with a degree of responsibility for the nuisance (***Sedleigh-Denfield v O'Callaghan*** [1940] AC 880), including the creator of the nuisance and the occupier of the land from which the nuisance emanates. Thus John and Bashitt Ltd (as creators) may be sued even though they have no interest in the land (***Southport Corp v Esso Petroleum Ltd*** [1953] 3 WLR 773). The occupier can also be sued in respect of a nuisance committed by an independent contractor. Where the nuisance is an inevitable consequence of the work undertaken (e.g. dust from the building operation) the occupier cannot escape responsibility by passing the work to the contractor (***Matania v National Provincial Bank*** [1936] 2 All ER 633). However, temporary building works will not generally give rise to an action in private nuisance unless they are carried out in an unreasonable manner. Generating sufficient dust to clog a car engine would tend to suggest a want of care on the part of the builders, so Desmond may succeed in claiming damages for his car repairs. Furthermore, a landlord can be sued where he lets premises and in doing so authorizes an activity which amounts to a nuisance. In ***Tetley v Chitty*** [1986] 1 All ER 663 a local authority letting a piece of land which they knew was to be used for go-carting were held liable, so the same should apply to Desmond in letting for the purpose of holding a rave at which loud music is played, provided he is aware of the planned activity.

Private nuisance is based on the principle of give and take and the role of the court is to try to reach a balance between the competing interests of the neighbours (***Kennaway v Thompson*** [1981] QB 88). The relevant factors in this process are whether there is a substantial interference with use or enjoyment of and whether the defendant can show that his use of the land is reasonable, although liability finally turns on whether the interference (rather than the acts which caused the interference) is reasonable or not. In ***St Helens Smelting Co v Tipping*** (1865) 11 HL Cas 642, and approved in ***Hunter v Canary Wharf Ltd***, nuisances were said to fall into three main categories: encroachments; physical damage (or 'sensible material harm'); and unreasonable interferences (or 'sensible material discomfort'). Of these three, the first two will almost always be automatically unreasonable, whereas the reasonableness (and thus lawfulness) of the third is a question of degree and calls for a complex balancing of a number of relevant factors.

So far as inconvenience nuisance, such as noise, is concerned, it is relevant to consider the locality within which the activity takes place. Thus it was said in *Sturges v Bridgman* (1879) 11 Ch D 852 that 'what would be a nuisance in Belgrave Square would not necessarily be so in Bermondsey'. In the question, the general locality is a rural area within which a noisy event such as a rave might not be regarded as falling within what is normally acceptable.

So far as Desmond's objection to the hospital is concerned, Atif might argue that he has planning permission for the changed use of the land; however, this will not afford him an outright defence (in the way that statutory authority would), though it may have the effect of altering the character of the neighbourhood so that what once would have been an intolerable interference may, due to the changed circumstances, become an acceptable state of affairs in the locality affected. In *Gillingham Borough Council v Medway (Chatham) Dock Co Ltd* [1992] 3 WLR 449, planning permission was granted to convert a naval dockyard into a commercial port causing a substantial increase in heavy traffic, especially at night. It was held that no nuisance was committed given the altered character of the locality. By contrast, in *Wheeler v JJ Saunders Ltd* [1995] 2 All ER 697, planning permission granted to a farmer to build two pig housing units on land next to the claimant's was held not to have changed the nature of the entire locality. It seems to be largely a question of scale, and the facts in the question offer no clear outcome—a change of use of a relatively small piece of property seems, on the face of it, unlikely to change a locality but one which brings with it a change in volume of traffic is rather more far-reaching.

One thing is clear, locality is irrelevant where material property damage is caused by the alleged nuisance (*St Helens Smelting Co v Tipping*), so Desmond's action for damage to his car should succeed, provided the damage occurred while the car was on Desmond's land.

A second important factor is the duration of the interference. Generally a 'one-off' event will not be sufficient to establish a nuisance since this is likely to be regarded as insufficiently substantial. What matters for private nuisance is the state of affairs created by the defendant. An isolated event may suffice but only if it arises from an underlying state of affairs (*Sedleigh-Denfield v O'Callaghan* [1940] AC 880; *Castle v St Augustine's Links* (1922) 38 TLR 615). In this case, the rave may be difficult to establish as part of a wider state of affairs, unless there is some indication that a series of similar events will be arranged in future. There is also authority to suggest that a temporary nuisance carried on at night, thereby causing sleep loss, is unreasonable (*de Keyser's Royal Hotel v Spicer Bros* (1914) 30 TLR 257), though the suggestion that the 'loss of a single night's sleep' should not be regarded as trivial should not be taken too literally. On balance, a single rave party is most unlikely to be actionable in private nuisance, though it could well be a public nuisance, as in *R v Shorrock* [1993] 3 All ER 917, in which case the residents would all benefit from any injunction to prevent a recurrence.

While malice is not usually relevant to liability in tort, it may convert an otherwise reasonable act into one which is unreasonable. This covers deliberately making a noise with a view to annoying one's neighbour (*Christie v Davey* [1893] 1 Ch 316) or in a manner calculated to cause damage (*Hollywood Silver Fox Farm Ltd v Emmett* [1936] 2 KB 468). On the facts of this scenario, Desmond, in deliberately firing guns all day and night, has created an unreasonable state of affairs. In line with the reasoning (and the facts) in *Hollywood Silver Fox Farm v Emmett*, although the sound of gunshots may be expected in a rural area, the fact that Desmond's activity is intended to cause a nuisance may be enough to make it actionable.

In *Miller v Jackson* [1977] 3 All ER 338, Lord Denning considered social utility to be an overriding factor sufficient to prevent conduct from being an actionable nuisance. This view was soundly rejected by the Court of Appeal in *Kennaway v Thompson* [1981] QB 88, though social utility is a relevant factor in assessing reasonableness because a person may be expected to put up with some degree of interference caused by activities necessary for the benefit of the public at large. Generally, the courts are more concerned with defending private rights than public interests when considering the primary question of whether there is a nuisance, but the more useful the defendant's activity, the less likely the court is to grant an injunction, or at least to structure it in such a way as to maximize the rights enjoyed by both parties (*Kennaway v Thompson*). Here, the construction of a private hospital seems to reflect the defendant's own commercial interest rather than offering any important public amenity.

Two remedies are available in the event of a private nuisance—damages and an injunction. A claimant such as Atif may well be seeking both: damages for past losses; and an injunction to order a continuing nuisance to cease and to prevent a recurrence in the future. Damages being the legal remedy, they will be awarded as of right once the nuisance is made out, but injunctions are a discretionary remedy. Although, in most circumstances, an injunction will readily be granted there are certain circumstances in which a court may decide it is equitable to withhold an injunction. In *Shelfer v City of London Electric Lighting Co* [1895] 1 Ch 287 four guiding principles were identified: damages will be awarded instead of an injunction if the injury to the claimant's legal right is (i) small; and (ii) can be estimated in money terms; and (iii) can be adequately compensated by a small money payment; and (iv) it would be oppressive to grant an injunction. It may be that the public interest is relevant to the granting of a temporary injunction, although the cases are divided on this issue. For example, the fact that heavy job losses might result from the closure of the factory was ignored in *Bellew v Cement Co* [1948] IR 61 and a temporary injunction on a factory was granted. But in *Miller v Jackson*, an injunction was refused against a cricket club at least partially on the ground that there was a public interest in preserving playing fields for recreation; another factor taken into account was the fact that the claimants were well aware of the proximity of the cricket ground before deciding to move into their house. In *Dennis v Ministry of Defence* [2003] EWHC 793 (QB), low-level training flights by military aircraft were held to be a nuisance but an injunction was withheld on the basis of public interest. None of this reasoning would seem to assist John.

? Question 2

Cockroach plc produce chemicals. As part of their operation, they use a fume-suppression device which is extremely noisy. The device is widely regarded as efficient and reliable but, occasionally, noxious fumes are nonetheless discharged into the atmosphere. Numerous residents in the locality have complained of the noise and the fumes produced by Cockroach plc's operations. These residents allege it is impossible to sleep with the windows open and that they cannot now sunbathe in their back gardens.

Ellen, one of the local residents, complains that her highly sensitive African violets, grown in her greenhouse, have all died as a result of the pollution caused by Cockroach plc. Moreover, Tom, a lodger in Ellen's house, complains that the combined effect of the noise and the fumes has caused him to suffer from a respiratory illness and extreme fatigue brought on through loss of sleep so that he has become permanently incapable of work.

Advise Cockroach plc.

Commentary

The question is concerned primarily with private nuisance, but it also raises the possibility of an action in public nuisance, negligence, and under the rule in **Rylands v Fletcher**. Once again, the range of potential actions should be considered in light of characteristics that might limit their usefulness to a claimant, e.g. due to lack of legal standing or the nature of the damage suffered.

Answer plan

- Who can sue and who can be sued in private nuisance?
- What factors indicate whether a private nuisance constitutes an unreasonable state of affairs?
- For the purposes of a private nuisance what is the relevant standard of care?
- Is personal injury damage recoverable in a private nuisance action and, if not, is an action in public nuisance a viable alternative?
- What remedies are available?
- Does **Rylands v Fletcher** apply to intangible escapes?

⇨ **Suggested answer**

Private nuisance is defined as an unreasonable interference with a person's use or enjoyment of land. In order to be able to sue for private nuisance, Ellen must have a proprietary interest in the land affected, e.g. as owner or tenant or a licensee with exclusive possession (*Malone v Laskey* [1907] 2 KB 141; *Hunter v Canary Wharf Ltd* [1997] 2 All ER 426). There is nothing in the question to suggest that Ellen lacks such an interest.

An action for private nuisance may be brought against anyone with a degree of responsibility for the nuisance, including the creator of the nuisance and, in certain circumstances, the occupier of the land from which the nuisance emanates (*Sedleigh-Denfield v O'Callaghan* [1940] AC 880). Since Cockroach plc is both the creator and the occupier, it appears to be the only possible defendant.

In *Kennaway v Thompson* [1981] QB 88, the Court of Appeal highlighted the point that private nuisance is based on the principle of give and take and that the role of the court is to try to reach a balance between the competing interests of neighbours, in order to maximize the rights of both. Usually the activity complained of is not in itself unlawful but will become so when it is carried out to an extent which the law regards as unreasonable, due to its negative effect on the claimant's property. Reasonableness is to be measured against a number of relevant criteria.

Although the issue of locality is often relevant, in *St Helens Smelting Co v Tipping* (1865) 11 HL Cas 642 a distinction was drawn between property damage and 'sensible personal discomfort'. Locality is relevant to the latter, but not the former since damage to property cannot be regarded as reasonable. Thus since Ellen complains of damage to property (her African violets), the character of the neighbourhood will be irrelevant.

Cockroach plc will also raise the argument that the African violets are 'hypersensitive'. Although the notion of hypersensitivity has in recent cases been absorbed within the fundamental question whether the interference complained of is unreasonable (*Morris (Soundstar Studio) v Network Rail Infrastructure Ltd* [2004] EWCA Civ 172), it is based on the proposition that the defendant's interference would not affect a person of ordinary susceptibilities (*Robinson v Kilvert* (1889) 41 Ch D 88) and is not, therefore, an actionable nuisance. So, if Ellen's violets are unusually sensitive and there is evidence that other plants would not be damaged in the same way, there is no nuisance. However, if Cockroach's activity would have interfered with ordinary land use, the fact the claimant is unusually sensitive will make no difference (*McKinnon Industries v Walker* (1951) 3 DLR 557). Plants which have to be grown in a greenhouse may appear to be sensitive, but many other plants require similar treatment. Moreover, if the extent of the pollution is such that other plant life also dies, the *McKinnon* approach seems to be the better one here. Evidence from other residents who have been affected by the fumes will assist Ellen's case.

Cockroach may well seek to argue that they have taken all reasonable steps to avoid creating a nuisance—specifically their choice of equipment that is widely regarded as efficient and reliable. While this might be enough to avoid liability in negligence, liability in nuisance differs. It was said in *Wagon Mound (No. 1)* [1961] AC 388 that negligence in the narrow sense is not necessary in a nuisance action. But negligence in the wider sense of foresight of harm under the remoteness test is a requirement. Thus if it is foreseeable to Cockroach that Ellen might suffer damage through the emission of fumes, an action may lie (*Wagon Mound (No. 2)* [1967] 1 AC 617). On this basis, it is probably foreseeable that the fumes emitted from Cockroach's factory could cause damage of the kind actually suffered.

These and other factors will also apply to the other local residents referred to in the question.

Tom is a lodger, which is a problem since a claimant must have a sufficient interest in the land affected. In *Hunter v Canary Wharf Ltd* [1997] 2 All ER 426, it was held that since the tort of private nuisance is directed at protecting the claimant's enjoyment of his rights over land, the action must be confined to a person with a sufficient interest. Often described as a proprietary interest, this is readily understood in light of their Lordships' emphasis on the role of private nuisance in protecting the amenity value of the land. In other words, if the value of the land is diminished by the fact that it cannot be freely used and enjoyed due to the effects of the nuisance, the only persons affected *in law* are those with an interest in the value of the land. However, none of the forms of proprietary interest would seem to cover Tom in his capacity as a lodger.

So far as the other residents' discomfort is concerned, locality is a factor. Where there is an inconvenience nuisance (e.g. noise, smells, etc.), it is relevant to consider where the alleged nuisance takes place. Thus it was said in *Sturges v Bridgman* (1879) 11 Ch D 852 that 'what would be a nuisance in Belgrave Square would not necessarily be so in Bermondsey'. The facts reveal that others in the area have had to close their windows, which establishes that the interference is widespread. If this is a quiet residential area, the fumes will probably be a nuisance, but if there are a number of other factories in the area, it may be that residents must put up with the inconvenience caused. However, even in an industrial area, if the extent of interference is great, it may still be a nuisance (*Rushmer v Polsue and Alfieri Ltd* [1907] AC 121). As for the noise, the courts have many times shown their willingness to regard loss of sleep as far from trivial (*Halsey v Esso Petroleum* [1961] 2 All ER 145; *Andreae v Selfridge* [1937] 3 All ER 255), which should further residents' claims.

Duration is another factor. What matters for private nuisance is that the defendant's activity must be capable of causing a continuing, unreasonable state of affairs. A dangerous underlying state of affairs which manifests itself in an isolated occurrence is still capable of being repeated in the future (*Castle v St Augustine's Links* (1922) 38 TLR 615) and the fact that there has been only one escape will not prevent this from being a continuing state of affairs, which will satisfy the duration requirement (*Sedleigh-Denfield v O'Callaghan* [1940] AC 880).

Generally, private nuisance is concerned with damage to an interest in land. Respiratory ailments and fatigue do not immediately come into this category, and it has been said that only land interests are protected (*Read v Lyons* [1947] AC 156). Although there are also cases in which it has been held that a personal injury associated with damage to a land interest is actionable (*Hale v Jennings* [1938] **1 All ER 579**), in *Hunter v Canary Wharf Ltd* the House of Lords affirmed the general rule established in *Read v Lyons*, namely that since private nuisance is a tort concerned with the amenity value of land there is no cause of action in nuisance for damages for personal injury. Personal injury is evidence that the land is affected, but the cause of action in this respect lies in the tort of negligence and fault must be proved. Thus any claims by residents in respect of personal injury, such as Tom's respiratory illness and extreme fatigue, are actionable only in negligence.

Lastly, Tom may have a claim in public nuisance. Public nuisance is a crime, which is actionable as a tort on proof of special damage and is defined as an act or omission which materially affects the reasonable comfort and convenience of life of a class of Her Majesty's subjects (*Attorney-General v PYA Quarries Ltd* [1957] **2 QB 169**). It is concerned with 'public rights', which are not clearly defined, although interferences with public health appear to be covered. A class of people has to be affected. The fact that other residents have complained suggests an effect on a class of people, but Tom, for damages, also has to prove special damage, i.e. damage over and above that suffered by others in the class (*Benjamin v Storr* (1874) **LR 9 CP 400**). Here the inconvenience caused by the fumes is suffered by everyone, but there are items of damage specific to Tom, namely the respiratory illness and his consequent loss of earnings. According to *Walsh v Ervin* [1952] **VLR 361**, the damage must be substantial, direct and not consequential, although it may cover general damage. There remains the question whether Tom's respiratory illness and collapse from exhaustion, being forms of personal injury, may be compensated under public nuisance. While such damage has, in the past, been recoverable (*Castle v St Augustine's Links*) more recently the House of Lords in *Hunter v Canary Wharf Ltd* observed that the now fully developed law of negligence available to claimants in modern times should mark an end to personal injury claims brought under *any* form of nuisance. If correct, this returns Tom to the position set out above.

Assuming a nuisance is established, which is more likely in Ellen's case than in Tom's, the appropriate remedy must be considered. The options are damages and/or an injunction, but an injunction would shut down a factory placing employees out of work. In general there are four guiding principles, as identified in *Shelfer v City of London Electric Lighting Co* [1895] **1 Ch 287**. Damages will be awarded instead of an injunction if the injury to the claimant's legal rights is: (i) small; and (ii) can be estimated in money terms; and (iii) can be adequately compensated by a small money payment; and (iv) it would be oppressive to grant an injunction.

Public interest may be relevant to the grant of an injunction, although the cases are divided on this issue. For example, the fact that heavy job losses might result from the closure of a factory was ignored in granting a temporary injunction on a factory in *Bellew v Cement Co* [1948] **IR 61**; but in *Miller v Jackson* [1977] **QB 966**, an injunction was refused against a cricket club on the ground that there was a public interest in preserving playing fields for recreation. The fairness and utility arguments may prevent a full injunction from being granted provided the interference is not excessive, though a partial injunction might be used to limit the timing of the defendant's activities and maintain a balance between the legitimate interests of both parties (*Kennaway v Thompson* [1981] QB 88; *Halsey v Esso Petroleum* [1961] 2 All ER 145).

There may be the possibility of an action under the rule in *Rylands v Fletcher* (1868) LR 3 HL 330, but generally this requires the accumulation of something tangible which is likely to do mischief if it escapes. Fumes and smells do not normally satisfy this requirement, which means that a *Rylands* action is most unlikely to apply.

? Question 3

Chromoshine Ltd, a cleaning firm, stores large quantities of a toxic industrial cleaning chemical on its land on an industrial estate close to a residential housing estate. Evidence shows that a group of badly behaved teenagers has been seen in the area on various occasions over the past two months. Mysteriously, a barrel of the toxic fluid is overturned and ruptures with the following results.

Mary, a catering assistant who works in Chromoshine's canteen, steps in the spilled fluid. Her legs are badly burned and her shoes are seriously damaged.

A quantity of the fluid seeps into an underground water supply used by the South Downs Water Company with the result that the latter must find an alternative source of supply in order to meet its statutory obligations to water consumers in the area.

The fluid flows into the street outside Chromoshine Ltd's premises. Traffic in the street sprays the fluid on to Alice's front garden rendering it in need of decontamination. The smell of the fluid causes Alice physical illness and she also has to vacate her house for two weeks while remedial action is taken.

Consider the liability of Chromoshine Ltd under the rule in *Rylands v Fletcher*.

Commentary

The tort which emerged from the decision of Blackburn J and the House of Lords in *Rylands v Fletcher* (1868) LR 3 HL 330 is heavily circumscribed by rules laid down not only in those decisions but in many authorities of the Privy Council and the House of Lords, most recently in *Transco plc v Stockport MBC* [2003] UKHL 61. This question calls for a detailed knowledge and application of those principles. It also allows for some comment upon the continued usefulness of the rule in *Rylands v Fletcher*, which was thoroughly discussed in the *Transco* case.

⭐ **Examiner's tip**

The question refers only to the rule in *Rylands v Fletcher* so you should not stray into the law relating to private nuisance generally or any other torts.

Answer plan

- Identify whether or not the substance is within the rule, i.e. was it brought on to the land and is it likely to do mischief?
- Consider whether there has been an escape.
- Discuss whether or not the defendant company was engaged in a 'non-natural use' of its land.
- Is the harm suffered an actionable loss?
- Suppose there has been the unforeseeable act of a third party causing the escape.
- What are the rules on remoteness of damage?

⇒ **Suggested answer**

The rule in *Rylands v Fletcher* (1868) **LR 3 HL 330** applies when a defendant, in the course of the non-natural user of his land, brings on to that land, and keeps or collects there something which, if it escapes, is likely to do mischief. In jurisprudential terms, the tort is one of strict, but not absolute, liability. This means that where an escape occurs and causes relevant harm, the defendant is *prima facie* liable for that harm, but may nevertheless successfully defend an action if he is able to raise one of several recognized defences.

First, there has to be an accumulation by the defendant for the defendant's own benefit of something likely to cause harm if it escapes. The stringency of this requirement was emphasized by Lord Bingham in the *Transco* case, and it is fairly clear that the 'something' has to be an accumulation which is recognized either subjectively, by the defendant, or objectively, as creating an exceptionally high degree of risk. The importing into the site of water for domestic purposes, even in bulk in a large diameter pipe, did not meet that criterion. A large number of things have been held to fall within this aspect of the rule, from water (*Rylands* itself) to gypsies (*Attorney-General v Corke* [1933] Ch 89) to a flag pole (*Schiffman v Order of St John* [1936] 1 KB 557), although the correctness of the latter two may be doubted following the decision in *Transco plc v Stockport MBC* [2003] UKHL 61. The core element appears to be accumulation rather than the operation of nature. Here there is a deliberate accumulation and if the product is known or ought to be known to carry a risk of exceptional harm, i.e. likely to do 'mischief' if it escaped, then liability may flow.

Secondly, according to Lord Cairns' formulation of the rule, the accumulation must involve a non-natural use of land. This point has proved to be the most crucial of the control mechanisms available to the courts in extending or reducing the scope of the rule. As interpreted, this phrase has been taken to refer not to a contrast between artificial and natural but as to the ordinariness or otherwise of the use, often within the context of its locality. This may well be to deviate too far from Blackburn J's formulation which included in his examples what were perfectly ordinary uses of land. *Rickards v Lothian* [1913] AC 263 is the leading case on the point and Lord Moulton made it clear that it was not every ordinary use of the land which would attract the operation of the rule but it must be some special use bringing increased danger. In that case the supply to the land of ordinary domestic water in small bore pipes was held to be not within the rule. Lord Bingham in *Transco plc v Stockport MBC* tried to keep distinct the elements of increased risk and ordinary/extraordinary use but the other members of the House of Lords rolled up the questions together. Lord Bingham thought that 'ordinary user' is preferable to 'natural user', and that the rule applied only where the defendant's use is shown to be extraordinary and unusual. In that case the use of a large bore pipe to take domestic water to a tower block was an ordinary user of its land. On the other hand, Lord Goff in the House of Lords in *Cambridge Water Co v Eastern Counties Leather plc* [1994] 1 All ER 53 made it clear that the storage of substantial quantities of chemicals on industrial premises was almost a classic case of non-natural use and that it could not be thought objectionable to impose strict liability for escape. Several cases including *Transco* and *Cambridge Water* have rejected the idea in *Read v Lyons* [1947] AC 156 that the manufacture of munitions in wartime could be a 'natural' or ordinary use of land. Applying these principles it would seem likely that a court would be entitled to hold that the storage of the chemicals by Chromoshine was a non-natural use of land. This would be so even though it was an industrial area, as was the land in the *Cambridge Water* case, and even though it provided employment in the area.

Thirdly, there has to be an escape. It is apparent from the House of Lords in *Read v Lyons* that a necessary pre-condition of the tort is that there must be an 'escape from a place where the defendant has occupation of, or control over, to land which is outside his occupation or control'. On this basis, it seems clear that Mary could not frame an action in *Rylands*, since, at the material time, she was still on the premises of Chromoshine Ltd, as was the claimant in *Read v Lyons* who was injured by exploding munitions whilst still on the defendant's premises. This requirement has been reaffirmed by the decision in the *Transco plc* case where one of the members of the House of Lords felt that there had been no escape of water from land under the control of the defendant on to other land. The reason for this aspect of the rule is closely connected to the next point: that the object of the tort is to protect interests in land.

Fourthly, the relevant type of harm must be suffered. Since *Rylands* involved damage caused to a neighbour's land the question might be asked whether damage to chattels and personal injury are protected by the tort. These points have been mooted in the past but the current trend in cases such as *Transco* and *Cambridge Water* would be towards equating *Rylands v Fletcher* liability with nuisance liability and concluding that it is a tort concerned with protecting the interest which someone has in the value of his land. In other words damages to chattels and personal injury harm would be beyond the scope of the rule. The *Transco* case contains the most recent comment on this point and although it is strictly *obiter* it nonetheless represents a clear indication that such damages will not be recoverable. Lord Bingham in that case drew support from *Cambridge Water* and *Hunter v Canary Wharf Ltd* [1997] 2 All ER 426. Thus, Mary will also be unable to recover for this reason. Alice, while not being able to claim for personal injury, will be able to recover for the diminution in value of her property and the loss of use of the land. The calculation will involve assessing the cost of reinstatement of the property and the cost of alternative accommodation.

Fifthly, recovery of damages is dependent upon reasonable foreseeability of the type of harm. The *Cambridge Water* case decided that the test for the remoteness of damage in *Rylands* is the same as that in negligence: *Wagon Mound (No. 1)* [1961] AC 388 (reasonable foresight of the kind of harm suffered). In *Cambridge Water* the impact of the escaping chemicals on the water supply of the claimant was unforeseeable in the light of scientific knowledge current at the time of the escape and there was no recovery for this unforeseeable harm. Despite the rather ambiguous language of Lord Goff in that case, it is the harm which has to be foreseeable and not the escape. With this in mind, it is arguable that the type of loss that Alice suffered would be regarded as not too remote a consequence of the spillage of some of the toxic fluid into a street down which motor traffic passes. The position of the South Downs Water Company will have to depend on the scientific evidence available. In the *Cambridge Water* case the type of chemical spilled was thought to evaporate into the atmosphere and that it could not be absorbed into the ground and thence the water bearing rocks. If this type of contamination is foreseeable then Chromoshine will be liable for the diminution in the value of the land which will reflect the consequential economic loss.

As regards the defences that may be open to Chromoshine Ltd the only one that might be available is 'act of a stranger'. A defendant may avoid liability where the escape is attributable to the act of a third party over whom the defendant had no control. The defence will fail if the claimant can show that the act which caused the escape was an act of the kind which the owner could reasonably have contemplated and guarded against. In *Rickards v Lothian*, property was damaged by water. The overflow of the water was caused by an unknown third party blocking the waste pipe in a sink. It was held that this provided a defence akin to the defence of 'act of God' or sudden overwhelming force such as an attack by enemies of the state. By contrast, in *Hale v Jennings* [1938] 1 All ER 579, the court held that the defendant should have foreseen the possibility of third-party interference with a fairground ride. The facts simply say the spillage occurred mysteriously, though it may not be unreasonable to suppose an element of human interference, in which case the defence may well be invoked.

Question 4

'A strong case can be made for the view that the rule in *Rylands v Fletcher* is but an application or instance of liability in nuisance.'

(Heuston and Buckley, *Salmond and Heuston on the Law of Torts*)

Discuss the interrelationship between the two torts in the light of this statement.

Commentary

The so-called rule in **Rylands v Fletcher (1868) LR 3 HL 330** has provoked much debate both as to its relationship with private nuisance and its continued usefulness. Discursive essay style questions will often focus on this controversial formulation of liability.

In particular this question requires discussion of the House of Lords' decisions in **Cambridge Water Co Ltd v Eastern Counties Leather plc [1994] 1 All ER 53** (in which Lord Goff subjected the interrelationship between these two torts to detailed examination), and, to a lesser extent, **Transco plc v Stockport MBC [2003] UKHL 61**. The answer also requires consideration of the principles underlying the imposition of liability in nuisance and under the rule in **Rylands v Fletcher** with emphasis being placed upon both shared and distinguishing features. The House of Lords' decision in **Hunter v Canary Wharf Ltd [1997] 2 All ER 426**, which addressed a number of important issues about the scope of the tort of nuisance is also highly relevant. You could also make the point that there are very few modern reported cases where the rule in **Rylands v Fletcher** has been the foundation for deciding a case in favour of the claimant other than in the context of damage by escape of fire.

Answer plan

- Identify the rule.
- Identify the similarities to private nuisance.
- Identify any distinctions.
- Deal shortly with the key elements of the rule.
- Demonstrate a good working knowledge of **Cambridge Water Co Ltd v Eastern Counties Leather plc**.
- Demonstrate a good working knowledge of **Transco plc v Stockport MBC**.

Suggested answer

Liability under the rule in *Rylands v Fletcher* (1868) **LR 3 HL 330** is imposed on a defendant where in the course of non-natural use of his land he accumulates upon it for his own purposes anything likely to do mischief if it escapes and which does escape and cause damage. Briefly, the facts of the case were that the defendants had employed independent contractors to construct a reservoir on their land in order to supply water to the defendant's factory. Due to the contractors negligently failing to discover and block a disused mine shaft, water from the reservoir burst through the shafts and flooded the claimant's mine. The defendants were held personally liable despite the absence of fault on their part. The existing law did not appear to provide a remedy in this situation. There was no trespass as the flooding was not direct and immediate. Neither was it certain that there could in law be a nuisance for an isolated escape which caused damage. Finally, on generally accepted principles there was no vicarious liability for the acts or omissions of the independent contractor amounting to negligence. None-theless, the defendant was found liable on the basis outlined, although the final version of liability was modified by apparently unintended differences between the formulation of Lord Cairns LC in the House of Lords and Blackburn J at first instance.

There are numerous instances where the overlap between this rule and the tort of nuisance is apparent. Liability in the tort of nuisance arises where there has been an unreasonable interference with the claimant's proprietary interest in land. In *Read v Lyons* [1947] AC 156, Lord Simonds pointed to Blackburn J's original formulation of the rule as recognizing that in most cases the law of nuisance and the rule in *Rylands v Fletcher* may be 'invoked indifferently'. Also, the principle of reasonable user in nui-sance means that a defendant acting reasonably (in the nuisance rather than the negli-gence sense) will not be liable for harm to his neighbour's enjoyment of his land. This is closely allied to the principle of natural use found in the rule in *Rylands v Fletcher* although in *Transco plc v Stockport MBC* [2003] UKHL 61 Lord Bingham considered that the principle would be better described as ordinary rather than natural, applying the Privy Council analysis in *Rickards v Lothian* [1913] AC 263. Lord Bingham also restated the proposition that Blackburn J had regarded the facts of *Rylands v Fletcher* itself as being a simple case of nuisance and that in *Ross v Fedden* (1872) LR 7 QB 661, itself a case on domestic water supply, he had rejected any notion to the contrary. To this extent the rule in *Rylands v Fletcher* was regarded by the House of Lords as no more than an application of well-known principles to an isolated and non-persistent interference, because an isolated event may be actionable in nuisance if it arises from a dangerous underlying state of affairs.

However, there are marked distinctions between the torts. *Rylands v Fletcher* is founded upon the non-natural accumulation of something by the defendant on his land which is likely to do damage if it escapes. By definition this excludes things naturally on the defendant's land. Thus, an occupier is not liable for damage caused by ordinary trees on his land given that growing a tree is a natural use of soil (*Noble v Harrison* [1926] 2 KB 332). On the other hand, in *Crowhurst v Amersham Burial Board* (1878) 4 Ex D 5, a yew tree on the defendant's land projected over land belonging to the claim-ant on which cattle grazed. The leaves of yew trees are poisonous, and the claimant's horse died after eating some of them. The defendants were held liable under the rule in *Rylands v Fletcher* on the basis that it was not a natural use of land to plant on it a poisonous tree. Liability in nuisance may, however, arise from acts of nature occurring on land. Thus, in *Goldman v Hargrave* [1967] AC 645 the Privy Council held that an occupier of land was under a duty to take reasonable steps to abate a fire started by lightning striking a tree on his land which had spread to his neighbour's property. This was followed by the Court of Appeal in *Leakey v National Trust for Places of Historic Interest or Natural Beauty* [1980] QB 485 where the defendants, who owned a hill which it was feared would slip on to the claimant's land due to natural weathering, were held liable in nuisance. In *Rylands v Fletcher* the water had been brought on to the land by the defendants, but where water is naturally on the land, the defendant will not be liable if it escapes. Thus, in *Smith v Kendrick* (1849) 137 ER 205 rain water had formed a subterranean lake surrounded by a coal seam. When the coal was mined the water escaped and flooded the claimant's mine. It was held that the defendant was not liable given that the adjoining mine owners each had a 'natural' right to work their respective mines in the manner best suited to them, even though the natural consequence of their work could be prejudicial to the other.

A further distinction is that nuisance covers damage caused by intangible escapes such as noise and so in *Rushmer v Polsue and Alfieri Ltd* [1906] 1 Ch 234, the claimant successfully brought an action in respect of noise at night caused by printing presses, even though he lived in the printing area of London. *Rylands v Fletcher* is confined to the accumulation of a tangible object on land which is likely to cause damage, either upon its own escape or upon its giving off fumes, electricity, or gas which escape.

A potential distinction that can be drawn between the rule in *Rylands v Fletcher* and the tort of nuisance relates to 'standing to sue'. With respect to the former, it was stated by Lawton J in *British Celanese v A. H. Hunt* [1969] 1 WLR 959 that once an escape is established, anyone who suffers damage as a consequence may claim irrespective of whether or not they are occupiers of adjoining land. As we have seen, nuisance is premised upon protecting proprietary interests in land and is therefore narrower in its scope of protected interests. Since the claimant must satisfy the requirement of having either a possessory interest or some other proprietary interest in order to bring an action in nuisance, members of his family who lack this interest will be precluded from suing even though they have suffered personal injuries as a result of the defendant's activity, as in *Malone v Laskey* [1907] 2 KB 141. The correctness of the decision in *Malone* was confirmed by the House of Lords in *Hunter v Canary Wharf Ltd* [1997] 2 WLR 684, in which it was held by a majority of their Lordships that an action in nuisance can only be brought by a person in 'exclusive possession' of the affected land, or by an owner without exclusive possession. Whether the approach in *British Celanese v A. H. Hunt* will survive the decision in *Hunter v Canary Wharf* may well be doubted, especially in the light of dicta in the *Transco* case which clearly align nuisance and *Rylands v Fletcher*.

It has been said that neither the rule in *Rylands v Fletcher* nor the tort of nuisance requires proof of fault on the part of the defendant. Yet it is apparent, particularly in more recent decisions culminating in *Cambridge Water Co Ltd v Eastern Counties Leather plc* [1994] 2 WLR 53, that the judges are steadily eroding non-fault-based liability. In his speech in *Read v Lyons* Lord Porter alluded to the concepts of 'justice' and 'reasonableness' when reviewing the judicial process for determining whether liability under the rule should be imposed. He pointed to the fact that judges have regard to all the surrounding circumstances including the time, place, and practice of mankind so that what might be regarded as non-natural may vary according to the circumstances. In *Mason v Levy Auto Parts of England Ltd* [1947] 2 QB 530, MacKenna J in equating 'non-natural' user with unreasonable risk recognized the similarities inherent in this approach with those considerations applicable in negligence. Moreover, the concept of 'unreasonableness' is central to the tort of nuisance, and fault is a concomitant of unreasonableness. Further, the importance of fault-based liability in nuisance was recognized by Lord Reid in *Wagon Mound (No. 2)* [1967] 1 AC 617 when he stated that 'fault of some kind is almost always necessary and fault involves foreseeability'.

Finally, the law of private nuisance does not extend to include recovery of damages for personal injury (*Malone v Laskey; Hunter v Canary Wharf*); despite conflicting decisions on the point it now seems likely that personal injury damages will not be recoverable under *Rylands v Fletcher*; it too is a tort concerned with land. This is stated clearly, though *obiter*, by Lord Bingham in the *Transco* case.

The decisions of the House of Lords in *Cambridge Water Co* and *Transco* have clarified the confusion which has marked the development of the tort. In the former the defendant operated a tanning business and had used large quantities of chemical. Much of this chemical had been spilt and contrary to scientific understanding current at the time, had seeped into the ground, though its effects at that time were considered to be harmless. The claimants purchased a well located over a mile away from the defendant's factory. At the time of purchase the water had been tested and found to be perfectly fit for consumption. Subsequently, an EEC Directive in 1985 governing water purity standards was passed and, after testing was carried out to the new standards, it became illegal to supply water from this source due to chemical contamination. The defendants successfully appealed to the House of Lords where, following the restrictive approach adopted in *Read v Lyons* with respect to the imposition of strict liability, it was held that strict liability under the rule in *Rylands v Fletcher* only arose if the defendant knew or ought reasonably to have foreseen that the escape would cause damage. Liability under the rule is strict in the sense that the defendant could be held liable for an escape resulting from the non-natural use of land despite having exercised all due care to prevent the escape occurring. But, given that the defendants could not have reasonably foreseen that the seepage of the chemical through the factory floor would cause the pollution to the claimants' borehole, they were not liable under the rule in *Rylands v Fletcher*.

The gist of Lord Goff's extensive treatment of this point was that *Rylands v Fletcher* and private nuisance derived from the same core and that since the authoritative cases on private nuisance led inevitably to the conclusion that reasonable foreseeability of damage was an essential element of private nuisance so too must it be an essential element of recovery under the rule in *Rylands v Fletcher*.

The judicial trend noted above which has heralded the erosion of non-fault-based liability was further reinforced by both the trial judge and the House of Lords in

Cambridge Water. The first instance judge and Lord Goff shared the view that any imposition of strict liability in respect of high-risk operations should be left to Parliament. It was stated that statute would be the appropriate means of ensuring that precise criteria were laid down governing the incidence and scope of such liability.

The House of Lords in the *Transco* case refused either to follow the trend set in other jurisdictions and jettison the rule entirely, or to extend it. Lord Bingham stated clearly that '[t]he rule in *Rylands v Fletcher* is a sub-species of nuisance'. This approach clearly reaffirms the place of *Rylands v Fletcher* within private nuisance, and is consistent with the rejection of earlier attempts to allow it to break free of its nuisance straitjacket.

? Question 5

Paresh owns a farm in the country and a disused plot of land in central London. The farm is situated near to an airfield used by a gliding club. Some of the gliders have occasionally landed in the fields of surrounding farms, damaging the crops, but the gliding club has always paid compensation to the farmers in such circumstances. The plot of land in central London is adjacent to a building site owned by Bipin and on which he is building a new office block. The jib of a tall crane constantly over-sails into the airspace above Paresh's plot. Bipin has offered to buy the plot of land from Paresh, but he has always asked for more than Bipin is prepared to pay.

Paresh is now seeking to obtain an injunction against the gliding club, preventing them from flying over his farm, and against the developers of the building site, preventing them from intruding into the airspace above his land with their crane, even though it will be very difficult for them to redevelop their land without doing this.

Advise Paresh as to any actions he may have in trespass to land.

Commentary

This question is concerned primarily with the tort of trespass to land (and in particular airspace). Trespass to land is an ancient and relatively straightforward tort and its characteristics may be simply stated at the outset. The problem really raises the issue of invasion of land in the possession of the claimant. You are not asked to consider the application of private nuisance here, so keep any reference to it (as an option) to the bare minimum. In most cases what the claimant wants is an injunction preventing the activity. While in nuisance there is some flexibility over the terms of the injunction (see e.g. ***Kennaway v Thompson* [1981] QB 88**), in trespass the right to possession is absolute and to deny an injunction may well result in depriving the claimant of his property rights. This question does ask for a description and application of the rules which apply to the discretionary remedy of an injunction. There is also some scope for comment on the statutory immunity for aircraft although a detailed statutory knowledge would not normally be required.

Examiner's tip

Deal with the cases on airspace fully, so as to establish the key legal reasoning behind the rules. A stronger answer will not simply assume that as there is a crane in the problem (for example) they should consider only the two crane cases.

Answer plan

Introduction Definition Rationale Core elements	→ Identify rules for airspace *Kelsen* *Bernstein* *Anchor Brewhouse* Structure or plane?	→ Remedies Legal damages Injunction Equitable damages *Shelfer*

Suggested answer

Trespass to land involves direct and intentional invasions by the defendant of land in the possession of another, although the intention relates to the voluntariness of the invasion rather than knowledge that the land belongs to someone else or the mistaken belief that the land is the trespasser's. Like all trespasses, trespass to land is actionable per se, i.e. it is complete without proof of actual harm. This makes it very useful in the resolution of boundary conflicts or as a mechanism for asserting rights, e.g. to exclude people from land. It may also be used to raise issues of constitutional importance, such as entry by executive officers: see e.g. **Entick v Carrington** (1795) **19 St Tr 1029**. Although at one early stage in the development of the law it was said that the land of the claimant extends to the heavens above and the earth below (*usque ad coelum, usque ad inferos*), this rather out-dated concept (described as 'fanciful' by one judge) no longer represents a statement of the law, if it ever did. Conflicting dicta as to whether or not there might be invasion of the airspace above a claimant's land were resolved in **Kelsen v Imperial Tobacco Co** [1957] **2 QB 334** where an overhanging advertising sign that intruded by no more than a few centimetres well above the claimant's roof was held to be capable of amounting to a trespass and that the claimant need not rely on nuisance. The court then had to decide whether or not to grant an injunction ordering it to be removed, which it did on the basis that the invasion, though small, had reduced into the defendant's actual possession airspace to which the claimant was entitled. So, on the authority of this case it can be safely said that Paresh has an interest in the airspace above his land which can be protected against invasion by structures adjoining or nearby his land. But the invasion was at a relatively low height in **Kelsen** and was by a fixture and not an aeroplane.

In *Bernstein v Skyviews & General Ltd* [1978] QB 479, it was held there would be no trespass by an over-flying aeroplane unless the aeroplane flies so low that it penetrates the airspace at a height which is within the 'normal user of the land'. As an aspect of ownership any occupier is entitled to bring within his control the airspace above his land (subject to normal regulatory procedures or covenants), but above the height at which such control is possible the landowner enjoys no greater rights than anyone else. Griffiths J in *Bernstein* concluded that there had to be a balance drawn between the private rights of the owner and the interests of the general public to take advantage of scientific developments in travel and communications. Therefore an owner has rights in the land extending only to such height as is necessary for the ordinary use and enjoyment of the land. There is scope for questioning whether this refers to the current use of the land, or to an objective assessment based on potential future use. Arguably, the latter is the better view as it ensures all land enjoys the same rights, a position supported in the case of *Bliss v Hall* (1838) 132 ER 758 in private nuisance. In *Bernstein* there was held to be no trespass and, subject to important questions as to the height of the gliders, here there may be no trespass into Paresh's airspace.

Note that Griffith J used language carefully and he did not require there to be an *actual* interference with the use of enjoyment of land, which draws a crucial distinction between trespass and nuisance. Where there is actual interference with the use and enjoyment of the land, e.g. by noise, then a nuisance by over-flying aircraft may be made out, even where there is a pressing military need: *Dennis v Ministry of Defence* [2003] EWHC 793 (QB). There is nothing here to suggest that the activities of the club amount to an actionable nuisance.

The question arises whether the intrusion of the jib of Bipin's crane into the airspace above Paresh's plot amounts to a trespass to that airspace. There is no suggestion that there is any interference with the use and enjoyment of the land, e.g. by noise or danger of items dropping, so there will not be a nuisance on that basis. There is an encroachment which could be an actionable nuisance if damage ensued. It has not here, though if a nuisance or trespass is threatened then an injunction may lie and the claimant does not have to wait for actual damage.

In *Anchor Brewhouse Developments Ltd v Berkley House Ltd* [1978] 2 EGLR 173, the defendant company had sought to argue that their cranes, which overhung the claimant's land, were not a trespass because of the public interest in developing a major site in London and the unreasonable cost to them of re-siting them and constructing a building with a smaller 'footprint'. It was held that the decision in *Bernstein v Skyviews* had not altered the law, so that where there was an invasion by a structure adjoining the land of the claimant then there would be a trespass. The defendant was taking into possession, no matter how briefly, airspace which the claimant was entitled to reduce into actual possession. There was no scope for balancing interests in the way adopted in *Bernstein v Skyviews*, since that case was concerned with protecting the interests of society at large rather than the interests of an individual airline operator. Accordingly, the invasion by Bipin's crane will amount to a trespass.

The defences in trespass are matters such as necessity and consent, neither of which seems to be applicable to this problem. Over-flying and possible noise nuisance may be subject to immunity under the **Civil Aviation Act 1982, ss. 76** and **77**. This immunity extends both to trespass to airspace and to nuisance, but it only arises if the club was complying with an air navigation order made under **s. 60**. There is no such immunity against claims arising from damage caused by an aircraft falling from the air, or by people or things falling from aircraft on to land below, even where negligence cannot be proved (**Civil Aviation Act 1982, s. 76(2)**). Any such claim would equate to a claim for trespass to land, although it is a statutory cause of action in its own right.

Suppose that there is a trespass in the instance of the crane jibs. What remedy is available in the absence of any actual damage? Paresh seems to be using his land in London as a 'ransom site', i.e. a strip of land which frustrates development on neighbouring land unless it is bought for whatever price the owner cares to name. There is no remedy against this at common law, since generally in the exercise of rights of ownership a person may make whatever lawful use of his own land he chooses (**Bradford Corp v Pickles [1895] AC 587**). The only statutory remedies are those which relate to the compulsory purchase of land by a local authority and those procedures made available to private landowners by the **Access to Neighbouring Land Act 1992**. The developers in this case do not possess any powers of compulsory purchase and the **Access to Neighbouring Land Act 1992** is confined to cases in which access is necessary for the purpose of the preservation of neighbouring or adjacent land. The Act does not apply to works for the alteration, adjustment, improvement, or demolition of any buildings or other land unless those operations are incidental to works of 'preservation'. In any event, even if the developers are entitled to rely on the **1992 Act**, they cannot go ahead with any entry onto the neighbouring or adjacent land without first obtaining a court order. Since Bipin is building something completely new he cannot take advantage of the legislation.

Normally an injunction will be granted as a matter of course but not as a matter of right and subject to the normal equitable rules such as the behaviour of the claimant, e.g. he must not have encouraged the defendant to believe that the work was permitted, nor must he have delayed. The suspension of the operation of the injunction in **Woolerton & Wilson v Costain [1970] 1 WLR 411** in which an injunction to restrain a developer from trespassing with a crane was effectively denied to a claimant who had adopted a wholly unreasonable attitude towards consenting to the proposed aerial invasion was disapproved of in later cases, including **Anchor Brewhouse**. This case confirmed that the claimant was entitled to an injunction as a matter of course if the trespass was going to be repeated. It does not seem to matter that the claimant might be acting as a 'dog in a manger' (*per* Scott J in **Anchor Brewhouse**).

But it would be open to Bipin to argue that damages would suffice. By virtue of statute, equitable damages in lieu of an injunction may be granted and the general principles governing the grant of damages were set out in **Shelfer v City of London Electric Lighting Co [1895] 1 Ch 287**. These were that the injury to the claimant's rights is small; the injury can be estimated in financial terms; the injury can be adequately compensated in money terms; and it would be oppressive to the defendant to grant an injunction. The grant of damages in such a case is intended to compensate for future invasions and represents a judicial removal of the claimant's bargaining tool.

The grant of an injunction is discretionary within these general principles and there is ample scope for the judges to give differing weight to the factors. Certainly there is nothing in principle to prevent the court granting an injunction to prevent the continued over-sailing of the crane jib, and the Court of Appeal's recent decision, in *Enfield LBC v Outdoor Plus Ltd* [2012] EWCA Civ 608, shows that damages should be calculated by reference to the factors which would have influenced any negotiation for the use. In that case, the defendant had benefited commercially from the use of the hoarding for advertising purposes. One might suppose the commercial profits to be made by a building developer might equally suggest a substantial sum.

Further reading

Bagshaw, R., 'Rylands Confirmed' (2004) 120 LQR 388.

Buckley, R. A., *The Law of Nuisance* (London: Butterworths, 1996).

Gearty, C., 'The Place of Nuisance in the Modern Law of Torts' (1989) 48 CLJ 214.

Heuston, R. F. V., and Buckley, R. A., *Salmond and Heuston on the Law of Torts*, 21st edn (London: Sweet and Maxwell, 1996).

Ingman, T., 'Continuing Trespass and Breach of Covenant: Injunction or Damages' [1995] Conv 141.

Lee, M., 'What Is Private Nuisance?' (2003) 119 LQR 298.

McNall, C., 'Holding Back the Tide of Negligence, Rylands Resurgent' [2004] Conv 240.

Morgan, J., 'Nuisance and the Unruly Tenant' (2001) 60 CLJ 382.

Murphy, J., 'The Merits of Rylands v Fletcher' (2004) 24 OJLS 643.

Newark, F. H., 'The Boundaries of Nuisance' (1949) 65 LQR 480.

Nolan, D., 'The Distinctiveness of Rylands v Fletcher' (2005) 121 LQR 421.

Palmer, R., 'Personal Injury in Private Nuisance: The Historical Truth about Actionability of "Bodily Security"' (2009) 21 ELM 302.

Wightman, J., 'Nuisance—The Environmental Tort' (1998) 61 MLR 870.

Liability for statements not made negligently

Introduction

This chapter is principally concerned with defamation, which offers a person the means to clear his name where the defendant has made a statement attacking the claimant's reputation. Defamation takes two forms: libel, in which the statement is of an enduring nature, e.g. written; and slander, where the statement is in a transitory form, e.g. spoken.

In either form, defamation requires a publication of a statement which tends to subject the claimant to ridicule or contempt or tends to lower the claimant in the minds of right-thinking members of the public. For the most part, it is a tort which does not require proof of damage unless the statement is made in a merely transitory form. The core elements of the tort have remained much the same over the years: the statement must be defamatory, it must refer to the claimant, and it must be published. Most emphasis in recent years has been on the development of the defences and in particular the defence of qualified privilege has received extensive consideration and expansion by the higher courts.

Defamation does not attract legal aid, with the result that a person who wishes to protect his reputation but who cannot afford to fund a defamation action may choose to sue for malicious falsehood. Although this tort is not primarily concerned with protecting reputation, it may sometimes be used to clear the claimant's name. The ingredients of malicious falsehood differ in a number of respects from the elements of defamation. In the first place, malicious falsehood protects a person's economic interests, and does require proof of economic damage. Secondly, the defendant's statement must be false, whereas a defamatory statement may be literally true, but may contain some actionable innuendo. For the purposes of malicious falsehood, there must be an intention to disparage, whereas there can be an entirely innocent defamation.

? Question 1

Fatima is a student of the Du Maurier College of Melodrama. She believes that she is being sexually harassed by Omar, one of the lecturers at the college. She writes a letter, addressed to all the governors and lecturers at the college, which includes the statement: 'Omar sexually harasses female students'.

Fatima takes the letter to the public library, in order to make 200 copies of it. By mistake, she leaves the original letter in the photocopier, where it is found by Nosey, who reads the letter and posts it, anonymously, to Omar's wife.

Fatima sends copies of her letter to every governor and lecturer at the college, using the internal post. Each letter is in a brown envelope, addressed to the recipient and marked 'confidential'. Two days later, one of these letters is found pinned to a noticeboard in the students' common room. Omar denies the allegation of sexual harassment.

Advise Omar as to his cause of action, if any, in defamation. You should ignore any issues of vicarious liability.

Commentary

Very often problem questions on defamation require a broad treatment both of the substantive law required to establish what defamation involves and of the available defences. Although you should identify the tests for when a statement may be defamatory in law, do not go overboard on demonstrating when a statement is defamatory unless the question demands it. For example, in this problem it will be necessary to establish that the statement is defamatory but the answer should seek to address this bearing in mind that the real thrust of this scenario is to establish the range of possible publications. Although the answer should reflect on why most of the defences do not apply do not take too long to do this; move as quickly as possible to look at the issue of qualified privilege raised by the problem. Unless the problem demands it, it is rarely necessary to speculate at length on the issue of the appropriate remedy.

Answer plan

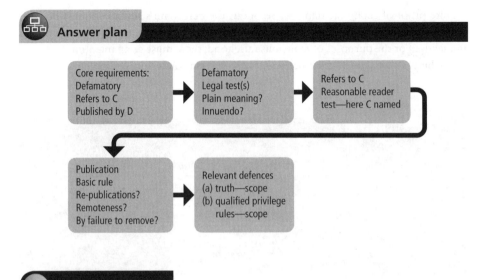

Suggested answer

Omar will have to establish the three core elements of defamation; these are the same whether the statement is written (libel) or oral (slander). He will have to show that words used were defamatory, that the statement referred to him, and that it was published to a third party. The judge will first determine whether the words are capable as a matter of law of bearing a defamatory meaning, then it is for the jury to determine whether the words are defamatory in fact. **Section 7 of the Defamation Act 1996** allows either party to apply for an order to determine, before trial, whether the words are capable of bearing a defamatory meaning.

There is no single test for when words are defamatory but one commonly accepted test is whether the statement would tend to 'lower the claimant in the estimation of right thinking members of society': *Sim v Stretch* **[1936] 2 All ER 1237**. This is not always useful; e.g. in *Berkoff v Burchill* **[1996] 4 All ER 1008** the claimant succeeded on the basis that he had been held out to ridicule by a newspaper review that described him as hideously ugly. First the plain meaning of the statement is examined, and then any secondary meaning (innuendo) alleged by the claimant. It is suggested that given Omar's profession, the statement that he sexually harasses female students is defamatory. It is in written form, and therefore an action will lie for libel which is actionable per se, i.e. without proof of actual harm.

The statement clearly refers to Omar by name, but the third requirement—publication—is not straightforward in the present case. In defamation, publication means simply the communication of the statement to a third party, i.e. other than the claimant.

Each fresh publication is a new libel and will be a major factor for the jury to take into account when assessing the amount of any damages to be awarded. Fatima has clearly published the defamatory material to the governors and lecturers at the college, but what about the letter left in the photocopier? The library authorities will not be liable since they played no part in its publication. Omar will argue the letter has been published to Nosey because a publication may occur even if the maker of a statement negligently allows a third party to read it. For example, in *Theaker v Richardson* [1962] 1 WLR 151, the writer of a letter was held to have published it to the addressee's spouse because he had sent it in a business envelope and did not make it clear that the contents were intended for the addressee only. Similarly, in *Weld-Blundell v Stephens* [1920] AC 956, where the claimant wrote a letter to his accountants about the financial affairs of a particular company, the letter was negligently left at the offices of the company where it was seen by the manager who noted it made defamatory remarks about two individuals. These individuals successfully sued the claimant for defamation, who in turn successfully sued the accountants for failing to take reasonable care of the letter. This should apply to Fatima.

Omar may also allege that the college is responsible for the publication of the letter on the students' noticeboard. It is not clear how the letter appeared on the board, but Omar will allege that the college is responsible because the college authorities should have removed the copy and that, by failing to do so, they adopted the defamatory statement and published it to the users of the common room. To remove the letter would involve no expense, and no damage to the structure of the building. This accords with the reasoning in *Byrne v Deane* [1937] 1 KB 818, in which the manager of a clubhouse had failed to remove an allegedly defamatory notice. Omar must show, however, that the college authorities had a reasonable opportunity to discover the letter and to remove it from the noticeboard.

Who should be responsible for the publication to Omar's wife? Although there is no 'publication' of a statement between a husband and wife when they communicate with each other, the law does not take the same approach when the communication is made by a third person to one partner about his or her spouse (*Wenman v Ash* (1853) 13 Ch 836). Nosey has published the letter to Omar's wife, but will Fatima be liable for this unauthorized publication?

In *Cutler v McPhail* [1962] 2 QB 292, it was held that the author of a defamatory letter sent to a newspaper was also responsible for its subsequent publication by that newspaper. In *Slipper v BBC* [1991] 1 QB 283, it was held that the makers of a defamatory television programme should have foreseen that it would be reviewed in a national newspaper, thereby spreading the allegations to a wider audience. The Court of Appeal, however, took the view that the actions of an unauthorized person could break the chain of causation, thereby releasing the original maker of the statement from any responsibility for its further publication, i.e. as a matter of remoteness of harm. This argument may not apply, however, to a person who has negligently left a document in a public place. In *McManus v Beckham* [2002] EWCA Civ 939 the issue was slightly different. The defendant loudly attracted public attention during an argument in a shop and her defamatory comments were headline news. It was held that she should be liable for the extent of the loss caused by the press publication on the basis that liability for damage resulting from a further publication by a third party should be decided on according to whether it was just that the defendant should be held responsible. On the facts, the defendant must herself have been aware that the matter would be reported, and a reasonable person would have realized that it would. Normally, however, an unforeseen publication will break the chain of causation. The outcome in Fatima's case is not clear cut.

Several defences may be available. For the defence of justification it would be necessary for the defendant to prove the truth of the 'sting' of the defamatory statement. For example in *Alexander v North Eastern Railway Co* (1865) 34 LJQB 152, the defendant was able to show that the claimant had been convicted of an offence and sent to prison and had served two weeks. The jury was entitled to regard the original statement (that he had served three weeks) as having been justified. In *Wakley v Cooke & Healey* (1849) 4 Exch 511, the statement that the claimant journalist was a libellous journalist was taken to mean that he made a habit of writing libels and not that he had done so once (which was true)—the defendant could therefore not justify the statement. Demonstrating that Fatima herself had been harassed may very well not be enough to prove the 'sting' of the allegations.

Secondly, it is unlikely that fair comment would apply. This requires that there should be a comment on a matter of public importance where the underlying basis of fact is shown to be true. We are told only that there are allegations of fact and the scenario does not reveal any comment.

The governors and the lecturers of the college are the intended recipients of Fatima's letter. Fatima may invoke qualified privilege. In this defence the law recognizes that it is in the public interest to protect some communications provided there is no malice and the communication is published no more widely than is necessary. Usually this defence arises when A makes a statement to B, because she has a legal or moral duty to make it to him, or because she (A) has a legitimate interest to protect in bringing it to his attention. B should also have a corresponding duty or interest. In the absence of such reciprocity there will be no privilege. Fatima has an interest to protect in complaining about Omar to the proper authorities within the college, and the college authorities have a reciprocal duty or interest to receive it. More recently the courts have taken the view that where there is a pre-existing relationship then there is no need to establish the exact nature of the duty-interest involved: *Kearns v General Council of the Bar* [2003] EWCA Civ 331.

Here, the question arises whether Fatima has circulated her allegations too widely. In *Adam v Ward* [1917] AC 309 it was suggested that a publication to the public at large could be protected by the defence of qualified privilege if it related to a matter of the widest public importance. The general rule is that the defence of privilege will be lost if the defendant exceeds the privilege by communicating the allegations to persons who have no legitimate interest in hearing them. Thus in *Chapman v Lord Ellesmere* [1932] 2 KB 431, it was held that the publication of a disciplinary decision of the jockey club was privileged when it appeared in *The Racing Calendar*, but not privileged when it appeared in *The Times* newspaper. Likewise in *De Buse v McCarthy* [1942] 1 All ER 19, a town clerk sent out a notice convening a meeting of the council to consider a committee report about the loss of petrol from one of its depots. The report was attached to the notice which was posted in public libraries. The claimants sued in defamation. The defendants claimed qualified privilege on the ground that there was a common interest between the council and the ratepayers. The court held that since the report was only a preliminary stage of the investigation there was no common interest and the report had been circulated too widely. The defence was examined in *Kearns v General Council of the Bar* [2003] EWCA Civ 331. Here the Bar Council, which has responsibility for the professional conduct of barristers, had circulated to all barristers incorrect and defamatory material about a firm of solicitors. This was retracted two days later but the claimants sued. The Court of Appeal held that the communication was between parties in an established relationship which required the flow of free and frank communications and that qualified privilege applied.

Any communication between a student and the governors of the college ought to entitle the student to rely on the defence of qualified privilege if it relates to the conduct of a member of staff. There is a clear incidence of the duty/interest relationship identified in *Adam v Ward*. The fact that the governing body might be a large number of people does not matter. In *Horrocks v Lowe* [1975] AC 135, the House of Lords held that qualified privilege extended to a complaint made against a town councillor published to all the other councillors. The vital question is whether Fatima had any right to circulate her allegations amongst the academic staff, most of whom would not have had any powers of management over Omar. If the articles of government of the college show that all the lecturers have the right to participate in the running of the college the net of qualified privilege will reach further, but it will not be enough for Fatima to show that the allegations would be of some interest to the academic staff, in the sense simply of being newsworthy.

It has been suggested in some cases that there may be a qualified privilege in communications to one spouse about the activities of another. In *Watt v Longsdon* [1929] All ER Rep 284 this question arose. The court refused to set down broad guidelines on this matter but found on the facts that there had been no privileged communication to the wife about the husband's alleged unpaid bills and alleged extra-marital affair. It seems unlikely that this defence would assist the sender, should he be identified.

The defence of qualified privilege will be defeated by malice. If Omar can show that Fatima was motivated by malice, she will not be able to invoke the defence, no matter to whom the allegations were sent (*Horrocks v Lowe*). But there is no evidence of the ill-will or spite which would suggest malice required by this case.

Finally, the **Defamation Act 1996, ss. 8–10** introduced significant reforms into the conduct of defamation proceedings but the jury continues to play a very important role. The so-called 'fast-track' procedure enables the court, in the absence of a jury, to dispose summarily of a case if it appears that the action has 'no realistic prospect of success'. Conversely, the procedure enables the court to provide 'summary relief' in a case if it appears that there is no defence and the claim has 'a realistic prospect of success'. By **s. 9(1)(c)** of the Act, summary relief is restricted to actions which can be adequately compensated by an award not exceeding £10,000. Perhaps Omar might be tempted to opt for a jury trial given that, by the nature of his vocation, he would hope for an award in excess of that figure and juries have been notoriously generous in assessing damages for libel though excessively large awards are now subject to review. Until **s. 8** of the **Courts and Legal Services Act 1990** was enacted, the Court of Appeal lacked the power to reduce jury awards unless they were completely 'divorced from reality'. Now, however, that power is available generally: see e.g. *Kiam v MGN Ltd* **[2002] EWCA Civ 43**.

Question 2

Sanjay, the Member of Parliament for Wessex North, is in the process of introducing a private member's Bill in Parliament authorizing the redesignation of agricultural lands in his constituency for industrial development. This would allow Wover Cars Ltd to build a manufacturing plant in the area. During the Parliamentary debate, the MP for a neighbouring constituency, Peter Piper, who belongs to the Wessex Alliance Party, emerged as the Bill's most vociferous opponent.

On hearing of the debate, Nick Whippet, the chairman and chief executive of Wover, wrote to Sanjay stating:

> Wover Cars' principal opponent in the House is a hypocrite like the party he belongs to and whose opposition to the scheme has more to do with the fact that he has recently purchased several farms in Wessex North which he stands to lose than with his apparent concern for the preservation of the countryside.

Sanjay confronts Piper with the allegations during a Parliamentary debate and accuses him of abusing his position by failing to disclose his personal interests. The *Wessex Daily Globe* is interested in this matter and publishes a detailed report of the debate. Sanjay has also written to the *Wessex Daily Globe* stating that 'Peter Piper MP is a liar whose only interest is to protect his own property at the expense of bringing employment into the region'. Using this information which it does not check with Peter Piper, the newspaper prints an editorial criticizing Peter Piper in similar terms. In fact Peter Piper does not own property in the Wessex North constituency.

Consider the law of defamation as it applies to the potential liability of the parties.

Commentary

This question requires consideration of the core requirements to establish what amounts to defamation together with the defences, whether common law or within the **Defamation Act 1952** or the **Defamation Act 1996**. The distinction between libel and slander can also be introduced. The answer should try to balance the amount of material devoted to each of these topics given that there is no obvious focus on any single issue relating to demonstrating the substance of a defamatory statement. On the other hand the particular defence emphasized is privilege (absolute and qualified), but it should be briefly explained why the other defences do not apply.

☆ Examiner's tip

Qualified privilege in this problem does extend to the **Reynolds** defence (**Reynolds v Times Newspapers [1999] 4 All ER 609**) and a strong answer will examine the relevant post-**Reynolds** case law for a current understanding of the courts' approach to the question of 'responsible journalism'.

Answer plan

- Distinctions between libel and slander.
- Explain the meaning of defamation.
- Identify and explain the core elements of defamation.
- **Defamation Act 1952; Defamation Act 1996**.
- Publication.
- State the available defences and consider in particular absolute and qualified privilege.
- Explain and consider the application of the **Reynolds** privilege.
- Refer briefly to the **Defamation Act 1952** and the **Defamation Act 1996**.

Suggested answer

Peter Piper may be able to bring an action in the tort of defamation against Nick Whippet, Sanjay, and the *Wessex Daily Globe*. A defamatory statement will usually be spoken or written but it may take another form of representation such as a photograph. As a broad rule, if the defamatory statement is conveyed in a permanent form it is libel, whereas if it is in a temporary form, it is slander. At present, the distinction between the two forms of action is important because libel is actionable per se (without proof of damage) whilst slander is actionable only upon proof of actual damage, though this may change with the Defamation Bill currently under debate. The proof requirement in slander is subject to certain exceptions, including, for the purposes of Peter Piper's action, an imputation of unfitness for office or professional incompetence. The **Defamation Act 1952, s. 2** provides that where the words are calculated to disparage the claimant in any office, profession, calling, trade, or business carried on by him there is no need to prove special damage, 'whether or not the words are spoken of the claimant in the way of his office, profession, calling, trade or business'. It is therefore not necessary for Peter Piper to prove defamation in the context of his office provided the words are likely to injure him within it. It should be noted that on grounds of public interest in freedom of expression, the courts will not allow free speech to be fettered by permitting government bodies, whether local or central, to sue for libel (*Derbyshire County Council v Times Newspapers* [1993] **AC 534**: a local authority; *Goldsmith v Bhoyrul* [1997] **4 All ER 268**: a political party). However, persons within such organizations may bring proceedings for defamation in their personal capacity if individually identified.

Peter Piper must prove the three elements of the tort of defamation: that the particular words used were defamatory; that they referred to him; and that they were published to a third party by the defendant.

Nick Whippet's letter is potentially a libel. Peter Piper will have to prove that the words are defamatory. Although there is no single test for this, a classic definition of defamation was suggested by Parke B in *Parmiter v Coupland* (1840) **6 M & W 105**, in which he said that a defamatory publication is one which 'is calculated to injure the reputation of another by exposing him to hatred, contempt or ridicule'. This formula has been criticized as being too narrow and a wider test was formulated by Lord Atkin in *Sim v Stretch* [1936] **2 All ER 1237**: 'Would the words tend to lower the claimant in the estimation of right-thinking members of society generally?'

If the judge considers that the words are capable of bearing a defamatory meaning they are put to the jury as 'right thinking members of society' to determine whether or not the words are in fact defamatory. By virtue of the **Defamation Act 1996, s. 7** either party may apply for an order to determine before trial whether the words are actually capable of bearing a defamatory meaning. The description of Peter Piper as a 'hypocrite' would appear to be libellous on its ordinary meaning and evidence will not be needed to elaborate on that meaning.

Although the words do not refer to Peter Piper by name he can introduce extrinsic evidence to show that he was the person referred to in the letter as in *Morgan v Odhams Press Ltd* [1971] **1 WLR 1239** where the claimant was unnamed. Sanjay's special knowledge would be relevant here. The test was said in the *Morgan* case to be the impression that would be conveyed to an ordinary sensible man having knowledge of the circumstances.

The third element of the tort is publication which has been defined as the communication of defamatory words to a third party, i.e. to some person other than the claimant. It is evident, therefore that Nick Whippet has published the statement to Sanjay

The defence of justification is not available to Nick Whippet, as he would have to prove the truth of the 'sting' of the defamatory statement. For example in *Alexander v North Eastern Railway Co* (1865) **34 LJQB 152**, the defendant was able to show that the claimant had been convicted of an offence and sent to prison and had served two weeks. The jury was entitled to regard the original statement (that he had served the three weeks) as having been justified. In *Wakley v Cooke & Healey* (1849) **4 Exch 511**, the statement that the claimant journalist was a libellous journalist was taken to mean that he made a habit of libels and not that he had done so once (which was true)—the defendant could therefore not justify the statement. Given that Peter Piper does not own the farm land claimed, and therefore has no vested interest in opposing the scheme, there is no truth in the statement that he is a hypocrite seeking to protect his property.

Similarly, fair comment is not available to Nick as a defence since there must be a comment and this must be a comment about facts that are true.

There is a defence of qualified privilege in situations where inaccurate information may be passed on but where the public interest in maintaining the free flow of information (even inaccurate information) outweighs the interest in the reputation of the claimant wronged by such a statement, provided that there is no malice behind the statement. This may well be available provided Nick is able to demonstrate that he has a legitimate interest in bringing the matter to the attention of the MP and that Sanjay has a corresponding duty to receive the information, or that there is a common interest and a reciprocal duty. There must be a reasonable belief in the truth of what is said although the actual truth need not be established. Qualified privilege may be defeated by demonstrating that there is no privileged occasion, or that there was malice on the part of the defendant. An example of a privileged occasion may be seen in *Watt v Longsdon* [1930] 1 KB 130 where correspondence between a director of a company and the chairman of the company concerning the behaviour of one of its overseas managers was protected. The director was under a moral or business duty to inform his chairman of the behaviour and there was a corresponding interest in receiving the information. Here, communicating with an MP with a view to raising matters in debate would seem to be protected by qualified privilege even though the statement was factually inaccurate.

As to the proceedings in debate, the allegation made by Sanjay that Peter Piper abused his position is prima facie slanderous in that it disparaged him in the conduct of his office. Further, under **s. 2 of the Defamation Act 1952**, special damage need not be proved. However, as the statement was made during a Parliamentary debate it enjoys absolute privilege both at common law (*Ex parte Wason* (1869) LR 4 QB 573) as stated in the **Bill of Rights 1688, art. 9**, and under statute (**Defamation Act 1996, s. 13(4)**), so no action will lie in respect of it. The categories of absolute privilege are quite narrowly drawn and reflect the policy of the law that in rare instances the need for a free flow of information in the general public interest is such as to allow even maliciously motivated statements to be protected.

Normally Parliamentary privilege will be used by MPs against litigants to stifle civil actions as in the *Church of Scientology of California v Johnson-Smith* [1972] 1 QB 522 where it deprives claimants of the right to use material from *Hansard* as evidence of malice. **Section 13** was subsequently passed in the light of several prominent actions by MPs against newspapers and in order to permit MPs to waive privilege so allowing their own actions to proceed relying on extracts from *Hansard*—not the situation here.

No action will lie against *Hansard* when the debate is published, since any statement in a paper published by the authority of Parliament is privileged by the **Parliamentary Papers Act 1840**.

By statute and at common law there is qualified privilege in newspaper or other reports of proceedings in Parliament providing that the reports are fair and accurate. Proof of malice would remove the privilege.

Sanjay's letter to the *Wessex Daily Globe* calling Peter Piper a liar is clearly libellous. It has been published to a third party, the newspaper and, as with Whippet, since the statement is based on the false assertion that Peter Piper is motivated by protecting his property interests, the defences of justification and fair comment are not available to him. Qualified privilege would depend upon the existence of a duty/interest relationship. Relationships which fall within this defence are narrowly confined. For example, in *Beach v Freeson* [1972] 1 QB 14 an MP wrote to the Law Society and the Lord Chancellor and his letter repeated defamatory statements made to him by a constituent about a solicitor. It was held that he had a duty to make the statement and that the recipients were under a duty to receive these. Sanjay's letter to the paper may not be justified on this basis.

In respect of the *Globe's* story, referencing a statement as a rumour offers no protection as it is taken by the courts to be an assertion that the rumour is true. Similarly, the newspaper will be liable for libel even if it has expressly stated in the editorial that it is merely reproducing what the editors have been told by Sanjay. Accordingly, the writer of the editorial, the newspaper proprietor, and its printers will each be held liable for its publication. One possible defence here might be for the newspaper to try to bring itself within the wide view of qualified privilege upheld by the House of Lords in *Reynolds v Times Newspapers* [1999] 4 All ER 609, now often called the *Reynolds* defence. There it was held that in exceptional circumstances there might be a duty on a newspaper to disseminate information to the general public who had a corresponding interest in receiving it. The Court of Appeal in *Loutchansky v Times Newspapers Ltd (No. 2)* [2001] EWCA Civ 1805 held that in deciding whether there had been a duty to publish defamatory words to the world at large the standard to be applied was that of responsible journalism. Lord Nicholls in *Reynolds* had indicated a list of factors which should be taken into account in deciding this. These included such matters as the seriousness of the allegation, the extent to which the subject matter is a matter of public concern, the steps taken to verify the information, the urgency of the matter, whether comment was sought from the claimant, and whether the article contained the gist of the claimant's side of the story. The principles were confirmed in *Jameel v Wall Street Journal* [2006] UKHL 44 and applied in *Seaga v Harper* [2008] UKPC 9 by the Privy Council, which said Lord Nicholls' criteria were not individual hurdles to be overcome. They should be applied pragmatically to reflect the real world of journalism. In the latter case the failure to check sources when there was plenty of time available put the speaker in breach of the standard of responsible journalism. Applying these factors it is unlikely that there would be a qualified privilege in the article; see the example of *Galloway v Telegraph Group Ltd* [2006] EWCA Civ 17 where the newspaper embellished its account and went beyond the standard of responsible journalism. Merely reporting allegations that are made by someone may not be defamatory repetition where the newspaper makes it clear that it is not adopting the statements as true; this is 'reportage'. But, going beyond the allegations and adopting them as true or embellishing them (as occurred in *Galloway*) will render the newspaper liable, as was the case in *Charman v Orion Publishing* [2007] EWCA Civ 972 where the publishers of a book were liable where the book went beyond the reporting of allegations and investigated the background to the statements in a piece of undercover investigative journalism.

The newspaper may make an 'offer of amends' to Peter Piper by offering to publish an apology or correction and pay him damages even before the writ is served (**Defamation Act 1996, ss. 2–4**). If Peter Piper accepts such an offer the issue must be settled by agreement between him and the newspaper. The court will only intervene, if necessary, to adjudicate as to the amount of compensation or on the nature of the apology or correction. Acceptance of an offer will operate to terminate the defamation proceedings.

The **Defamation Act 1996, ss. 8–10** introduced significant reforms into the conduct of defamation proceedings. The so-called 'fast-track' procedure enables the court, in the absence of a jury, to dispose summarily of a case if it appears that the action has 'no realistic prospect of success'. Conversely, the procedure enables the court to provide 'summary relief' in a case if it appears that there is no defence and the claim has 'a realistic prospect of success'. By **s. 9(1)(c)** of the Act, summary relief is restricted to actions which can be adequately compensated by an award not exceeding £10,000. It is suggested that Peter Piper may wish to opt for a jury trial given that by the nature of his vocation, he would hope for an award in excess of that figure. Juries have been notoriously generous in assessing damages for libel and until **s. 8** of the **Courts and Legal Services Act 1990** the Court of Appeal lacked the power to reduce jury awards unless they were completely 'divorced from reality'. Now, however, that power is available generally: see e.g. *Kiam v MGN Ltd* [2002] EWCA Civ 43. A last consideration for Peter is that there have been significant and newsworthy examples of politicians 'shooting themselves in the foot' and being hugely embarrassed by other matters revealed in the course of their own libel actions.

? Question 3

During a local radio phone-in programme Bill Birch, the leader of the majority party on the Council for the city of Bilchester, announces that he intends to push through his plans to deregulate gambling in the city and its suburbs. He explains that he wishes to see Bilchester become a second Las Vegas.

Mary Priggish, a well-known member of the 'Moral Crusade Party', telephones the programme and is put on the air. She states that: 'Birch is an immoral clown who wants to see law and order disintegrate in our city. If he were to marry he might give up his hedonistic lifestyle and start pushing for family virtues.'

In fact Bill Birch is married to Primrose Hill, a charity worker who is also a governor of the local primary school. Shortly after the broadcast, Bill's wife is told that the chairman of the school governors wishes her to resign. He feels that it is inappropriate for someone who is cohabiting outside of wedlock to hold such a position.

William Birch is a professional clown who is unmarried and who is often employed at children's parties. Some friends have said that they thought the comments referred to him.

Advise Bill Birch, Primrose Hill, and William Birch.

Commentary

This question requires consideration of the three elements of the tort of defamation but with particular emphasis on the meaning of defamatory and reference to the claimant where the words are capable of applying to more than one person. Typically the question demands that you identify these core elements with considerable care and by reference to a good selection of relevant cases. The available defences must also be considered.

Answer plan

- **Section 166** of the **Broadcasting Act 1990**.
- Innuendo.
- The defence of unintentional defamation (**Defamation Act 1952, s. 4**; and **Defamation Act 1996, ss. 2–4**).
- The defence of fair (honest) comment.
- The defence of qualified privilege.
- Reference to the claimant.

Suggested answer

Bill and Primrose Birch, and William Birch (the clown) may each have an action in defamation against Mary Priggish and the radio company. **Section 166** of the **Broadcasting Act 1990** provides that the publication of any words during the course of a broadcast programme, on television or radio, shall be treated as publication in permanent form. Their action will therefore lie in libel which is actionable per se (without proof of actual damage), and thus the request for Primrose to resign from the school governors is not crucial to her claim (though it is relevant to the calculation of damages). It is necessary for each claimant to prove the constituent elements of the tort, namely that the statement was defamatory, that it referred to them, and that it was published to a third party by the defendants.

Bill Birch has two possible claims. First, that the statement that he is an 'immoral clown' is capable of being defamatory since it would tend to lower him in the estimation of right-thinking members of society (*Sim v Stretch* **[1936] 2 All ER 1237**, *per* Lord Atkin), or the words could expose him to 'hatred, contempt or ridicule' (*Parmiter v Coupland* (1840) 6 M & W 105, *per* Parke B). A good illustration of words exposing someone to ridicule is to be found in *Berkoff v Burchill* **[1996] All ER 1008** where describing a well-known actor and director in terms which suggested he was hideously ugly were held to be defamatory as exposing him to ridicule.

Whether or not the statement is capable of bearing a particular meaning is a question for the judge to determine: it is then for the jury to decide if the actual meaning of the statement falls within that permissible range. It is submitted that an accusation of immorality is capable of being defamatory within the tests laid down by Parke B and Lord Atkin, particularly in light of the nature of Bill Birch's public office. Secondly, although the suggestion that he is unmarried is not prima facie defamatory, it must be considered against the fact that he is married to Primrose. Even if the people who know he lives with Primrose conclude they are unmarried but still do not think any less of him, the test for determining whether the statement is defamatory is dependent upon its effect on 'right-thinking members of society', who may well regard his apparent pretence of marriage as a hypocritical lie. Although the courts do not permit actions for defamation by local and central governmental bodies since there is a public interest in free speech on matters relating to government (*Derbyshire County Council v Times Newspapers Ltd* [1993] AC 534), proceedings by individuals such as councillors, MPs, and candidates are nonetheless allowed (*Goldsmith v Bhoyrul* [1997] 4 All ER 268).

Bill Birch will need to introduce extrinsic evidence to establish the meaning of this true innuendo, i.e. words not defamatory on their face but made so by virtue of knowledge or understanding of facts known to others. In *Tolley v Fry* [1931] AC 333 the suggestion that a person might have been paid to lend his name and image to an advertisement would not usually be defamatory but the claimant was well known as an amateur golfer barred from receiving payments in any way connected with his image as a sportsman.

The decision of the Court of Appeal in *Cassidy v Daily Mirror Newspapers Ltd* [1929] 2 KB 331 is clearly pertinent to Bill's claim, and that of his wife Primrose. In *Cassidy* the defendant newspaper published a picture of Mr Cassidy, also known as Michael Corrigan, and a woman. The caption stated that it was 'Mr M Corrigan, the race horse owner, and Miss X, whose engagement has been announced'. Mrs Cassidy sued for libel claiming that the caption and photograph were capable of meaning that her husband was a single man, and that therefore she was living in immoral cohabitation with him. Several of her female acquaintances gave evidence that they had assumed from the article that Mrs Cassidy was unmarried and had no legal right to bear that name. It was held that in the light of evidence that Mr Cassidy was in fact married, the publication was defamatory. It was immaterial that the defendant was unaware of the true facts, provided that the paper had been read by those who did and who knew that it applied to the claimant. The same reasoning will apply in this case, and the fact that Primrose is not referred to will not affect her claim given that ordinary sensible people, proved to have special knowledge of the facts, might reasonably believe that the statement implicated her. In *Morgan v Odhams Press Ltd* [1971] 2 All ER 1156, the House of Lords held that there was no requirement that the words themselves should expressly refer to the claimant by name provided evidence could be adduced to show that she was referred to. Thus the key factor is the inference which an 'ordinary sensible' listener would draw from the statement.

When making her statement on the phone-in Mary knew that it would be broadcast contemporaneously and is therefore liable for its publication (*Adams v Kelly* (1824) **Ry & M 157**). Similarly, the radio company as the 'publisher' of the statement is also liable (*M'Pherson v Daniels* (1829) **10 B & C 263**). Further, the programme's production staff may also be found liable on the basis that they disseminated the defamatory statement. Other than Mary, the defendants may raise the defence of unintentional defamation provided by the **Defamation Act 1996, s. 1**, in relation to the innuendo. However the defence is available only if a person innocently publishes words alleged to be defamatory *and* has exercised all reasonable care in relation to the publication. Had this been a recorded programme, one might have argued that as a public figure it would not have been difficult to ascertain Bill's marital status, and therefore reasonable care had not been taken to avoid defaming him and, by implication, Primrose. In the absence of reasonable care, it is immaterial that the defendants were unaware of the external facts which turned a presumptively innocent statement into one which is defamatory (*Newstead v London Express Newspaper Ltd* [1940] **1 KB 377**). This problem, however, concerns a live radio broadcast and so offered no such opportunity for checking.

As regards the defence of fair comment on a matter of public interest (or, as the Supreme Court in *Spiller v Joseph* [2010] **UKSC 53** has suggested it be renamed, 'honest comment') the law recognizes that one aspect of freedom of speech is to allow robust criticism in public matters. The notion of what is a matter of public interest has been generously applied by the courts so as to promote freedom of speech and it would extend to the suitability for office of politicians and their policies. But, it has to be shown that the statement is a matter of comment, or opinion, on a matter of fact and not an assertion of fact. It may be difficult to distinguish a statement of fact from a comment but there has to be some underlying fact(s) about which a comment may be made. There was such underlying fact in *Kemsley v Foot* [1952] **AC 345** (the standard of reporting of a newspaper group and the type of story covered) but not in *London Artists v Littler* [1969] **2 QB 375** where the assertion that there was a conspiracy to oust an impresario from a theatre was not comment about a fact since there was no factual evidence of such a conspiracy. The allegations about Bill Birch may amount to comment but there is an incorrect statement of facts so the defence will not be available.

In addition the defence can be defeated by a plea of malice, i.e. that the statement was motivated by ill will or spite. Malice outweighs the suggestion that the comment was fair, i.e. a statement that an honest person could make 'however prejudiced he may be or how obstinate his views' (*per* Lord Phillips in *Spiller*). According to the Court of Appeal in *Telnikoff v Matusevitch* [1992] **2 AC 343**, generally, once the defendant has shown that the opinion is one that a reasonable man could hold he does not have to go on to prove that he actually held it. It is for the claimant to show that the statement is unfair and that the opinion was motivated by malice, one aspect of which may be that it was not an opinion genuinely held. In the case of newspapers or other broadcasters reporting the statements of others (and where they will not usually be able to show such genuine belief) this approach protects the newspaper from liability unless malice is shown in some other way. In the problem there is no evidence of malice.

Given the breadth of the assertions and the general context in which they are made it is unlikely the broadcast will satisfy the requirements laid down by the House of Lords in *Reynolds v Times Newspapers* [1999] 4 All ER 609 for the defence of qualified privilege. In this context, where the broadcast is very wide and by the press, the test is one of responsible journalism. This involves giving the claimant an opportunity to comment upon the allegations and depends, among other things, on the urgency of the matter. These conditions are not the requirements of a statute and must be applied sympathetically according to the House of Lords in *Jameel v Wall Street Journal* [2006] UKHL 44 and the Privy Council in *Seaga v Harper* [2008] UKPC 9.

Finally, as regards William Birch (the clown), the question is whether or not the statement can be said to refer to him. In *Newstead v London Express Newspapers* [1940] 1 KB 377, the text of a newspaper story referred to a Harold Newstead, 30-year-old man from Camberwell. This description fitted the claimant who was entitled to sue in respect of the defamatory statement that he was a convicted bigamist, even though it was true of another person intended by the newspaper to be the subject of the story. Similarly, in *Hulton v Jones* [1910] AC 20 a story referring to a fictitious Artemus Jones, churchwarden of Peckham, was held to refer to Artemus Jones, a barrister from Manchester (there being evidence that friends had believed the account to be about him). Subject to the other elements of the tort being made out as described above then there is no reason why William Birch cannot sue. In *Newstead*, damages were set at one farthing (the smallest coin possible) as few of his acquaintances had been convinced by the story, while in *Hulton* damages were substantial due both to the claimant's professional standing and his wider social circle. So, subject to any offer of amends, damages will depend on the jury's perception of the effect on William's livelihood.

Further reading

Barendt, E., 'Libel and Freedom of Speech in English Law' [1993] PL 449.

Descheemaeker, E., 'Protecting Reputation: Defamation and Negligence' (2009) 29 OJLS 603.

Gatley, J. C. C., *Gatley on Libel and Slander,* 11th edn (London: Sweet & Maxwell, 2008).

Loveland, I., '*Reynolds v Times Newspapers* in the House of Lords' [2000] PL 351.

Trindade, F. A., 'Defamatory Statements and Political Discussion' (2000) 116 LQR 185.

Williams, K., 'Defaming Politicians: The Not So Common Law' (2003) 63 MLR 748.

Interference with chattels and business interests

Introduction

One purpose served by the law of torts is to protect members of society against harm to the person, but it also protects property rights and, to a much lesser extent, a person's legitimate business interests.

The first of the questions that follow is primarily concerned with the tort of conversion which requires consideration of the claimant's right to possession of goods. Both conversion and the tort of trespass to goods require proof of an intention, on the part of the defendant, to interfere. Moreover, since these are intentional torts, the remedies available to the claimant differ from torts which require a lesser state of mind.

The other question considers the economic tort of intentional infliction of harm by unlawful means. While this provides some protection against intentional interference with economic interests, it also illustrates a strain in the law in that they compete with the right of another to make a living. A balance has to be struck between legitimate business competition or hard bargaining and unacceptable interference with the interests of another. In some way, the law has to attempt the difficult task of identifying those unlawful acts which interfere with the trade or business of another without unduly restricting the right of others to engage in free competition. This is not easy.

(1) Trespass to goods and conversion

? Question 1

Paresh, a keen golfer, while looking for a lost golf ball, finds a heavy gold chain round the neck of a skeleton at the bottom of a lake on the Victoria Park golf course, a site owned and run by Graspshire County Council. The clasp on the chain is imperfect with the result that Paresh asks Harold, a jeweller, to carry out repairs. Harold sells the chain to Atika for £500, claiming that it belongs to a friend of his who has given him authority to obtain the best possible price. Paresh lends the skeleton to Patrick, a friend who is a medical student, for the period of his degree studies. The skeleton is deliberately damaged by Vijay, Patrick's flat-mate during a party. Atika then gives the chain to her boyfriend, Albert, as a birthday present. Albert, a dealer in jewellery, has now displayed the repaired chain in his shop window at a price of £1,500.

Advise the parties whether there is any action for conversion.

 Commentary

This question requires consideration of the proper scope of the tort of conversion and the defences available to a person alleged to have converted chattels in respect of which another person has a higher claim. Other relevant factors include the problem posed where a person does some act which has the effect of increasing the value of goods that are later claimed to have been converted.

Answer plan

- Define conversion.
- Is a finder of goods someone who has standing to sue?
- What effect does the existence of a bailment relationship have on the liability of the bailee?
- What effect does the common law defence *jus tertii* have in the light of the **Torts (Interference with Goods) Act 1977, s. 8**?
- What remedies are available in respect of the tort of conversion in the light of the **Torts (Interference with Goods) Act 1977, s. 3**?
- What are the rights of an improver under the **Torts (Interference with Goods) Act 1977, s. 6**?

Suggested answer

Conversion is the intentional dealing with goods, rather than intangible personal property rights (*OBG Ltd v Allan* [2007] UKHL 21), which is seriously inconsistent with the possession, or right to immediate possession, of another person. Trespass to goods involves a direct interference with goods in the possession of the claimant, whether the interference is intentional or careless.

Whether the chain and the skeleton are goods that may be converted requires the items to be moveable chattels that may be owned and possessed. The chain fits this description, but the skeleton may cause some difficulty. It has been held that while there can be no property in a corpse (*Dobson v North Tyneside Health Authority* [1996] 4 All ER 474 and *A and others v Leeds Teaching Hospital NHS Trust* [2004] EWHC 644 (QB)) it may be possible to obtain property in a preserved specimen (*R v Kelly* [1999] QB 621). However, this is a skeleton found at the bottom of a lake in a public area with a chain around its neck and could be the remains of a victim of crime or an accident, so that it is unlikely to be a preserved specimen and therefore not an item of personal property that can be converted.

If the skeleton is capable of possession, it is technically in the possession of both Paresh (bailee) and Patrick (possessor), but only one of them can sue, and whichever of the two elects to sue Vijay first will have to account to the other possible claimant in respect of his interest (*Nicolls v Bastard* (1835) 2 Cr M & R 659; *O'Sullivan v Williams* [1992] 3 All ER 385).

If Vijay is to be liable, he must have committed an act of conversion and merely damaging the goods will not be enough (*Fouldes v Willoughby* (1841) 8 M & W 540), unless Vijay is shown to have intentionally destroyed the goods.

As the chain was found at the bottom of a lake on land owned by another, it has to be established that Paresh has a right to possession. The common saying 'finders, keepers' may have some value as the fact of possession is sufficient to create an interest in the goods. In *Parker v British Airways Board* [1982] QB 1004, it was held that the finder of a chattel acquires rights over it if the true owner is unknown, the chattel appears to be abandoned or lost, and he takes the chattel into his care or possession. In such a case, the finder acquires a right to the goods which is valid against everyone except the true owner, or a person who asserts a prior right to the goods which subsisted at the time the finder took possession, so if a customer finds banknotes on the floor of a shop, the customer will have a better claim to the notes than the shopkeeper, since until informed of their presence by the customer, the shopkeeper is unaware that they are there (*Bridges v Hawkesworth* (1851) 21 LJQB 75; see also *Amory v Delamirie* (1722) 1 Stra 505).

The facts suggest that the chain has been found below the surface of the water but on the bed of the lake, which may allow Graspshire County Council to assert a superior interest. Things embedded in land appear to belong to the landowner: *Elwes v Briggs Gas Co* (1886) 33 Ch D 562 (prehistoric boat embedded six feet below the surface). In *Waverley Borough Council v Fletcher* [1995] 4 All ER 756 the local authority that owned a park in which the defendant found a medieval gold brooch nine inches below the surface was considered to have a superior right to that of the defendant as he had no right to dig up the ground. In the problem case, Paresh has not had to dig in order to find the chain, but on the other hand the surface of the water may be regarded as the top of the County Council's land, in which case the chain may be regarded as equivalent to being buried, as was the case in *South Staffordshire Water Co v Sharman* [1896] 2 QB 44 where two gold rings found at the bottom of a pool were said to be owned by the local authority who owned the pool rather than their employee who found the rings.

The finder has a better interest in the goods if they are merely on the land rather than being attached to it, provided the owner has not shown an intention to exercise control over the land and things upon it. Thus in *Parker v British Airways Board* there was no evidence to show that the defendants had any intention to exercise control over a bracelet found by the claimant on the floor of the departure lounge at an airport. But in *London Corp v Appleyard* [1963] 2 All ER 834, the discovery of banknotes in a box in a wall safe showed that the owner of the land did have an intention to exercise control over the property. In the present case, there appears to be little evidence of an intention to control the chain on the part of Graspshire County Council, which may be taken to suggest that Paresh has a greater interest.

After finding the chain, Paresh hands it to Harold for repair, so as to create a bailment relationship under which Harold, as a bailee, has a lien over goods entrusted to him for repair, but only in respect of his right to payment for the work he has done. Once a bailee wrongly parts with possession, he loses his lien, which he does by selling the chain to Atika. Moreover, his act also amounts to conversion, thereby entitling the owner to sue him (*Mulliner v Florence* (1878) 3 QBD 484).

The **Torts (Interference with Goods) Act 1977, s. 8(1)** allows a third party to plead his better title at the time of conversion as a defence (*De Franco v Metropolitan Police Commissioner* (1987) *The Times*, 8 May). So if Graspshire County Council have a better title to the chain, an action in conversion against Harold, Atika, or Albert is likely to fail.

Conversion requires an intentional act which results in an interference with the claimant's goods (*Ashby v Tolhurst* [1937] 2 KB 242). However, if the defendant intends to deal with the goods in such a way as to interfere with the claimant's right of control, it does not matter that he is unaware that he has challenged the true owner's right to property or possession (*Caxton Publishing Ltd v Sutherland Publishing Ltd* [1939] AC 178). It follows that there is no defence of mistake or acting in good faith (*Hollins v Fowler* (1875) LR 7 HL 757 and see also *Kuwait Airways Corp v Iraqi Airways Co (Nos 4 and 5)* [2002] UKHL 19). Harold intends to deal in the chain in a manner which is inconsistent with Paresh's right of possession and as Harold has possession only for the purposes of repair, there will not be a sale with the consent of the owner for the purposes of the **Factors Act 1889, ss. 1(1)** and **2(1)** (*Pearson v Rose & Young* [1951] 1 KB 275). Moreover, Atika has also acted intentionally by delivering the chain to Albert and the fact that she is unaware that she has challenged Paresh's right to possession is irrelevant.

Albert has merely invited offers for the purchase of the chain, so there is no sale or agreement to sell, with the result that there is no transfer of possession and, therefore, no conversion (*Lancashire Wagon Co v Fitzhugh* (1861) 6 H & N 502). If Albert has 'used' the chain as his own, e.g. by wearing it, this may be conversion: *Petre v Hemeage* (1701) 12 Mod Rep 519. The same may be true of a person who tries to sell an article, as Albert has.

A claimant can recover damages to the extent of the value of the goods converted, namely, the market value of the converted goods at the date of conversion:

Uzinterimpex JSC v Standard Bank plc [2007] **EWHC 1151 (Comm)**. In this case, if Albert's price for the chain represents its market value, that amount will be £1,500. However, the relevant date for assessment of damages is the date of conversion (*BBMB Finance Ltd v Eda Holdings Ltd* [1991] 2 All ER 129). In *Kuwait Airways Corp v Iraqi Airways Co (Nos 4 and 5)*, Lord Nicholls drew a distinction between a person who converts in good faith and one who converts deliberately. The former would be liable for consequential losses only to the extent that those losses were reasonably foreseeable, whereas the latter will be liable for damage flowing 'directly and naturally' from the tort.

By repairing the chain, Harold may have increased its value, but the enhanced value is not normally recoverable (*Caxton Publishing Ltd v Sutherland Publishing Ltd*). If the act of conversion occurs after the improvement, as in Harold's case, the **Torts (Interference with Goods) Act 1977, s. 6(1)** applies, allowing a defendant who has improved the goods in the mistaken belief that he has a good title to recover an allowance, but this is unlikely to assist Harold. Under **s. 6(2)** a similar allowance may also be made in favour of subsequent purchasers, such as Atika, provided they act in good faith. Albert is unlikely to be able to use **s. 6** in his favour, since it only applies to a subsequent purchaser, and as Atika gave him the chain as a present, he is a volunteer.

(2) Interfering with business by unlawful means

? Question 2

'Although no branch of the law of torts has a higher proportion of decisions of the House of Lords...the scope of the tort is as obscure as its history.'

(Heuston and Buckley, *Salmond and Heuston on the Law of Torts*)

How far is this an accurate reflection on the tort of conspiracy?

Commentary

One of the difficulties associated with the torts concerned with interference with contract or trade, is that the courts have to seek to achieve a balance between conduct that oversteps the bounds of what is acceptable and the right of a person to pursue his trade or livelihood. While a person has a right to pursue his own business, he must not do so if his conduct impinges on the rights of other traders to do the same. Broadly speaking the torts of intentional infliction of harm by unlawful means, conspiracy, and inducement to breach of contract are all connected by the common thread that they apply in circumstances in which the conduct of the defendant has wrongly interfered with the right of another to carry on his lawful business.

This question requires a critical examination of the scope of the tort of conspiracy, including where it came from and the present range of unlawful acts capable of falling within the definition of the tort.

Answer plan

- Define the tort.
- Show its links with the criminal law.
- Differentiate between the tort of intentional infliction of harm by unlawful means, conspiracy to injure, and unlawful means conspiracy.

Suggested answer

Conspiracy amounts to the commission of a tort when two or more persons agree to commit an act which would be lawful if committed by one person acting alone. In order for there to be an actionable conspiracy, there must be an intention to cause damage and actual damage. There can be a 'simple' conspiracy or an 'unlawful means' conspiracy. The first requires a conspiracy to injure another in his trade and the second requires a conspiracy to carry out an unlawful act such as a crime or a tort. There have been those who argued that 'unlawful means' conspiracy was a redundant concept, but the House of Lords in *Customs & Excise Commissioners v Total Network SL* [2008] **UKHL 19** has confirmed that this tort is not a variety of accessory liability and remains a valuable tool in dealing with groups of people working in combination to harm another.

In addition to the two named varieties of conspiracy, the courts have also developed a 'genus' tort of using unlawful means to cause loss to another (see *OBG Ltd v Allan* [2007] **UKHL 21**), which appears to be easier to establish than conspiracy per se, since there is a much broader definition of unlawful means.

In *Allen v Flood* [1898] **AC 1**, it was held that motive alone does not turn a lawful act into something that is unlawful, but 'simple' conspiracy must be viewed as an exception to the rule, since the motive of injuring a person in his trade is the central feature of this form of conspiracy.

It is possibly questionable why the deeds of two people acting in combination should be actionable when the actions of a multinational corporation, as a single juristic person, are not. Indeed, for this very reason, doubts have been expressed by the House of Lords as to the rationale of the tort of conspiracy, although on each occasion the existence of the tort has been confirmed (*Lonrho Ltd v Shell Petroleum Co* [1982] **AC 173**; *Lonrho plc v Fayed* [1992] **1 AC 448**).

The tort requires an agreement, so that an order by a superior to an employee to cause harm to the claimant will not amount to a conspiracy as there has been no agreement (*Crofter Hand Woven Harris Tweed Co v Veitch* [1942] **AC 435, 468** *per* Lord Wright). Moreover, if the act is done for a good reason, such as furthering one's business interests, no tort is committed: even if the claimant is excluded from a lucrative business market (*Mogul Steamship Co v McGregor, Gow & Co* [1892] **AC 25**). Likewise, an agreement between two trade union officials will not be a conspiracy, provided there is evidence that the agreement they have reached is intended to further the legitimate interests of the union or its members (*Crofter Hand Woven Harris Tweed Co v Veitch*).

In contrast, an agreement intended to punish the claimant for holding an opinion is likely to be treated as having been made for good reason (*Quinn v Leathem* [1901] AC 495), although this might be criticized as inconsistent with *Allen v Flood* where a non-interventionist position was adopted.

Following *Quinn v Leathem* it was thought that malice was an ingredient of the tort, but it is clear since *Crofter Hand Woven Harris Tweed Co Ltd v Veitch* that this is not the case, although it may actually be present in some cases. The decision in *Crofter* made it necessary to consider the predominant purpose of the defendants' actions, which should be to injure the claimant (*Metall und Rohstoff AG v Donaldson, Lufkin & Jenrette* [1990] 1 QB 391), although the emphasis should be on intention rather than motive (*Lonrho plc v Fayed* [1992] 1 AC 448). In *Crofter* the defendant's (a trade union) predominant purpose in placing an embargo on the importation of woollen yarn to the Isle of Lewis was the protection of the interests of its members, but in *Quinn v Leathem* there was a desire to punish the claimant.

A conspiracy to injure occurs where there is a wilful act which is intended to and does cause damage to the claimant in the course of his trade or business. For these purposes, there is still a conspiracy if the defendants know all the facts and intend to cause damage even if they are unaware of the illegality of their actions (*Pritchard v Briggs* [1980] Ch 388). It is important to emphasize that the gist of the action is actual pecuniary loss. Accordingly, it has been held that injury to reputation, including injury to business reputation in the form of damage to goodwill, is not a recoverable head of damage in an action for conspiracy (*Lonrho plc v Fayed (No. 5)* [1994] 1 All ER 188). Such losses are the proper province of the tort of defamation in which justification may be pleaded by the defendant.

If conspiracy is viewed as a crime and a tort, the burden of proving absence of justification for the defendant's actions may lie on the claimant; however, as a civil action alone the burden of proving justification of an intentional act sits better with the defendant. What is clear, however, is that the defendant who proves that his principal aim was to further his legitimate trade interests will succeed.

The second kind of actionable conspiracy, namely unlawful means conspiracy, requires a combination between two or more people to engage in criminal conduct at common law or by statute, whether or not that conduct also gave rise to an independently actionable civil wrong, with the result that the claimant suffers damage (*Customs & Excise Commissioners v Total Network SL* [2008] UKHL 19).

For these purposes, 'unlawful means' includes conduct that goes beyond something that would be independently actionable as a civil wrong, but the opinions in *Total Network SL* are unclear on how much broader the definition should be. The unlawful means must be employed in order to intentionally inflict harm on the claimant, such as a fraud intended to avoid liability to pay VAT in the UK by importing goods from another country via a company that was VAT exempt in that other country, as in *Total*

Network SL. Through this practice the Customs & Excise Commissioners had been deprived of a balancing payment which ought to have been due to them. Although there was no independent tort committed by the defendants, the crime of cheating the public revenue had been committed, so the companies concerned in this fraud had, by unlawful means, combined to intentionally inflict harm on the claimants by depriving them of the taxation revenues due to them.

It does not follow from this that all agreements to commit a crime will amount to unlawful means conspiracy as there are indications in the opinions of Lords Walker, Mance, and Neuberger that special significance was attached to the fact that the crime in *Total Network SL* related to protecting the revenue. It may be the case that the tort will only apply where the criminal offence has been created in order to protect the claimant's interests.

For the purposes of this tort, proof of a predominant intention to injure the claimant is not an essential element (*Lonrho plc v Fayed* [1992] 1 AC 448). In *Lonrho Ltd v Shell Petroleum Ltd (No. 2)* [1982] AC 173, the defendants intentionally agreed to import oil into Southern Rhodesia from South Africa, in breach of a statutory prohibition. By acting in this way, the defendants substantially increased their profits at the expense of the claimants. On these facts, it was held that there was no intention to injure the claimants since there was no tort unless the defendants acted for the purpose not of protecting their own interests but of injuring the interests of the claimants. However, since *Lonrho plc v Fayed* [1992] 1 AC 448, the fact that a reason or even the predominant reason for acting unlawfully is the furtherance of one's own interests is not to be regarded as a defence.

The 'genus tort' of using unlawful means to cause loss to another, confusingly, requires the unlawful means employed by the defendants to amount to an independently actionable tort or, at least, something that would have been actionable as a tort had damage been caused (*OBG Ltd v Allan* [2007] UKHL 21). For the purposes of this tort, 'unlawful means' may include an action amounting to a tort, a breach of contract and a crime.

If the defendant intentionally causes the claimant to suffer loss by committing a tort in relation to X, so that X finds his freedom to deal with the claimant is interfered with, the defendant will have committed the genus tort whether or not the defendant's acts cause X to suffer any kind of actionable loss (*OBG Ltd v Allan* [2007] UKHL 21 at [49]–[50], *per* Lord Hoffmann; *Lonrho v Fayed* [1990] 2 QB 479).

A breach of contract is also regarded as 'unlawful means' despite the fact that an order for compulsory performance is not available for every breach of contract. Thus, a threat to break a contract is regarded as no different to a threat to commit a tort (*Rookes v Barnard* [1964] AC 1129; *OBG Ltd v Allan* [2007] UKHL 21 at [48] *per* Lord Hoffmann).

Where the conduct of the defendant amounts to both a crime and a tort at the same time, there should be no difficulty in treating this as 'unlawful means', but there is more difficulty where the crime is only regulatory in nature. In **OBG Ltd v Allan** the House of Lords was divided on this issue but, in the event, a majority accepted Lord

Hoffmann's view that a crime should only count as unlawful means if it was actionable in tort at the instance of the third party.

In order for the tort to be committed, the defendant's act must interfere with the freedom of a third party to deal with the claimant. According to Lord Hoffmann in **OBG** this will be the case where the defendant's act makes it impossible to perform a contract, where he threatens the third party if he performs a contract, or where he misleads the third party so that he acts otherwise than had he not been misled.

Finally, the genus tort requires, on the part of the defendant, an intention to cause loss to the claimant. This requires a distinction to be drawn between something that is part of the defendant's means and what is merely a consequence of using those means. If it transpires that the defendant intended to cause the loss suffered by the claimant, it will make no difference if the defendant would have preferred that the loss did not result. For example, in **Rookes v Barnard [1964] AC 1129** the defendant would have preferred the claimant to resign from his position rather than be sacked, but as the defendant's actions were intended to produce the end result, they had committed the tort.

In **OBG** both Lord Hoffmann and Lord Nicholls opined that an outcome will be intended if the defendant knows that it is the 'other side of the same coin' as the loss complained of. Thus in **Douglas v Hello! (No. 3) [2007] UKHL 21** the claimants (the owners of **OK!** magazine) had exclusive rights to publish photographs of a celebrity wedding and the defendants were the publishers of a magazine (**Hello!**) that managed to procure and publish illicit photographs of the same wedding taken by a member of the paparazzi. The defendants argued that they did not intend to reduce the sales of **OK!**, but that they merely wished to protect the market position of **Hello!**. However, in the House of Lords, the two positions were regarded as opposite sides of the same coin, so that the defendants could be said to have intended the loss suffered.

There may also be cases in which the defendant intends one kind of loss, but actually causes a different type. In **OBG** Lord Hoffmann stated on more than one occasion that what the tort requires is an intention to cause loss, not the particular type of loss suffered by the claimant.

Further reading

Bagshaw, R., 'Can the Economic Torts Be Unified?' (1998) 18 OJLS 729.

Carty, H., 'The Economic Torts in the 21st Century' (2008) 124 LQR 641.

Stilitz, D., and Sales, P., 'Intentional Infliction of Harm by Unlawful Means' (1999) 115 LQR 411.

General defences

Introduction

This chapter deals with the general defences available to a defendant who is faced with an action in tort. While a number of torts carry with them a range of specific defences, there are defences which apply across the whole range of tortious liability. In particular, this chapter considers the application of the defences of contributory negligence, *volenti non fit injuria* (otherwise known as the defence of consent or, in the context of negligence, voluntary assumption of risk), and the defence of illegality encapsulated in the latin maxim *ex turpi causa non oritur actio* (a man cannot benefit from his own misdeeds). This last defence is most closely linked to public policy.

The first of the questions that follow considers the confused state of the defence of *volenti non fit injuria* and considers what are its true requirements and what purpose the defence serves in light of the other available defences which may adequately explain the claimant's lack of complete success.

The second question illustrates the extent of overlap between the defences of contributory negligence, *volenti,* and public policy; while the third, another problem, places the role of each of the defences within a more complex negligence scenario.

? Question 1

The confused state of the defence *volenti non fit injuria* is 'partly due to a considerable overlap with other conceptual techniques employed to limit or reduce a defendant's liability'.

(Jones, *Textbook on Torts*)

Discuss.

Commentary

This question requires an explanation of the main ingredients in the defence of *volenti non fit injuria*, and a consideration of its relationship with the other available defences and with duty of care. Because the operation of *volenti* deprives the claimant completely of a remedy, and the defendant of responsibility, the conditions for its application are quite stringent, and contributory negligence might be seen by the court as a fairer option. Also, although *volenti* is classed as a defence, it is often expressed in terms that no duty is owed to a person who willingly accepts a risk.

⭐ **Examiner's tip**

When dealing with an essay question such as this, first try to get to grips with the underlying key point. Here it states the defence is in a confused state, and offers suggestions why. Some of the decisions on this defence may seem quite illogical, so a strong answer will focus on the judges' reasoning in the relevant cases.

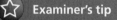 **Answer plan**

- Voluntary choice.
- Agreement to accept the legal risk of harm.
- Knowledge of the existence, nature, and extent of the risk of harm.

➡️ **Suggested answer**

Roughly translated, *volenti non fit injuria* means, 'to one who is willing, no harm is done'. It is a defence based on consent which operates to displace the duty which would otherwise be owed by the defendant. The principal ingredients of the defence are that the claimant must have made a voluntary choice to accept the risk of harm with full knowledge of the nature and extent of that risk. It is therefore necessary to examine three elements: the legal meaning of voluntary; how we determine the claimant has accepted the risk; and the degree of knowledge required before the defence is made out.

The requirement of voluntary choice means that the claimant must be in a position to make a free choice. It follows from this that an employee is not *volens* to the risk of injury at work merely because he is aware of a dangerous practice. In *Smith v Baker* [1891] AC 325, for example, the House of Lords recognized there may be other reasons why he continues to work, such as economic compulsion—the need to earn a living. Moreover, as a matter of policy the courts may recognize that certain people such as rescuers act in a manner which exposes them to a risk of injury because of the dictates of some social or moral duty rather than because they have voluntarily assumed the risk of injury (*Haynes v Harwood* [1935] 1 KB 146). This approach may be seen both as a recognition of the reality of the situation, within which free will gives way to moral compulsion, and of the public interest in encouraging such selflessness rather than deterring it by withdrawing the protection of the law.

Another situation in which voluntariness falls into question relates to suicides. The defence has been defeated in a number of so-called 'custody cases', in which a negligent failure on the part of the defendant has created an opportunity for suicide (*Kirkham v Chief Constable of Greater Manchester Police* [1990] 3 All ER 246; *Reeves v Metropolitan Police Commissioner* [2000] 1 AC 360) both on grounds, in most cases, of impaired autonomy, and also on the policy ground that a duty to guard against potential suicide should not be negated by the act itself.

Similarly, in cases of suicide consequent on negligently caused physical injury (*Pigney v Pointers Transport Services Ltd* [1957] 2 All ER 807; *Corr v IBC Vehicles Ltd* [2008] UKHL 13) the courts have recognized that an impairment of autonomy may be such as to defeat *volenti*, even though the deceased had been able, in many ways, to function fairly normally.

Based as it is on consent, it has been said that the defence of *volenti* requires some degree of agreement. If the notion of agreement is taken in its contractual sense, a person can be said to agree to the presence of certain terms in a contract only if he has been made aware of those terms before the contract is made and agreement is reached. If one were to substitute the notion of legal risk of harm for 'the terms of the contract' this would seem to suggest that in order to be *volens* the claimant must be aware of the risk of harm and consent to run that risk before it arises. The analogy of contract works well in relation to the intentional torts, where consent on the part of the claimant may be expressed (as in the case, for example, of medical treatment) or implied from their conduct (as in the case of participants in contact sports). In other words, in contract or the intentional torts it would be clear to an observer precisely what had been consented to whereas it is in the very nature of negligence that the boundaries of the risk are uncertain. Given the very precise connotations of the word 'consent', it is therefore generally more appropriate in negligence to describe the defence in terms of 'voluntary assumption of risk'.

Despite the terminology, however, any defence which deprives the claimant of a remedy is a serious matter and the defendant is required to prove that the claimant's conduct amounts to a clear demonstration of his intention to waive any legal rights that may arise from the harm that is risked—in effect a kind of estoppel. This may be described in terms of an agreement, as for example in *Wooldridge v Sumner* [1963] 2 QB 43 in which it was said that *volenti* should not be available in the absence of express consent to the legal risk of harm. In *Nettleship v Weston* [1971] 2 QB 691, Lord Denning said that: 'Nothing will suffice short of an agreement to waive any claim for negligence.' On the facts of that case, the claimant's enquiry about insurance cover was evidence of his knowledge (and, perhaps, acceptance) of risk, but equally of his intention to seek compensation should the risk materialize. By contrast, there are cases in which it has been held that the defence is available in cases where the claimant merely encounters an existing danger, as in *Titchener v British Railways Board* [1983] 3 All ER 770, where the presence of a 15-year-old on a railway track was taken as evidence of her willingness to undertake the risk of being hit by a train.

In reality, the word 'agreement', in its usual sense, is rarely applicable in negligence cases but may be inferred from the claimant's conduct, most often manifesting itself by their willing participation in some kind of risky joint venture. In *ICI Ltd v Shatwell* [1965] AC 656, for example, two experienced shotfirers were injured following a joint decision to use detonators against all safety rules. The House of Lords inferred from the claimants' equal knowledge and joint decision that the defence was made out, despite any apparent 'agreement'.

To be met by the defence of *volenti* the claimant must be aware of the nature and extent of the risk of harm. In *Dann v Hamilton* [1939] 1 KB 509, knowingly (and willingly) travelling in a car whose driver was intoxicated was not held to be sufficient for the defence of *volenti* as the range of possible outcomes was too wide for the claimant to be taken to have accepted all of them. Asquith J said that *volenti* should operate only in respect of a risk so glaringly obvious as 'intermeddling with an unexploded bomb'. By contrast, the claimant in *Morris v Murray* [1990] 3 All ER 801 was a passenger in a plane (a rather more glaringly obvious risk), and had actively participated in the venture, having spent the afternoon drinking with the pilot and assisted him in preparing the plane for take-off and so on.

One difficulty created by the defence of *volenti* is that it sometimes appears to have been applied in circumstances in which some other limiting device might have been more appropriate. This may well have been due, at least in the older (pre-Act) cases such as *Dann*, to the fact that common law contributory negligence was a complete defence, so little was to be gained by arguing the defences in the alternative. It must be appreciated that *volenti* is a defence which displaces the primary duty and that before it can be invoked, an actionable tort must have been committed. Thus, if a reduced standard of care is expected of the defendant, there may be no actionable tort and to use the language of *volenti* is misleading and unnecessary. In *Wooldridge v Sumner* [1963] 2 QB 43 it was held that a photographer at a showjumping event who takes photographs from within the jumping arena is not truly *volens* to the risk of harm when he is struck by a horse, because it can hardly be said that he has consented to the risk that he might be injured. Instead, it is probably better to say that the event organizers owe a lesser duty of care to such people, because of the competitive nature of the activity, so that the standard of care is more easily satisfied.

This reduced standard of care reasoning also works in other contexts. Thus one explanation for the application of the defence *ex turpi causa non oritur actio* is that it is difficult or impossible to ascertain what standard of care is required of the defendant in the light of the claimant's own illegal or immoral conduct. In *Pitts v Hunt* [1990] 3 All

ER 344, the claimant failed in an action for damages against the deceased's estate where he had encouraged the deceased in driving a motorcycle in a dangerous fashion. Although it could have been argued that the claimant had consented to the injuries he suffered (by his willing participation in a risky joint enterprise), the defence was specifically rendered ineffective by the **Road Traffic Act 1972, s. 148(3)** (now **s. 149(3)** of the **Road Traffic Act 1988**) and an alternative argument was needed if his claim was to fail. The interpretation favoured by Balcombe LJ was that the claimant's involvement in the series of events leading up to the accident was such that it was impossible to say what level of care was required of the deceased, and one could not say a duty was owed whose scope could not be determined.

The defence of *volenti*, if it succeeds, is a complete defence and absolves the defendant from all liability. The possibility of a more equitable compromise is offered by the **Law Reform (Contributory Negligence) Act 1945**, which replaces the common law approach in which contributory negligence was a complete defence; instead it confers on the courts a discretion to reduce damages to take into account the partial responsibility of the claimant in failing to take reasonable care for his own safety. A good example of this approach in operation is in relation to the willing passengers of drunken drivers, where it seems that the normal judicial response will be to treat the claimant as merely contributorily negligent (*Owens v Brimmell* [1977] QB 859—20 per cent reduction; see also *Donelan v Donelan and General Accident Fire & Life Insurance* [1993] PIQR P205—75 per cent reduction). It is suggested that the latter approach is legally correct since if *volenti* is properly understood, the claimant must assent to the legal risk that the defendant's actions will cause him harm but waives his right to sue for damages. Only in extreme cases such as *Morris v Murray* [1990] 3 All ER 801 should the claimant be denied damages altogether. Moreover, where the denial of liability is considered necessary, in most cases this is justified by public policy rather than by the fact that the claimant has assented to the risk of injury. Case law seems to indicate a general unwillingness on the part of the courts to see a negligent defendant's liability altogether extinguished.

? Question 2

Anya and Tomas, two students, having completed their final examinations, decide to spend a night out at the Mucky Duck, a public house. Anya meets Tomas at the Mucky Duck. At the end of the evening, Tomas offers Anya a lift home at a time when both of them are extremely drunk. Tomas drives his car down the middle of the road, occasionally swerving to frighten other road users. Anya enthusiastically encourages Tomas in this venture.

Tomas drives through a red traffic light at speed and collides with a car driven by Gary. Gary who is not wearing a seat belt is crushed behind the steering wheel of his car. Anya is also seriously injured in the collision.

When taken to hospital, Gary refuses a blood transfusion on religious grounds. Because of this refusal and the seriousness of his injuries, Gary's arm has to be amputated.

Advise Tomas of his potential liability in tort.

Commentary

This is an example of a wider question concerning liability for negligently caused personal injury, the issues of causation remoteness, and puts contributory negligence and the availability of the general defences into context.

Answer plan

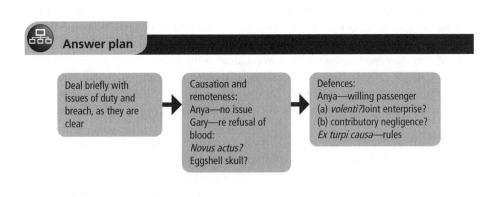

Deal briefly with issues of duty and breach, as they are clear

Causation and remoteness:
Anya—no issue
Gary—re refusal of blood:
Novus actus?
Eggshell skull?

Defences:
Anya—willing passenger
(a) *volenti?*Joint enterprise?
(b) contributory negligence?
Ex turpi causa—rules

Suggested answer

There is no doubt that, as a road user, Tomas, in normal circumstances, would owe a duty of care to Anya, since any person who uses the road owes a duty of care to other road users. Moreover, the manner in which Tomas drives also suggests that he has failed to exercise reasonable care since he has not reached the standard ordinarily expected of a reasonably competent driver (**Nettleship v Weston [1971] 2 QB 691**). However, Anya's own involvement in the events of the evening may allow Tomas to plead one of a number of possible defences which may serve to reduce or negative his potential liability.

Tomas might argue that the defence of *volenti non fit injuria* applies. This defence requires a tort to have been committed, and where it operates, it serves to displace any duty which otherwise would have existed. What seems to be required is that the claimant should have assented to the legal risk of injury created by the defendant's negligence. In **Nettleship v Weston** Lord Denning said the claimant should have expressly or impliedly agreed to waive any claim against the defendant, though in *Titchener v British Railways Board* [1983] 3 All ER 770 the House of Lords took the view that a 15-year-old on railway tracks consented to the risk of injury from a train, holding it is sufficient that the claimant encounters a known and existing danger created by the defendant. In the present case, it may be difficult to find an express agreement to run the legal risk since at the time the lift is offered to Anya, she is extremely drunk. There are instances in which the courts have been prepared to find an implied agreement from the parties' conduct, though generally this requires some sort of joint enterprise in which the defendant and claimant operated as equal partners. So, in *Dann v Hamilton* [1939] 1 KB 509, knowledge and apparent acceptance of the range of risks inherent in travelling with a drunk driver in a car was held to be insufficient to support a defence of *volenti*, though Asquith J said it may apply where the risk was so glaringly obvious as to be the equivalent of 'intermeddling with an unexploded bomb'. That test was met in *Morris v Murray* [1990] 3 All ER 801, in which the vehicle employed in the drunken escapade was an aircraft and the claimant had participated fully in the events leading to the crash.

A further difficulty is that the claimant must have subjective knowledge of both the existence of the risk and its nature and extent (*Smith v Austin Lifts Ltd* [1959] 1 WLR 100). This might suggest that a passenger who is sufficiently drunk does not have the necessary knowledge. In *Morris v Murray* the claimant was drunk, but not so drunk that he did not realize what he was doing, so the defence applied. It was accepted by the Court of Appeal that the question was whether the claimant was so drunk as not to realize what he was doing, which produces the paradox that a person may be better off if he is extremely drunk rather than just a little! Although this may be so, in *Insurance Commissioner v Joyce* (1948) 77 CLR 39, an Australian case cited with approval in *Owens v Brimmell* [1977] QB 859, Latham CJ neatly sidestepped the paradox, at least in relation to contributory negligence, by noting that a mildly intoxicated passenger was partially at fault for travelling with a drunk driver, while a very drunk passenger was at fault for allowing himself to become incapable of making a sensible decision.

The question states that Anya and Tomas are both extremely drunk, which might mean that Anya is unable to give the necessary assent required for the purposes of the defence of *volenti*. In any event, Anya is injured in a road traffic accident and, in this regard, the **Road Traffic Act 1988, s. 149** prevents reliance on the defence of *volenti* where the compulsory insurance provisions of that Act apply. Here Tomas is driving on a public highway so he is subject to the requirement of compulsory third-party insurance and so there can be no reliance on *volenti*.

Intoxicated driver cases are generally better dealt with under rules on contributory negligence (*Owens v Brimmell*). If Anya accepts a lift from a person who is incapable of driving safely, she appears not to have acted as a reasonably prudent person would (*Jones v Livox Quarries Ltd* [1952] 2 QB 608).

In order to establish contributory negligence, Tomas must prove that Anya has failed to take reasonable care for her own safety. In this respect, there are two principal issues.

First, it must be asked whether harm to the claimant was reasonably foreseeable. The test is objective so that even if Anya is so drunk as to be incapable of making a rational judgement, this will not matter for the purposes of this defence (*Owens v Brimmell*).

While the claimant's conduct does not have to be the cause of the accident, it must be causally connected to the harm suffered. It will be sufficient if the claimant places herself in a dangerous position which increases the chance that harm of a foreseeable kind will be caused (*Jones v Livox Quarries Ltd* [1952] 2 QB 608).

Where the defence applies, **s. 1(1)** of the **Law Reform (Contributory Negligence) Act 1945** provides that the court must apportion damages to such extent as it thinks just and equitable, having regard to the claimant's share in the responsibility for the damage. Key factors are damage, causation, and blameworthiness. The language used by the **1945 Act** is said to be mandatory in that there must be an apportionment, which means the court cannot hold the claimant wholly responsible for the damage (*Pitts v Hunt* [1990] 3 All ER 344).

Although reductions for contributory negligence may often seem relatively low, there are instances in which the claimant's degree of blameworthiness is great, in which case a large percentage reduction may be justified. For example, in *Donelan v Donelan and General Accident Fire & Life Insurance Co Ltd* [1993] PIQR 205 a 75 per cent reduction was applied where the defendant drove the car at the claimant's insistence when the claimant knew that the defendant was inexperienced and drunk. Similarly, in *Barrett v Ministry of Defence* [1995] 3 All ER 87, the defendants were held liable for failing to take proper care of the deceased once he was highly intoxicated (though not for allowing him to become so in the first place) but damages were reduced by two-thirds under the Act, to take account of his own fault.

If the court wishes to bar Anya's claim altogether, the most likely way of doing this is through an application of the 'illegality' defence, *ex turpi causa non oritur actio*—no action arises from a bad deed. In negligence cases, the basis on which the defence works is that the claimant's 'illegal' involvement is such that the court may choose not to recognize the existence of a duty of care. For example, in *Ashton v Turner* [1981] QB 137, no duty of care was owed by the driver of a get away car to his partner in crime. An alternative way of approaching the problem in negligence cases is to say that the claimant's action will fail where the illegal nature of the venture in which the parties are engaged is such that the court feels unable to set an appropriate standard of care, as in *Pitts v Hunt* [1990] 3 All ER 344, in which the claimant was a pillion passenger on a motorcycle driven by the defendant, who was drunk. The vehicle was driven recklessly, but the claimant had encouraged him to drive in that fashion. The Court of Appeal held that the claimant's injuries arose directly out of the illegal venture and were not merely incidental. Accordingly, at least on one analysis, it was impossible to set an appropriate standard of care to be expected of the defendant. Alternatively, since it is not all illegal acts that trigger *ex turpi causa*, the court has to balance the negative consequences of *granting* relief against the negative consequences of *refusing* relief, which inevitably involves a value judgement as between the parties. According to Lord Hoffman in *Gray v Thames Trains* [2009] UKHL 33, the maxim 'expresses not so much a principle as a policy' which 'is not based upon a single justification but on a group of reasons which vary in different situations' because, where two parties are involved in an unlawful transaction, the court 'faces the dilemma that by denying relief on the ground of illegality to one party, it appears to confer an unjustified benefit illegally obtained on the other'.

Either way, it is arguable that Anya's claim in respect of her injuries might be rejected on the basis of the illegality defence, following *Pitts v Hunt*.

Tomas clearly owes Gary a duty of care and his driving is such that there is probably a breach of that duty, but problems may arise in relation to an award of damages. First, it should be noted that Gary is not wearing a seat belt. This is a well-established example of contributory negligence since it involves a failure by Gary to take reasonable care for his own safety (*Froom v Butcher* [1976] QB 286). Moreover, the failure to wear the seat belt is very likely to materially increase the risk of injury should there be a traffic accident, except in circumstances where the nature of the accident, e.g. where a vehicle is crushed by a falling object, makes the role of a seat belt irrelevant.

In determining how damages should be apportioned, the Court of Appeal has sought to lay down guidelines, since seat belt cases are fairly common. In *Froom v Butcher*, it was held that if wearing a seat belt would have prevented altogether the damage suffered, an appropriate reduction in damages would be 25 per cent. If the injury would have been less severe, the reduction should be 15 per cent, but if the injury would have been the same whether a belt was worn or not, there should be no reduction at all. The fact that *Froom* was decided before the wearing of seat belts was made compulsory is irrelevant, since the defence is based on a failure by the claimant to take proper care for his own safety and not simply a failure to abide by the law (*Capps v Miller* [1989] 2 All ER 333).

Gary is crushed behind the steering wheel. Whether he was wearing a seat belt or not, this is a kind of injury likely to be suffered by the driver of a car hit, at speed, by another vehicle. This would seem to suggest a maximum reduction in damages of 15 per cent, but if it is shown that the extent of injury would have been the same whether a seat belt was worn or not, then Gary's damages should not be reduced at all.

When Gary is taken to hospital, he refuses a blood transfusion, with the result that his arm has to be amputated. It must be decided whether Gary's refusal to have a blood transfusion is a *novus actus interveniens*, such as to break the chain of causation between Tomas' negligence and the loss of Gary's arm.

An unlawful or unreasonable act of the claimant is capable of breaking the chain of causation (*McKew v Holland Hannen & Cubitts (Scotland) Ltd* [1969] 3 All ER 1621), but only in circumstances in which it would be fair to say that his act was such as to absolve the negligent defendant. Here, the emphasis is on whether the claimant has acted reasonably in the circumstances. It is less important to consider whether the claimant's act is foreseeable or not. In *Wieland v Cyril Lord Carpets Ltd* [1969] 3 All ER 1006, it was said to be foreseeable that an injury caused by the defendant's negligence may affect the claimant's ability to cope with the vicissitudes of life and thereby lead to (and be the legal cause of) another injury.

The difficulty in this case is that Gary's refusal is based on religious grounds. This will face the court with the daunting prospect of deciding whether it is reasonable for a person to hold a particular belief! The likely approach in these circumstances is that Tomas will have to take Gary as he finds him and that Gary's refusal will not break the chain of causation. In criminal law, a defendant has been found guilty of murder where his victim refused a blood transfusion on religious grounds (*R v Blaue* [1975] 3 All ER 446). The tort law equivalent of this approach is the 'egg-shell skull rule' under which unusual or unforeseeably extensive injury is not regarded as too remote where it results from some peculiarity of the claimant himself (*Smith v Leech Brain & Co* [1962] 2 QB 405). An alternative approach might be adopted by analogy with the case *Emeh v Kensington and Chelsea and Westminster AHA* [1985] QB 1012, in which the court rejected an argument that a woman's failure to terminate an unwanted pregnancy after the defendant's negligent treatment was a *novus actus*. Although partly underpinned by policy relating to the sanctity of life, this is a good example of the courts' general unwillingness to disregard genuinely held moral or religious beliefs. The same policy reasoning should defeat any argument that Gary's refusal amounted to contributory negligence.

? Question 3

Adam arranges to meet his girlfriend, Sally, at the Roxy cinema. As he is walking to the cinema he is day-dreaming and steps into the road. He is struck and seriously injured by a car driven negligently and at grossly excessive speed by Ranjit, a 16-year-old, who has taken a car without the owner's consent and who is showing off to Manjit, his nine-year-old sister who is a passenger in the car.

Sally visits Adam in hospital as soon as she hears of the accident, six hours after the incident. Sally is extremely upset and depressed after observing Adam's facial injuries.

Manjit is crushed against the dashboard of the car and is seriously injured. Manjit was not wearing a seat belt at the time of the accident.

Advise Ranjit of his potential tortious liability.

Commentary

This question raises the principal issues of recovery by a secondary claimant for psychiatric damage, contributory negligence, and the public policy defence of *ex turpi causa non oritur actio*. It is complicated by the age of the participants. The answer should consider the application of the control mechanisms applicable to secondary claimants. There has been some activity in the fields dealt with by the problem, e.g. there has been a Law Commission report relating to liability for negligently caused psychiatric damage and a consultation paper on the principle *ex turpi causa*.

Answer plan

- What standard of care can be expected of a 16-year-old driver?
- What is contributory negligence and what rules attach to this defence?
- What are the restrictive rules on recovery of damages for psychiatric harm?
- Is Manjit's involvement in the joy-riding incident sufficient to disentitle her to an award of damages under the principle *ex turpi causa non oritur actio*?
- How does the defence of contributory negligence apply to her?

Suggested answer

It is likely that the Motor Insurers' Bureau under its agreement with the Department of Transport, in respect of uninsured drivers, will stand in the shoes of the uninsured Ranjit. It is well established that one road user owes a duty of care to anyone who also uses the road—this includes pedestrians such as Adam. In order to succeed, Adam will have to show that Ranjit was in breach of that duty. The test is to ask what a reasonable man would do or would not do in the circumstances: ***Blyth v Birmingham Waterworks Co* (1856) 11 Ex 781**. The standard to apply is that of the reasonably competent qualified driver (***Nettleship v Weston* [1971] 2 QB 691**) and the fact that he is somewhat young and inexperienced will make no difference, though common sense dictates that this standard could not realistically be applied to a much younger child.

Ranjit was negligent and as regards Adam there is the issue of contributory negligence.

Under the **Law Reform (Contributory Negligence) Act 1945** contributory negligence ceased to be a complete defence and became a partial defence allowing for an apportionment of responsibility. It applies where a person has suffered damage partly as a result of his own fault and partly as a result of the fault of another person. The Act permits the court to reduce the damages to the extent the court thinks just and reasonable having regard to the claimant's share in the responsibility. The Act applies where the claimant has failed to take reasonable care for his own safety, thereby contributing to the damage suffered or the extent of the damage suffered, but there is no need for the claimant to owe the defendant a duty of care because the Act operates as a shield and not as a sword.

Contributory negligence requires fault on the part of both Adam and Ranjit. Adam's fault requires consideration of two issues. First, has Adam failed to take reasonable care for his own safety (*Jones v Livox Quarries* [1952] 2 QB 608)? Day-dreaming in the middle of the road, for whatever reason, seems to suggest this is true.

The second issue relates to causation as to the harm suffered. It must be asked whether, but for the day-dreaming, Adam would have been injured. In *Jones v Livox Quarries*, the claimant was injured in a collision when he was riding on the back bumper of a slow-moving quarry vehicle. Lord Denning made the point that if he had been (coincidentally) injured by a shot fired by a negligent sportsman the Act would have had no application because his fault would have had no connection with the injury and the means by which it occurred. Again, there seems little doubt since a person who was not day-dreaming would have stayed on the pavement; it would have been otherwise had Ranjit driven the car on to the pavement.

The third issue in contributory negligence cases is the matter of apportionment of damages. There is considerable scope for the courts to reach an equitable solution with a flexible approach looking at issues of causation of damage and blameworthiness. If the blameworthiness of Adam is small, as seems to be the case, even if he is in the road, a low reduction of, say 10–20 per cent may be likely under the **Law Reform (Contributory Negligence) Act 1945, s. 1(1)**. Alternatively, if Adam's fault is great one might analyse the incident in terms of joint causation, as in *Fitzgerald v Lane* [1988] 2 All ER 961 in which a negligent pedestrian was struck and injured by two negligent motorists. This could be significant in relation to Sally's claim (see below).

Sally is upset and suffers depression at the sight of Adam's injuries. This raises the issue of negligently inflicted psychiatric damage. The law has evolved slowly in this area from a position where 'nervous shock' in negligence was not recoverable, e.g. *Victorian Railway Commissioners v Coultas* (1888) 13 App Cas 222, to the present day where such actions are recognized but are hedged about with control mechanisms designed, as a matter of policy, to restrict the potential for an unmanageable volume of possible claims. The law distinguishes between a primary claimant (someone who is involved in an incident and who could foreseeably have been injured or who reasonably fears for his own safety) and secondary claimants (those who witness the event or come upon the immediate aftermath of it). As Lord Lloyd said in *Page v Smith* [1995] 2 All ER 736, in regard to secondary claimants, the law insists on control mechanisms 'in order as a matter of policy to limit the number of potential claimants'.

First, it must be established that the depression Sally suffers is a medically recognizable psychiatric illness. This has been a consistent theme of all the decisions in this area such as *McLoughlin v O'Brian* [1983] AC 410 and *Alcock v Chief Constable of South Yorkshire Police* [1991] 4 All ER 907. In Sally's case the mere fact that she is upset will not suffice though her depression will provided it amounts to a diagnosable psychiatric illness.

The result from *McLoughlin v O'Brian* and *Alcock* is that the control mechanisms amount to three elements: (1) the claimant must fall into the relevant class of persons whose claims should be recognized; (2) the claimant must have proximity in time and space to the accident; and (3) the court must have regard to the means by which the shock has been caused.

A person may sue provided that he has a close tie of love and affection with the injured victim of the defendant's negligence. This may be presumed to exist, e.g. in cases of spouses, children, and parents, or (perhaps) as between engaged couples, though in all other cases would have to be proved.

In relation to the requirement of proximity in time and space, *McLoughlin v O'Brian* extended the law by permitting recovery where the claimant saw not the accident or event itself but came upon the immediate aftermath of the event. Since Sally was not at the scene of the accident, but only visits Adam in hospital the following morning, it must be decided if she is present at the *immediate* aftermath. In *McLoughlin v O'Brian* a period of two hours was short enough to come within the aftermath principle, but in *Chester v Waverley Corp* (1939) 62 CLR 1, a six-hour delay before the victim's body was found was considered too long. So also in *Alcock*, visits by relatives of the victims of the Hillsborough tragedy to a mortuary some eight to nine hours after the initial incident, for the purposes of identifying bodies, was considered to be too long a period to fall within the definition of the 'immediate aftermath'. Other factors may well be the state of the victim and the purpose of the visit. In *McLoughlin v O'Brian* the victims were still in a very distressed state and had not yet been fully treated or cleaned up after the accident. The reference in the question to 'the following morning' suggests a very long time, during which Adam has probably been cleaned up and installed in a hospital bed, so Sally has probably come too late to fall within the rule. The essence of recovery for psychiatric injury in this type of case is shock and in the absence of something equivalent to a sudden assault on the senses recovery will not usually be possible.

A further obstacle to Sally's claim could be posed by the decision in *Greatorex v Greatorex* [2000] 4 All ER 769, in which it was held that a defendant will not be liable for psychiatric injury to another arising from the defendant's own negligently self-inflicted injury. In part, the justification for this was said to be that a legal responsibility to take care of oneself to avoid psychiatric harm to others would unduly curtail the right to self-determination. The impact of this principle on Sally's case would seem to hinge on the extent of Adam's own contribution to his injuries.

Since Manjit is a passenger in the car, she is owed a duty of care in the same way as any other road user. As this is a road traffic accident, the defence of *volenti*, even if its ingredients were satisfied, is ruled out statutorily where the vehicle must be compulsorily insured against third-party risks: **Road Traffic Act 1988, s. 149(3).**

Manjit's involvement in the joy-riding incident may be sufficient to invoke the public policy defence of *ex turpi causa non oritur actio* (although strictly it is a bar to an action proceeding rather than a defence). The precise scope of the *ex turpi causa* defence is difficult to ascertain. One view is that the defence amounts to a more or less automatic bar on the recovery of damages where the claimant is involved in a joint criminal enterprise with the defendant (*Ashton v Turner* [1981] QB 137), but this does seem rather draconian. In *Pitts v Hunt* [1990] 3 All ER 344, the claimant had actively encouraged the defendant to drive in an extremely dangerous manner and the principle was applied, though members of the Court of Appeal did not agree on any single clear explanation. A second approach was identified, as based on whether it is possible to determine what standard of care should be owed by the defendant to the claimant. A third possible approach was that the principle would be applied if the behaviour offended the public conscience, though this rather vague test was rejected by the House of Lords in *Tinsley v Milligan* [1993] 3 All ER 65, in which emphasis was placed upon the public policy basis of the defence and the extent of the court's discretion. According to *Tinsley*, it is necessary to weigh the adverse consequences of giving a remedy against the consequences of refusing that remedy.

More recently in *Vellino v Chief Constable of Greater Manchester* [2001] EWCA Civ 1249, the claimant had attempted to evade arrest by jumping from a second-floor window but he was severely injured. He claimed that the police officers had acted negligently. In the Court of Appeal the majority found that escape from custody was a sufficiently serious criminal offence to permit the principle to be applied. Therefore the police did not owe an arrested person a duty to take care that he was not injured in a foreseeable attempt to escape police custody. Sir Murray Stuart-Smith said that:

> The operation of the principle arises where the claimant's claim is founded upon his own criminal or immoral act. The facts which give rise to the claim must be inextricably linked with the criminal activity. It is not sufficient if the criminal activity merely gives occasion for tortious conduct of the defendant…this has to be sufficiently serious to merit the application of the principle.

On the facts of the problem, there is no suggestion that Manjit has actively encouraged Ranjit or participated save as passenger. In the circumstances, it seems likely the fact that Manjit is only nine years old may be significant, since she may be considered too young to appreciate the risks involved, and that the *ex turpi causa* defence will not operate against her.

A second issue is whether Manjit is contributorily negligent in getting into the car with an unlicensed, uninsured, and probably incompetent driver. Manjit's age, once again, will be relevant, as the courts are disinclined to hold that a person so young could have foreseen the risk of harm: *Yachuk v Oliver Blais* [1949] AC 386. In *Gough v Thorne* [1966] 1 WLR 1387, Lord Denning suggested that very young children would not be guilty of contributory negligence and that as they got older whether they would be guilty was a question of degree. More recently, in *N (A Child) v Newham LBC* [2007] CLY 2931, a seven-year-old schoolboy who was injured when he punched the glass panel in a classroom door was held 60 per cent to blame. This was because N knew right from wrong, that it was wrong to punch, and that when punched glass was likely to break and injure him. On this reasoning, perhaps Manjit is old enough for the defence to apply since the need to wear seat belts is well known, even to very young children.

While Manjit has not caused the accident by her conduct, she has materially increased the risk of injury by not wearing a seat belt. A formula for compensation stated in *Froom v Butcher* [1976] QB 286 suggests a 25 per cent reduction if no injury would have been suffered had the seat belt been worn, a 15 per cent reduction if the injury would have been less severe had the seat belt been worn, and no reduction at all if the same injury would have been suffered whether or not a seat belt was worn. Being thrown out of her seat suggests at least a 15 per cent if not a 25 per cent reduction in damages, but this is subject to the issue of Manjit's age.

Further reading

Fulbrook, J., 'Alcohol and Third Parties—"Dram Shop Liability" and Beyond' [2007] JPIL 220.

Hudson, A.W., 'Contributory Negligence as a Defence to Battery' (1984) 4 LS 332.

Jones, M. A., *Textbook on Tort Law*, 8th edn (Oxford: Oxford University Press, 2002).

Law Commission No. 219, *Contributory Negligence as a Defence to an Action for Breach of Contract* (1993).

O'Sullivan, J., 'Employer's Liability for Injured Employee's Suicide' (2008) 67 CLJ 241.

Ritchie, A., and McAllister, R., 'Damages for Self Harm after Suffering Tortious Injury (Suicide and Contributory Negligence)' (2009) 1 JPIL 20.

Spowart-Taylor, A., 'Contributory Negligence—A Defence to Breach of Contract' (1986) 49 MLR 102.

14

Remedies

Introduction

This final chapter considers an important issue as far as a tort claimant is concerned, namely what remedy is available in the event of a tort on the part of the defendant. The two major remedies in tort law are an award of damages and the grant of the equitable remedy of injunction. This chapter concentrates on the issue of damages, but questions concerning the rules which apply to injunctions can be found in **Chapter 10** (Torts relating to land), where the injunction plays an important role in providing a remedy for continuing torts such as private nuisance. As far as the remedy of damages is concerned, it is important to consider not just the issues raised in this chapter but also related issues such as the rules on causation and remoteness in negligence actions (see **Chapter 6**).

The three principal types of damage for which a remedy may be available include personal injury (death and psychiatric harm included), property damage, and economic loss. The primary purpose behind an award of damages is to compensate the claimant for the loss or damage actually suffered and not, generally, to punish or deter the defendant from his wrongdoing. The principle which lies behind an award of tort damages is, so far as money can do this, to return the claimant to the position he was in before the defendant's wrong was committed. In personal injury actions, it is sometimes difficult to achieve this result, particularly where harm such as pain and suffering is concerned, since these heads of loss are difficult to quantify in monetary terms.

In property damage cases there is sometimes a problem in identifying the appropriate basis for assessment of damages. For example, it might be appropriate to give the cost of repair, whereas in other cases the fairer measure of damages may be based on the diminution in value of the damaged property.

? Question 1

Hector has been warned by his doctor that he must not drive. Since his wife has been taken seriously ill, he decides to rush her to hospital by car rather than wait for an ambulance. Tamara, Hector's daughter, has recently telephoned the police to inform them that Hector sometimes drives a car despite the fact that he has been advised not to, but the police have done nothing about this. On the way to the hospital, Hector collapses at the wheel, and the car swerves off the road. Dougal, who is painting a second-floor window, is injured when he jumps from his ladder in an attempt to get out of the way of the car. The car comes to a halt after demolishing part of a shop owned by Zebedee. Twenty minutes later, while the police are attempting to remove the car, part of a wall collapses on Florence and Ermintrude, two spectators. Ermintrude, who has recently been divorced from her husband, Dylan, is crushed to death in the space of three minutes and Florence is so badly injured that she suffers from depression and commits suicide three months later. Florence's live-in lover, Brian, is distraught at the death of his partner. Ermintrude's ex-husband, Dylan seeks to recover damages in respect of Ermintrude's death, including damages for the pain and suffering endured by her before she died.

Advise Dougal, Zebedee, Brian, and Dylan.

Commentary

This question concerns the duty of care owed by a road user to other road users and the question whether there has been a breach of that duty. In relation to the remedy of damages, consideration has to be given to the effect of death on an award and how this affects dependants of the deceased and those representing the deceased's estate. In relation to pre-death injuries it is also necessary to consider the form of an award of damages for pain and suffering.

Answer plan

- Is there a breach of duty?
- How relevant is the dilemma which Dougal faces?
- Do the actions of the police amount to a *novus actus interveniens*?
- Who is a dependant and what damages may be recovered in respect of such dependency?
- How do dependency damages differ from 'survival' damages?
- Is suicide a *novus actus interveniens*?

⇨ **Suggested answer**

All road users owe a duty of care to other road users (*Nettleship v Weston* [1970] 2 QB 691), so Dougal and Zebedee will be owed a duty of care in respect of the physical injury and property damage they suffer.

Whether Hector is in breach of the duty of care he owes to Dougal and Zebedee requires consideration of the magnitude of risk, the seriousness of the harm suffered, the utility of the defendant's conduct, and any precautions which might have been taken to guard against the risk. As Hector has been warned by his doctor that he should not drive there seems to be a substantial risk that he may be the cause of an accident if he collapses while driving, but he drives in order to ensure that his ill wife gets to hospital as early as possible. In *Watt v Hertfordshire County Council* [1954] 1 WLR 835 (see also *S (a child) v Keyse* [2001] EWCA Civ 715) a relevant factor in deciding that the defendant was not in breach of duty was the objective of the journey (to save life) that exposed the claimant, a fire fighter, to a substantially increased risk of injury by riding on the back of a lorry not suited to carrying a piece of lifting gear. Nevertheless, where there is a risk to other road users, e.g. where an ambulance driver ignores a red traffic light, there may still be a breach of duty (*Griffin v Mersey Regional Ambulance* [1998] **PIQR P34**). Hector has taken a risk by driving a car when advised not to do so, but he has done so in order to avert the risk of more serious harm to his wife. However, Hector has alternatives such as ordering a taxi or waiting for an ambulance. Whether these alternatives are feasible depends on the seriousness of the risk to his wife's life, but it is generally accepted that the defendant must take only reasonable precautions to guard against the risk, not all possible precautions (*Latimer v AEC Ltd* [1953] AC 643).

Dougal jumped from the ladder so as to avoid being struck by an oncoming vehicle. In *Jones v Boyce* (1816) 1 Stark 493 it was held that a person who risks harm to himself in order to avoid reasonably perceived greater harm created by the defendant's actions may still hold the defendant responsible. If Dougal reasonably believes that Hector's car is about to strike the ladder on which he is standing, it may be reasonable for him to jump, even though this may result in injury.

Whether Hector or the police are liable for the death of Ermintrude and the injuries to Florence will depend on whether the actions of the police amount to a *novus actus interveniens*. It has been held that the police should not be subject to a duty of care in relation to the conduct of investigations (*Hill v Chief Constable of West Yorkshire* [1988] 2 All ER 238), but it does not follow that the police cannot be liable for their negligence in the course of ordinary operations: see *Rigby v Chief Constable of Northamptonshire* [1985] 2 All ER 985 and *Knightley v Johns* [1982] 1 All ER 851.

The immunity suggested by some cases may be displaced for reasons of public policy, such as the proper protection of the public. Thus, in *Swinney v Chief Constable of Northumbria Police* [1996] 3 All ER 449, the claimant supplied the police with confidential information about a group of known violent criminals, who obtained the information by breaking into a police vehicle. As a result of this, the claimant was subjected to violence and consequently suffered psychiatric harm. Because of the special relationship which existed between the claimant and the police, which set him apart from the general public, a duty of care was owed. The facts indicate that the police failed to take action after Tamara informed them that Hector was still driving his car. However, the principle in *Swinney* appears to be one which is personal to the informant, and since Tamara is not injured because of the failure of the police to take action, it is unlikely that the principle established in *Hill*, that a duty is not owed to the general public, will be displaced.

Although Hector's negligent driving caused the car to collide with the wall of Zebedee's shop, the way the police act subsequently may break the chain of causation, but not if the response is perfectly reasonable: *The Oropesa* [1943] P 32. Where the act of the third party is reckless, it is likely to be viewed as a *novus actus interveniens*: *Wright v Lodge* [1993] 4 All ER 299. In *Knightley v Johns* [1982] 1 All ER 851, it was held that it should be asked whether the whole sequence of events is a natural or probable consequence of the defendant's negligence and whether it was more than just foreseeable as a mere possibility. In order to decide the question, it might sometimes be helpful to consider whether the third party's positive act is deliberate or whether he is guilty of no more than an omission or an innocent mistake or miscalculation. In the case of the accident caused by Hector, there does not appear to be any evidence of a negligent act on the part of the police, and the initial damage to the wall has resulted from Hector's driving. This might seem to suggest that the actions of the police do not amount to a *novus actus interveniens* and that Hector will also be responsible for the death of Ermintrude and the injuries to Florence.

There are likely to be two actions for damages; one will be brought by Florence's lover, Brian, and another is likely to be brought by Dylan, Ermintrude's former husband. Both Dylan and Brian may have an action for dependency damages under the provisions of the **Fatal Accidents Act 1976**, despite the fact that Dylan is no longer married to Ermintrude. This is because the list of dependants set out in the **Fatal Accidents Act 1976, s. 1** includes spouses and former spouses, including those who have remarried (*Shepherd v Post Office* (1995) *The Times* , 15 June). Brian, as a cohabitee, will also be regarded as a dependant if he has lived with Florence for at least two years, although it is possible for a person to live in more than one household at the same time (*Pounder v London Underground Ltd* [1995] PIQR P217).

This is a new action which arises where death is caused by a wrongful act or default which is such as would have entitled the person injured to maintain an action and recover damages in respect of it. The person who would have been liable, had death not ensued, will be liable to an action for damages, notwithstanding the death of the person injured (**Fatal Accidents Act 1976, s. 1(1)**). The relatives covered by the action include spouses and persons who have lived with the deceased as husband or wife for a period of two years prior to the date of death (**Fatal Accidents Act 1976, s. 1(2)**), although persons falling into the latter category will be unable to recover set bereavement damages of £10,000, in the same way as a spouse may (**s. 1A(2)**). The action for dependency damages is brought by the executor or administrator or the dependant personally, but can only be brought if the deceased could have sued in his own right had he only been injured. The purpose behind the **Fatal Accidents Act 1976** is to give the dependant sufficient to represent the loss of a breadwinner, so that assessment of damages starts with a quantification of the wages the deceased was earning, subject to a deduction in respect of the deceased's own living expenses. This will produce a figure representing the deceased's earning capacity which is then subjected to a multiplier running from the date of death and representing the probable length of the deceased's earning period. The award is subdivided into two parts covering, respectively, the period from death to the date of trial, and from the date of trial on into the future (*Cookson v Knowles* [1979] AC 556). In order to be considered for dependency damages, the dependant must show financial loss as a result of the death, and in the case of Ermintrude, this will include the value of any domestic services she might have provided as a wife.

Brian and Dylan may also have a 'survival' action under the **Law Reform (Miscellaneous) Provisions Act 1934** if they represent the estate of the deceased person. This represents the pecuniary and non-pecuniary loss suffered by the deceased as a result of the defendant's tort and is dependent on whether the deceased could have maintained an action against the defendant had he survived. To be able to use the **1934 Act** both Brian and Dylan must represent the estate of the deceased, which will depend on the terms of the will or relevant rules on intestacy. If, as an ex-husband, Dylan is excluded from Ermintrude's will, he will not be able to sue under the **1934 Act**.

If the period between the tort and the date of death is so short as to be treated as part of the death, no award will be made for pain and suffering: *Hicks v Chief Constable of South Yorkshire Police* [1992] 2 All ER 65. This may suggest that the period of three minutes between the collapse of the wall whilst the police are attempting to remove Hector's car from Zebedee's shop and Ermintrude's death is too short to allow an award of damages for pain and suffering.

Assuming Brian represents Florence's estate, it will have to be shown that had Florence lived she could have sued Hector. Florence's suicide, brought on by depression resulting from the accident caused by Hector's negligence, may amount to a break in the chain of causation that prevents Brian from maintaining an action under the **1934 Act**. *Pigney v Pointer's Transport Services Ltd* [1957] 1 WLR 1121 suggests that insane suicide does not amount to a *novus actus interveniens* so that an action under the **1934 Act** by a surviving spouse will not be prejudiced. However, this case was decided when suicide was a crime and the applicable remoteness test was then based on recovery of all losses flowing directly from a defendant's tort. Since then the House of Lords in *Reeves v Commissioner of Police for the Metropolis* [2000] 1 AC 360 has held that public policy should not deny a remedy, but that it should be asked whether the suicide was caused by the breach of duty using the 'but for' test. In *Reeves*, however, the defendants were under a duty to prevent the deceased from committing suicide, as he was in police custody. Here Florence's state of depression is traceable to the injuries she has suffered in the accident caused by Hector's careless driving.

In *Corr v IBC Vehicles Ltd* [2008] UKHL 13 it was held that all the claimant has to do is to show that if her husband suffered an injury at work those injuries might lead to depression. As the depression suffered by the claimant's husband was a logical consequence of the defendants' negligence, there was no break in the chain of causation. If Florence's sight of the accident, caused by Hector's negligence, is what has brought on the depressive state then the suicide will not be a *novus actus interveniens* and the death will not be regarded as damage that is too remote.

In *Reeves* the claimant's damages were reduced by 50 per cent for contributory negligence so as to take account of the fact that the deceased had committed suicide while of sound mind. Surprisingly in *Corr* Lords Bingham and Walker thought that no such deduction should be made, despite what had been decided in *Reeves*, since, on the facts, Mr Corr was not really to blame for his own death. However, a majority of the House of Lords did agree that, in principle, it would be right to reduce damages payable to the next of kin under the **Fatal Accidents Act 1976** where the person committing suicide bears some responsibility for his own death. Accordingly, the chain of causation emanating from Hector's breach of duty may not have been broken, thereby leaving Brian in a position to be able to maintain an action for damages, but those damages might be reduced to take into account the fact of suicide.

? Question 2

Donald, aged 35, is badly injured in a road traffic accident caused by the admitted negligence of Charles. Donald's car, valued at £10,000, is written off. The extent of his injuries is such that prior to the date of trial Donald incurs private medical expenses of £12,500, but has also spent a number of weeks in a NHS Trust hospital at public expense, with the result that the household costs incurred by Rebecca, Donald's wife, are less than usual for part of the time, but greater than usual once Donald returns home for convalescence. During the period of hospitalization and medical treatment, Donald is unable to work as a research chemist at a salary of £30,000 per annum.

The extent of Donald's injuries is such that for the future he will be unable to continue in his employment for a further three years after trial and will be unable to continue his pastime as an amateur cricketer. Moreover, there is a distinct prospect that his injuries may worsen in years to come, although this is by no means certain. Donald took out a personal accident insurance plan a number of years ago, which will pay substantial benefits following the accident. Moreover, Donald has also received state benefits and will continue to do so after the date of trial.

Advise Donald.

Commentary

This question is concerned mainly with personal injury damages and the different heads of damage under which an award may be made. A distinction must be drawn between pre-trial expenditure and future loss. Account must also be taken of any deductions which should be made from an award of damages so as to ensure that the claimant is not over-compensated. There is also a minor issue in relation to damages for harm to property.

Examiner's tip

If you are told that one of the parties admits negligence, you do not need to discuss the duty issue or whether there is a breach of duty.

Answer plan

- What pre-trial expenditure is recoverable and what off-sets must be made?
- How is loss of future earnings to be quantified?
- Instead of a lump sum award, is there the possibility of an award of provisional damages?
- What deductions from the award are to be made in respect of social security and insurance payments?
- How are damages for pain and suffering and loss of amenity to be assessed?
- Is the appropriate basis for damages in respect of the car the cost of repair or the diminished value of the vehicle?

Suggested answer

In an action for damages for personal injury, there are two distinct heads of damage. The first is expenditure incurred as a result of the tort of the defendant and the second is loss of earnings.

Any expenditure prior to the trial is recoverable if actually and reasonably incurred. This will include private medical expenses such as the £12,500 paid by Donald, but there is a deduction to be made in respect of any savings made through maintenance at public expense in a NHS Trust hospital, but these savings must be offset against any loss of income (**Administration of Justice Act 1982, s. 5**). Moreover, the household expenditure incurred by Rebecca is reduced compared with what is the norm, so a deduction in respect of expenditure which would have been incurred in maintaining

Donald may be made (*Harris v Empress Motors Ltd* [1984] 1 WLR 212). However, after Donald returns home for convalescence, household expenses increase, in which case this increase may be taken into account. Rebecca may feel morally obliged to give up work in order to tend to Donald in which case she has a recognized pecuniary claim since the decision in *Hunt v Severs* [1994] 2 All ER 385 and Donald will hold any award in this respect in trust for Rebecca as a provider of the services.

Donald will be able to recover the amount he would have earned between the date of the tort and the date of trial, subject to deductions in respect of tax liabilities (*British Transport Commission v Gourley* [1956] AC 185).

The award will take into account his future pecuniary loss, such as lost future income, identified by calculating his net annual loss multiplied by a figure which, as far as possible and if properly invested, will produce an overall amount equivalent to the lost income. This can be a substantial amount if the claimant, like Donald, is well-educated and has very good job prospects (*Dixon v John Were Ltd* [2004] EWHC 2273 (QB)). Furthermore, if Donald is handicapped in the labour market, an award can be made even though it may be speculative (*Doyle v Wallace* [1998] PIQR P146). Taking account of investment is an important factor since the court must have regard for the fact that the damages are paid in the form of a lump sum. Accordingly the multiplier used will not equate exactly with the number of lost working years. The fact that Donald's injuries may worsen in years to come may affect his earning capacity in the future. This is a factor which may be considered when assessing damages if it is likely to serve as a handicap in the job market (*Moeliker v A. Reyrolle & Co* [1977] 1 WLR 132). However, the rule seems to be confined to complete loss of job prospects, whereas Donald will be unable to work for three years, but may be able to work thereafter. Nonetheless a person who is out of work for three years may find it difficult to find replacement employment after that period.

A well-established problem with the lump sum system of paying damages is that it is not easy to deal with future uncertainties, but an award of provisional damages may be made to allow the claimant to return later to recover an additional payment, if warranted: **Senior Courts Act 1981, s. 32A**. There must be more than a fanciful chance that at some definite or indefinite time in the future, the injured person will develop some serious disease or suffer some serious deterioration that is capable of measurement (*Willson v Ministry of Defence* [1991] 1 All ER 638). The availability of this option is now a factor the courts will take into account in determining whether they should refuse to order a lump-sum payment, particularly if the degree of likely deterioration might result in death (*Molinari v Ministry of Defence* [1994] PIQR Q33).

There is no certainty that Donald's injuries will worsen so a court may feel unable to make an award of provisional damages under **s. 32A**. Moreover, it is clear that continuing deterioration, such as the onset of osteo-arthritis after injuries consisting of broken limbs, will not fall within the ambit of **s. 32A** (*Willson v Ministry of Defence*).

The lump sum method of compensation can be ineffective if it fails to accurately reflect the claimant's loss if his condition worsens in the future. To cover this possibility, a court has a power to make a periodic payment order in relation to future income loss (see **Courts Act 2003, ss. 100 and 101** and **Damages Act 1996, s. 2(1).**) Where such an award is made, the court will determine the frequency and the amount of the payments based on current needs at the time of the order without regard to longevity. Moreover, the court should have regard to the best interests of the claimant rather than give effect to what the claimant (or his family) wants (*Thompstone v Tameside & Glossop Acute Services NHS Trust* [2008] EWCA Civ 5.)

When an award of damages is made in respect of pecuniary loss, the court must take account of any relevant offsets, so that the award does not over-compensate the claimant. As with liability to taxation, the court will also have to have regard to sources of financial support other than the award of damages itself. The question states that Donald has received and will continue to receive state benefits and that he is due to receive a payment under a personal accident insurance plan. The insurance policy moneys will not be deducted from the award of damages (*Bradburn v Great Western Railway* (1874) LR 10 Ex 1), since the claimant has paid for the benefit and courts do not wish to discourage the making of insurance provision.

The rule on state benefits is different since these and tort damages are designed to compensate the same losses. The **Social Security (Recovery of Benefits) Act 1997** now provides that the amount of any relevant benefit paid or likely to be paid to or for the claimant is to be disregarded, but the compensator is not permitted to pay any compensation until the Department for Work and Pensions has issued a certificate detailing the total amount of benefit. Once this has been issued, the amount certified must be deducted in respect of a period of five years following the date of the accident and is payable to the Secretary of State. The deduction is made from the whole of the award which includes any element in respect of non-pecuniary loss, such as pain and suffering which is not compensated by social security benefits.

In addition to pecuniary losses, an award of damages may also cover less easily quantifiable losses such as pain and suffering and loss of amenity. Provided it can be assumed that the claimant has endured pain, an award of damages for pain and suffering may be made. The one instance in which such an award is unlikely is where the claimant is and will remain permanently unconscious (*H. West & Son Ltd v Shephard* [1964] AC 326). Here there is nothing to suggest that Donald is comatose, in which case the award of damages may include an element in respect of pain and suffering. Donald is unable to continue his pastime as an amateur cricketer. This is a factor which may be reflected in any award of damages. Thus if the claimant loses the joy of life and cannot ride a bicycle or kick a football, he is entitled to damages representing his loss of enjoyment of life (*Heaps v Perrite Ltd* [1937] 2 All ER 60). Finally, Donald's car is damaged in the accident caused by Charles' negligence. The question states that it has been written off and that it is valued at £10,000. Where a vehicle has been written off, it is considered uneconomic to repair it and the court is likely to treat this as a case of constructive total loss (*Darbishire v Warran* [1963] 1 WLR 1067). In the circumstances there is said to be no difference between the cost of repair and the reduction in market value of the damaged chattel. It follows that an award of damages will represent the replacement value of the damaged article; in Donald's case, £10,000.

? Question 3

Tom, through his admitted negligent driving, damages a vintage Bentley car owned by Algernon. The car is so badly damaged that in normal circumstances it would be written off by an insurance company, but Algernon is so attached to it that he wants to have it repaired. Algernon has a badly paid job and has maintenance commitments to the children of his first marriage. As a result of his financial position he cannot immediately afford to arrange for the necessary repairs, with the result that he waits for six months before doing anything. In the meantime Algernon takes advantage of a credit hire arrangement in order to be able to obtain a replacement vehicle while the Bentley is off the road. For this arrangement Algernon is not required to make any payment 'up-front', but the credit hire company will present an account when Algernon's tort action against Tom is concluded. The charge for this credit facility and the replacement car is the equivalent of paying £50 per day for a hire car, when the normal daily charge for an equivalent hire car would be £33.

Subsequently Algernon discovers that the specialist in Bentley cars who is to carry out the necessary work has raised the cost of the work by £1,250 to a total charge of £4,500. This amount is £500 more than a general car repairer would charge for the same work.

A further consequence of the collision between the two vehicles is that Tom's own car, after Tom was thrown from his vehicle, collided with a propane gas tank, causing an explosion which damaged a derelict factory owned by Richmann Properties Ltd. Richmann had intended to clear this site for the purposes of future development.

Advise Tom of his potential liability in damages.

💬 Commentary

This question concerns the rules on an award of damages for property damage. A car is badly damaged in circumstances in which it would be normal to see an award of damages based on market depreciation, but there is also the possibility of damages based on the cost of repair. Other factors such as consequential expenses, the impecuniosity of the claimant, and rules on mitigation of damage must be considered. There is also a problem of damage to real property and the basis on which damages should be awarded.

Answer plan

- Explain the difference between repair costs and diminution in value in respect of damage to chattels and when the different measures apply.
- The effect of shortage of resources on the choices made by a claimant and how this relates to the rule on mitigation of damage.
- Whether the real property damage should be compensated on the basis of repair costs or diminution in value.

⇨ **Suggested answer**

Tom has admitted to driving negligently, there is no need to consider the issues of duty of care and breach of duty. Accordingly, the principal question concerns Tom's liability in damages for the harm suffered by Algernon and Richmann Properties Ltd.

Algernon's car is so badly damaged that in normal circumstances it would be written off by an insurance company, often called a constructive total loss (*Darbishire v Warran* [1963] 1 WLR 1067) and the award of damages will be based on the replacement value of the vehicle. Exceptionally, the claimant may be allowed the cost of repair where the damaged property is effectively unique: *O'Grady v Westminster Scaffolding Ltd* [1962] 2 Lloyd's Rep 238 (repair value given for an old but carefully maintained car that would be difficult to replace). It would appear that Algernon's position is very similar to that in *O'Grady* and that the cost of repair might be the appropriate measure of damages.

Consequential losses suffered as a result of the damage inflicted by the defendant, such as the cost of hiring a substitute, may also be recovered (*Darbishire v Warran*). Here Algernon has incurred no immediate cost in hiring a replacement, but will receive an account under the credit hire agreement. The problem this presents is that the hire charges are greater than the normal cost of hiring a car. However, Algernon may argue that he has been forced into doing this because of lack of resources as he cannot pay the 'up-front' cost of hiring a car on a daily basis.

In *Liesbosch (Owners) v Edison (Owners)* [1933] AC 449 it was held that losses resulting from the impecuniosity of a claimant are too remote to be recovered, despite the normal rule that the defendant has to take the claimant as he finds him. In the context of motorists who enter into credit hire arrangements, the House of Lords has considered the status of the *Liesbosch* principle twice in *Dimond v Lovell* [2002] 1 AC 384 and *Lagden v O'Connor* [2003] UKHL 64.

In *Dimond v Lovell* the claimant sought to recover the cost of a replacement vehicle provided by her insurers under a credit hire agreement which was more expensive than a 'daily hire' car. There was no question of shortage of resources, but the claimant took advantage of the insurance arrangement as it involved no up-front cost. The House of Lords held that the rule on mitigation of loss meant that damages in respect of the hire of a replacement car should be restricted to the normal daily hire rate and that the inflated costs (i.e. interest and administration charges) of the credit hire agreement should not be recoverable.

Algernon's position is different, since he is badly paid and has maintenance commitments towards the children of his first marriage. As a result of this, he may not have the resources immediately to hand to be able to pay the standard daily hire rate for a replacement car, while his own vehicle is off the road. In *Lagden v O'Connor* a similar, but not identical position prevailed. The unemployed claimant's car was damaged by the defendant's negligent driving, but he could not afford to hire a replacement without using a credit hire company, so that there was no initial outlay. A replacement car was a convenience, but not an absolute necessity for the claimant. A majority of the House of Lords departed from the *Liesbosch* principle because it conflicted with the rule that a defendant should take the claimant as he finds him. Accordingly, provided the extra cost incurred by the claimant was not unforeseeable, the impecuniosity of the claimant was a factor that a court could consider in determining what damages should be awarded against a defendant and his insurer. A further reason given for departing from the *Liesbosch* was that it was decided before *Wagon Mound (No. 1)* [1961] AC 388 which applied a reasonable foresight test for remoteness of damage in negligence cases and that the *Liesbosch* principle was a consequence of the old directness of damage test applied in *Re Polemis & Furness Withy & Co Ltd* [1921] 3 KB 560. Accordingly, whatever might be said of the correctness or otherwise of the decision in *Liesbosch*, at that time, the law had moved on, and it was time for the House of Lords to recognize reality in *Lagden v O'Connor*.

In *Lagden*, the majority concluded that, given the claimant's lack of means, they were not constrained by the decision in *Dimond v Lovell*. It was reasonably foreseeable that the claimant would require a replacement car. Since he was not in a position to make any initial outlay on hiring a replacement on the daily hire spot market, it was foreseeable that he might take advantage of a credit hire arrangement, even though this would increase the claim for damages against the defendant.

The decision in *Lagden v O'Connor* is not without its difficulties, as was recognized by the majority. It will necessitate drawing a distinction between those who are impecunious and those who are not. Lord Scott delivered a powerful dissenting judgment preferring the reasoning in *Dimond v Lovell*, so that the claimant would be confined to the standard daily charge for a hire car. Lord Scott observed that the car was not used for any particular business purpose, so how could it be said that the claimant had suffered any compensable loss through not having a car available to him. He could use public transport as an alternative. Lord Scott expressed the view that one of the main functions of the law of obligations is to construct a set of yardsticks for determining when legal injury has been suffered (*Lagden v O'Connor* [2003] UKHL 64 at [86]) and that the test of impecuniosity was over-complicated and too impracticable to be of service (ibid.).

In the hypothetical example, Algernon has a job, albeit not well paid, and has binding financial commitments towards the maintenance of his children, but he has also chosen to continue to own a vintage Bentley car, that in normal circumstances might be written off by an insurer. He could have sold the Bentley to another Bentley enthusiast with the means to pay for its restoration and so get more than the scrap value. There may also be other reasons for his lack of means, albeit not mentioned in the facts of the problem. Does he take regular holidays abroad, smoke cigarettes, and drink alcohol? As Lord Nicholls observed, lack of financial means is a question of priorities (*Lagden v O'Connor* UKHL 64 at [9]). It is arguable that Algernon may have made an unreasonable choice in the circumstances and may be confined to the measure of damages applicable in *Dimond v Lovell* and *Liesbosch*, namely, the market cost of a replacement vehicle, rather than the actual cost.

The *Liesbosch* principle only applies to the impecuniosity of the claimant, but if there are other reasons for the increased cost, they may be relevant. Thus in *Martindale v Duncan* [1973] 2 All ER 355, a taxi driver whose cab had been damaged due to the negligence of the claimant chose to wait until he had obtained authorization from his insurers before he had his vehicle repaired. While the vehicle was off the road, the claimant suffered loss of business profit. This loss was held to be recoverable despite the fact that the claimant's reason for waiting was that he could not afford to have the repairs carried out himself. However, since there was another reason for the delay, namely that the claimant was awaiting the decision of his insurers, the *Liesbosch* principle was held not to apply. Similarly in *Perry v Sidney Phillips & Son* [1982] 1 WLR 1297, the claimant was able to recover damages for anxiety and inconvenience even though this anxiety arose principally from the claimant's inability to pay for the cost of repairs to the property concerned. Both of these cases are distinguishable from *Liesbosch* since in *Martindale* something other than the claimant's impecuniosity could be said to be the cause of the loss and in *Perry* the loss suffered by the claimant could not be described as a business loss, in which case the rule that the defendant must take the claimant as he finds him can be applied.

The *Liesbosch* principle was also distinguished in *Dodd Properties Ltd v Canterbury City Council* [1980] 1 WLR 433, where the cost of repairing a damaged building had risen sharply due to the effect of inflation. The claimants had not had the property repaired immediately, partly because they claimed their resources would have been stretched and partly because they were awaiting the outcome of the trial before effecting the repairs. It was held that the increased cost was recoverable since the claimants' impecuniosity was only one reason for the delay, and secondly that the case should be approached on the basis of mitigation principles rather than rules on remoteness of damage. On this latter basis, the claimant cannot reasonably be required to do something he cannot afford to do in order to reduce his losses. However, this approach can be criticized on the ground that the rules on mitigation apply to steps taken to reduce losses for which damages are going to be awarded in the future. If the case is dealt with as one concerned with remoteness of damage, the defendant ought not to be held responsible for losses which result from an unreasonable failure by the claimant to act in his own best interests.

Apart from Algernon's impecuniosity, the question also indicates that Algernon has waited for some time before arranging to have his vehicle repaired, during which time the cost of repair has risen. Given the age and value of the car, it would appear perfectly reasonable to employ the services of a specialist in Bentley cars, despite the fact that they are more expensive than general car repairers. It would be reasonable to assume that the extra cost may be taken to represent the specialization in this type of vehicle. On the matter of the delay itself, it may be that the reason can be traced to the defendant and his insurer in seeking to delay the commencement of proceedings or taking their time in the process of agreeing a settlement. In this case the delay may be regarded as something brought about by the defendant rather than the claimant, in which case the *Liesbosch* principle does not apply: see *Alcoa Minerals of Jamaica Inc v Broderick* [2000] 3 WLR 23.

Applying all of this to Algernon, the principal issue appears to be whether or not he has acted reasonably in delaying the process of repairing the vehicle and in obtaining a hire car in the way he has done.

Algernon is a private individual, who appears to be treated differently from businesses. In such a case, it may be foreseeable that such a person might not immediately be able to rectify the damage caused by the defendant's negligence. Assuming the delay in effecting repairs is reasonable, the cost incurred by Algernon in hiring a replacement will be recoverable and this may even include the additional charges incurred through taking out a credit hire agreement, depending upon whether Algernon is taken to have no practical choice other than to acquire the car in this way due to his financial plight. Moreover, the additional cost in employing the services of a specialist in Bentley cars does not seem out of the way, given the value of the vehicle.

The damage to the property owned by Richmann Properties Ltd also requires consideration. The basic principle which applies to harm to real property is that the claimant should be put into the position he was in before the property was damaged. There are two ways in which this may be done. The first is to assess damages on the basis of the diminution in the capital value of the property and the second is to give the cost of effecting repairs. Generally, which is the appropriate measure will depend on the claimant's intended use of the property. For example, if the property is used by the claimant for the purpose of occupation or for the purposes of running a business, the appropriate measure will be the cost of repair, since it will be difficult for the claimant to sell the damaged property and purchase a replacement. This remains the case even where the cost of repairing the property is in excess of the depreciation in value and even where the effect of the repair is to give the claimant a better and more up-to-date set of premises (*Harbutt's Plasticine Ltd v Wayne Tank & Pump Co Ltd* [1970] 1 QB 447). Conversely, if the property has been acquired as an investment, it seems that the appropriate measure of damages is to be based on the diminution in value of the property (*CR Taylor Ltd v Hepworths Ltd* [1977] 1 WLR 659). This appears to be the more appropriate measure in the case of Richmann Properties as the question states that the land is intended for future development.

Further reading

Law Commission No. 257, *Damages for Personal Injury: Non-pecuniary Loss* (1999).

Rogers, W. V. H., *Winfield & Jolowicz on Tort*, 18th edn (London: Sweet & Maxwell, 2010), ch. 22.

Stapleton, J., 'The Gist of Negligence' (1997) 113 LQR 1.